FIELD GUIDE TO
COVERING
SPORTS

Joe Gisondi

Eastern Illinois University

CQ PRESS

A Division of SAGE
Washington, D.C.

CQ Press
2300 N Street, NW, Suite 800
Washington, DC 20037

Phone: 202-729-1900; toll-free, 1-866-4CQ-PRESS (1-866-427-7737)

Web: www.cqpress.com

Cover design: Matthew Simmons, www.myselfincluded.com
Cover photo: GettyImages.com
Composition: C&M Digitals (P) Ltd.

♾ The paper used in this publication exceeds the requirements of the American National Standard for Information Sciences—Permanence of Paper for Printed Library Materials, ANSI Z39.48-1992.

Printed and bound in the United States of America

16 17 18 19   7 6 5 4 3

SUSTAINABLE FORESTRY INITIATIVE

Certified Chain of Custody
Promoting Sustainable Forestry
www.sfiprogram.org
SFI-01268

SFI label applies to text stock

Library of Congress Cataloging-in-Publication Data

Gisondi, Joe.
Field guide to covering sports / Joe Gisondi.
    p. cm. — (Field guide series)
Includes bibliographical references and index.
ISBN 978-1-60426-559-0 (pbk. : alk. paper)
    1. Sports journalism. 2. Sports journalism—Authorship. I. Title. II. Series.

PN4784.S6G58 2010
070.4′49796—dc22

2010000050

For my parents, whose love knew no bounds.

CONTENTS

PART III. EXPLORING FURTHER

FOREWORD

by WILL LEITCH

In April 2008, I appeared on HBO's "Costas Now" program to talk about the future of Internet sports journalism with the eponymous Bob Costas, then-Cleveland Browns wide receiver Braylon Edwards and Pulitzer Prize-winning author of *Friday Night Lights,* Buzz Bissinger. I had not expected this to be a Socratic exchange of ideas – it is, after all, television, which is a medium that seems founded in a fundamental opposition to Socratic exchanges of ideas – but I had hoped that each side would be able to present its viewpoints for a few minutes, while the viewing audience, surely waiting for Michael Strahan to come back on stage, ran to the kitchen for a wedge of cheese. (And by "side," I mean "Bissinger's side" and "my side." I am not sure why Braylon Edwards was there, and I'm fairly certain he wasn't, either.)

If you saw the program, or have a few minutes to set aside this book to type "Bissinger vs. Leitch" into your computing device, you know the Socratic exchange of ideas is not what happened. Again: I blame this on television. Costas put together the panel as "Journalist Guy" (Bissinger) vs. "Internet Guy" (me), and encouraged sparks to fly. That they did. But it didn't bring us any closer to answering the question the panel was (theoretically, anyway) put together to answer: What does sports journalism (and all journalism, really) look like in the 21st century?

As I pointed out to everyone who talked to me about the show afterward – and there were many people; as I joked with Bissinger (who, however unlikely, has become a friend) later, the program will end up in both our obituaries, albeit a few paragraphs higher in mine than his – there is a massive middle ground here that Costas and his show refused to acknowledge. At the time the show was taped, Bissinger and I had both had pieces printed in seven magazines – once, in an issue of *Play,* on opposite pages from each other.

Bissinger and I obviously went about our careers in different ways, but in those magazines, and on bookshelves, they ended up in the same place. Certainly we have different styles and sensibilities, but readers and consumers do not care how the sausage is made. They just want quality work. They want to be informed, they want to be enlightened, they want to be entertained. They are the customer, and their tastes are always changing. It is our job, as journalists, as writers, as broadcasters, as humans, to pay attention to them. This book will help you, the journalist, do that for sports writing.

Sports journalism is a business, not an art project. Bissinger is popular and well-read because he has paid attention and produced great work. I am less popular, and less well-read, but still *somewhat* read because I have tried to do the same. It is an ongoing process.

This book is about that idea, a look at journalism in the new century, what works, what doesn't, tips, test cases, what you might need. It is a guide, but it's not comprehensive, nor is it meant to be. What this book teaches is something that you constantly have to work on. This book is a good start.

I highly recommend Braylon Edwards read it.

Will Leitch is a contributing editor at New York Magazine, *a columnist at* Sporting News *and the founder of Deadspin. He is also the author of four books,* Life as a Loser (2003), Catch (2005), God Save the Fan *(2008) and the upcoming* Are We Winning? *(May 2010).*

PREFACE

I'll never forget the anxiety I felt writing my first few stories for a daily newspaper – and the kindness shown to me by the sports editors on those late Friday nights. At the time, I was a cocky 17-year-old who had already covered games and written features for two weekly newspapers, and I was sports editor of my high school newspaper – making me a grizzled veteran. Or so I thought.

That first Friday night, I struggled for 15 minutes to craft a lead before an editor told me, "Just write anything. You've got about 20 minutes before deadline." I started to sweat – the warm kind you feel when you've forgotten to study for a test or are about to ask someone on a date. The kind that portends failure. I kept plugging away on that electric typewriter, fumbling over notes and writing play-by-play filled with way too many adjectives and far too few details, with quotes that were generic and a lead that was barely palatable.

Joe Arace, the longtime prep sports editor at *The News-Press* in Fort Myers, Fla., told me to sit next to him while he edited the story. He deleted adjectives, asked me questions so he could add vivid descriptions, inserted transitions, and moved up key plays and stats. Each keystroke was an execution. Each revision a slap in the face. Each edit proof that I had chosen the wrong career.

Like other kids, I had grown up idolizing sports figures, watching games, reading the sports pages to relive these moments and dreaming of making it to the big leagues. I hadn't yet accepted that if I got there, I'd be sitting in the press box. And in my early newsroom nights, even that scenario seemed unlikely.

After Joe sent the story to the copy chief, he turned to me, smiled, and said, "Good job. See you next week." What? They wanted me to write again? I was shocked. Clearly, I had done something right. But what?

The next morning, my spine tingled when I read the byline: Joe Gisondi. I was a little ashamed that I hadn't written every word myself. I hadn't realized yet that journalism is a team game where everyone – assignment editors, copy editors, designers, proofreaders – contributes to a story's success. That doesn't mean sports reporters should blithely expect others to correct their mistakes. But it's nice to know you have that support.

I determined not to repeat the same errors. So I made new ones, which were corrected and revised by editors while I sat and watched, listening to their suggestions and explanations as they worked on my copy. And each week I heard, "Good job. See you next week."

As I write this book, I hear those editors' voices, their suggestions and their encouragement. I hear the voices of the 90-plus sports journalists and coaches who offer advice in these pages on how to cover more than 20 beats, from auto racing to field hockey to wrestling. These voices come not just from *The New York Times,* ESPN and *Sports Illustrated,* but from newer outlets like Rivals.com and SpeedTV and from the small news organizations that employ the majority of sports journalists. In places like Cedar Rapids, Iowa, and Kennebec, Maine, sports coverage means local coverage, and local coverage means kids and schools.

For students and beginning sports journalists, this field guide serves as their portable editor: posing questions, suggesting new approaches and summarizing the basics needed to cover any game. It offers hands-on, practical advice, the kind given in sports departments across the country. Like the one I sat in so many years ago.

Training needed

Although Americans play dozens of sports, just a few – football, baseball, basketball – get most of the media coverage. Millions of people follow those sports, but that doesn't mean either fans or sportswriters understand them expertly. Teachers and editors know that their students and new hires know far less than they claim. Even so, few sports journalists receive formal training. So many young reporters cover games more like fans than professionals. They fumble through statistics, struggle to take proper notes, mishandle interviews and settle for both clichéd language and the same old leads. They're not sure how to identify, or write about, the most significant plays, trends or moments in a game.

This book provides even the most basic writers with the tools they need to succeed on their first assignments. It trains writers to answer, in advance, the questions their editors and readers will ask: What happened? How? Why? The running back ran for 200 yards. Any fan can see that, but a journalist needs to explain why. Did the offensive tackles drive back a smaller defensive line? Did the offensive coordinator scheme so well that the defense was confused? Did this running back follow his blockers well or display amazing athleticism?

A track runner broke the county record in the mile. How? Did she take the lead early, have to kick it in for the final lap, or get pulled along by a competitive field? And how did she train to prepare for this meet?

Just like athletes, journalists need training. The introductory chapters of this book start that training by providing the big picture, with tips on interviewing sources, writing game stories, acting professionally. Chapters on blogging and covering high school sports prepare writers for two areas that are booming as news organizations focus even more on local action and interactive approaches to news.

The core of the book, the middle section, takes beginning journalists step-by-step through every one of the 20 sports they're likely to be sent out to cover. Within each sport, four sections provide tips on how to prepare for the game, what to look for while you're watching, whom to interview, what to ask and, finally, how to write up what you've seen. PREPARE – WATCH – ASK – WRITE: You'll see those four sections in each sports chapter. In addition, experienced sports journalists chime in with their own advice, sharing what they've learned about how to observe events, take notes and keep score and interview players and coaches.

Of course, no book of field-guide size could possibly fit in every rule and every term for every sport a journalist might need to cover. Instead, these pages contain the basics a young reporter is most likely to need. Reporters will learn to:

▶ Keep score accurately and effectively. Illustrated scorecards show how to record scores and take notes on auto racing, baseball/softball, basketball, bowling and football.

▶ Understand the rules when covering an unfamiliar sport. Can golfers flick bugs off balls before hitting them? Are stock-car drivers legally allowed to bump other cars? How much tailwind nullifies a record-breaking track performance? What's the purpose of a drag flick in field hockey?

▶ Understand the necessary terminology. What's a "near fall" in wrestling, and what does a coxswain do in rowing? What does 6 – 4 – 3 mean in baseball? How many pins are recorded in a frame after a spare?

▶ Ask more informed questions after games. Did the safeties stay back, trying to prevent the deep pass? Did the pitcher have more spin on the ball?

USES FOR THE CLASSROOM

This field guide is designed as a companion "un-text" for sports-writing classes. Teachers can use the introductory chapters to review the basics: research, observation, interviewing and writing game stories. In addition, you can go over chapters on specific sports before covering a local or college team as a class. Do make sure to let the college sports information director or high school athletic director know before doing this, so they can assist. These hands-on activities strengthen students' abilities to take notes, keep score and focus on the most significant angles.

Inviting coaches to class to speak about their specific sports gives students not just good information but a chance to practice interviewing in a relaxed environment. Students can review the appropriate chapters before listening to a speaker, then ask questions and write up the session on deadline as if it were a press conference.

Since this book is devised as a practical guide, ask students to apply what they've learned, assigning them to cover games or beats. You can even set up a blog to cover college or high school teams in your region.

Reading great sports stories is the best way to provide a sense of options and inspire students to write better. Readers such as the *Best American Sports Writing* series or *The New York Times Sports Reader* acquaint students with the best of the best. Local and national newspapers, on paper and online, show how professionals in markets large and small go about their jobs.

Students, teachers and advisers can also regularly check in to my sports blog at either sportsfieldguide.com or onsports.wordpress.com – which has been favorably reviewed by Poynter's NewsU, Cyberjournalist, American Press Institute and College Media Advisers – for additional tips and insights into sports journalism issues.

Sports journalism is evolving

Will Leitch may seem like an unusual pick to write a foreword about sports journalism. He created a sports blog, Deadspin.com, with a motto that is anathema to sports journalism: "Sports news without access, favor or discretion." But Deadspin struck a chord with millions of sports fans who flocked to the site and made it the most popular independent sports blog on the Internet – at times even challenging ESPN for readership. Obviously, sports journalism is evolving and is no longer in the sole possession of those who write for newspapers. Leitch, who has covered the major league baseball playoffs for *The New York Times* and who writes a regular sports column for *Sporting News,* understands the challenges in straddling old and new media. Buzz Bissinger may have called him "low-life scum" in an infamous segment of HBO's "Costas Now," but others have countered by calling him iconoclastic. Either way, he's certainly innovative, a trait that will help all sports journalists.

Acknowledgments

Years ago, I learned that sports reporting, like anything in journalism, is a team effort. More than 90 professional journalists and college coaches generously shared their considerable experiences for this book, receiving nothing more than a thank you and a chance to help others become solid journalists.

I've learned that a writer needs an equally dedicated team to create a large project such as this. Thanks to Earl Pingel, who encouraged me to create the initial outline; Aron Keesbury, who helped develop the project; Charisse Kiino, who continued to support the project; Christina Mueller for keeping everything organized; Jane Harrigan, who brought it all together by keeping me on task and vastly improving the copy; Mary Marik, who further refined the copy; and to Sarah Fell, who saw the book through production and added last-minute suggestions. I'd also like to thank the professors and journalists who provided helpful feedback during the review process: Vince Benigini, College of Charleston; Lori Ann Dickerson, Michigan State University; Martin Dobrow, Springfield College; Bill Fleischman, University of Delaware; Marie Hardin, Penn State University; Melanie Hauser, University of Texas-Austin; Marie Kaufman, University of Miami; Robert Keohan, Merrimack College; Jim Killam, Northern Illinois University; Roland Lazenby, Virginia Tech; Mead Loop, Ithaca College; Donald Markus, American University; Mike Poorman, Penn State University; Jeff Shearer, Troy University; Ron Thomas, Morehouse College.

Thanks also to my mom and dad, who encouraged me to follow my heart, even if it meant living and breathing all things sports.

Most of all, thanks to my wife, Betsy, whose encouragement and patience enabled me to keep plugging away. Apollo never had a better muse. And thanks, girls, for putting up with your papa's crankiness during deadlines. Your grit, skills and desire on the playing fields are more than a match for anyone trying to get in your way.

Ultimately, I'll never forget editors like Joe Arace, Dave Renbarger, Gary Kicinski, Dick Schneider and Nick Moschella who took the time to help out a young kid, encouraging me, befriending me, and helping me become a better sports journalist.

Contributors

Journalists

Scott Andera, *The Palm Beach Post*
Erik Arneson, SpeedTV
Budd Bailey, *The Buffalo News*
Mike Beacom, Fantasy Sports Writers Association
Greg A. Bedard, *Milwaukee Journal-Sentinel*
Doug Binder, *The Oregonian* (Portland, Ore.)
Bryan Black, *The Virginian-Pilot* (Norfolk, Va.)
Rob Bolton, RotoWorld.com
Ed Bouchette, *Pittsburgh Post-Gazette*
Christine Brennan, *USA Today*

Robert Burghardt, TGFantasyBaseball.com
Rich Chere, *The Star-Ledger* (Newark, N.J.)
Pamela Colloff, *Texas Monthly*
Matt Daniels, *Ledger-Sentinel* (Oswego, Ill.)
Matt DiFilippo, *Morning Sentinel and Kennebec Journal* (Maine)
Doug Dull, media relations, University of Maryland
Bob Dutton, *The Kansas City Star*
Cameron Eickmeyer, USAHockey.com
Dick Evans, *The Daytona Beach News-Journal*
Jeff Evans, *The Bakersfield Californian*
Creig Ewing, *The Courier-Journal* (Louisville, Ky.)
Bruce Feldman, *ESPN The Magazine*
Doug Ferguson, Associated Press
Peter Fimrite, *San Francisco Chronicle*
Scott French, *Major League Soccer Magazine*
Jeffrey Gamza, USAFieldHockey.com
Steve Goff, *The Washington Post*
Chuck Gormley, *Courier-Post* (Cherry Hill, N.J.)
Merv Hendricks, director of student publications, Indiana State University
Dave Hyde, *Sun Sentinel* (Fort Lauderdale, Fla.)
Phil Jasner, *Philadelphia Daily News*
Bruce Jenkins, *San Francisco Chronicle*
Art Kabelowsky, *Milwaukee Journal-Sentinel*
Tyler Kepner, *The New York Times*
George Kirschbaum, Coxguide.com
Dejan Kovacevic, *Pittsburgh Post-Gazette*
Warren Koziresky, SUNY-Brockport
David Lassen, *Ventura County Star* (Calif.)
Will Leitch, Deadspin.com and *Sporting News*
Jim Leitner, *Telegraph Herald* (Dubuque, Iowa)
Jim Litke, Associated Press
Frank Litsky, *The New York Times*
Brian Logue, *Lacrosse Magazine*
Mary Lynly, California Bowling Writers
Jackie MacMullan, ESPN
Jason Marsteller, *Swimming World Magazine*
Mike Miazga, *Volleyball Magazine*
Vicki Michaelis, *USA Today*

Gary Mihoces, *USA Today*
Bryce Miller, *The Des Moines Register* (Iowa)
Jason Mucher, USATriathlon.com
Jim O'Connell, Associated Press
J.R. Ogden, *The Gazette* (Cedar Rapids, Iowa)
John Patton, *The Gainesville Sun* (Fla.)
Kim Pendery, *The Tampa Tribune*
Jon Rascon, FantasyFootballTrader.com
Jim Rossow, *The News-Gazette* (Champaign, Ill.)
Jim Ruppert, *The State-Journal Register* (Springfield, Ill.)
Michael Russo, *Star Tribune* (Minneapolis, Minn.)
Bob Ryan, *The Boston Globe*
Nate Ryan, *USA Today*
Drew Silva, RotoWorld.com
Craig Smith, *The Seattle Times*
Jason Sobel, ESPN.com
Eric Sondheimer, *Los Angeles Times*
Glenn Stout, *The Best American Sports Writing* series
Jared Turner, SceneDaily.com (NASCAR)
L. Jon Wertheim, *Sports Illustrated*
Andy Wilson, *The Guardian* (London)
Dan Woike, Rivals.com
Lynn Zinser, *The New York Times*

Coaches

John Barnes, Excel Aquatics (Gallatin, Tenn.)
Bebe Bryans, University of Wisconsin (rowing)
Donald Fritsch, University of Wisconsin-La Crosse (cross country)
John Fuchs, Western Washington University (rowing)
Frank Graziano, Eastern Illinois University (rugby)
Kelley Green, Loch Haven University (softball)
Mick Haley, University of Southern California (volleyball)
Kevin Hambly, University of Illinois (volleyball)
Rich Luenemann, Washington University in St. Louis (volleyball)
Geoff Masanet, Eastern Illinois University (cross country)
Missy Meharg, University of Maryland (field hockey)
Lynn Oberbillig, Smith College (chair of NCAA Softball Rules Committee)

Leslie Pfeil, Philadelphia Scholastic Rowing Association
Becky Robinson, Ithaca College (rowing)
Brady Sallee, Eastern Illinois University (basketball)
Jim Schmitz, Eastern Illinois University (baseball)
Kim Schuette, Eastern Illinois University (softball)
Greg Strobel, Lehigh University (wrestling)
Richard Sutton, Kent State University (field hockey)
Bob Warming, Creighton University (soccer)
Mark Wetmore, University of Colorado (cross country)
Claus Wolter, Franklin & Marshall College (rowing)

CHAPTER 1

FROM SPORTS
FAN TO
SPORTS REPORTER

You're a lifelong football fan who can recite the names of every single Super Bowl champion. You also know the intricacies of baseball's infield fly rule and the difference between major and minor penalties in hockey. Ty Cobb's lifetime batting average? Please. You can even name the Maple Leafs player in 1951 who scored in overtime to hand Toronto the Stanley Cup.

And now you've landed your dream job, covering sports. First assignment: field hockey. Suddenly, you don't have a clue. Can't tell the difference between a penalty shot and a penalty corner. You'll have to do some reporting, relying on your skills to learn more about this sport, these teams and the key players. Nobody, no matter how big a sports fan, is a born journalist. The transformation from fan requires training and education.

You don't need a license – or even a degree in the field – to be a journalist. But you do need to act like one. And journalism is a profession that requires reporters to seek truth and report it; to provide a fair, comprehensive account of events; and to verify information, act independently and be accountable for mistakes. In addition, sports journalists research, interview and observe thoroughly.

THERE'S NO CHEERING IN THE PRESS BOX

So how do fans and sports journalists differ? In more ways than most people realize.

For example, fans can make unsubstantiated comments without consequences, the kind that can be unjustifiably critical of those who coach and play. A sports fan can say the goalie sucks. But a sports reporter needs to be more detailed and more diplomatic. Had a defender moved out of position? Maybe the goalie's been playing hurt, diving at pucks despite a broken finger or severely sprained ankle. Or maybe the goalie has just had a few bad performances. That happens to all of us – even those who write for a living. Sources won't trust someone who's unwilling to verify the facts. And you'll lose sources rather quickly by making mean, lazy comments.

Fans can openly cheer for their favorite teams and players, high-fiving friends and joyously screaming after a game-winning score. But there's no cheering in the press box. Or in game stories. Or while interviewing players and coaches after a game. Cheering clouds perspective, preventing a sports reporter from discerning the plays, trends or strategies that enabled a team to win. In addition, you could lose some sources who might refrain from speaking with someone willing to spin everything for the home team.

In addition, sports reporters need to abide by professional codes of conduct, such as those outlined by the Society of Professional Journalists and the Associated Press Sports Editors (published later in this book). They can't accept free tickets or eat the free food that, as fans, they'd happily scarf down.

Fans can steal others' work, taking credit for a phrase or key argument when talking with friends or while blogging. Sports journalists report, finding new information that others use.

Fans can skip a game if the weather stinks or the team is hopeless or they have something else to do. Beat reporters faithfully cover games at night and on weekends and holidays, even when the job means missing important family events.

Fans can complain that nothing interesting happened in a midseason baseball or basketball game. Sports writers need to find something unique about a minor league baseball game in late July, an NBA game in mid-February, or a minor league hockey game in April

by taking detailed notes, asking precise questions and keeping score. They must know the game well enough to find these new angles and write a comprehensive account of the game.

Fans prepare for games by listening to talk radio, watching pregame shows and reading preview stories for their information. Sports journalists supply this information through exhaustive research and reporting.

Before behaving like a professional, you'll need to look like one by dressing properly, wearing slacks and collared shirts instead of T-shirts and jeans. For outdoor summer events, you can wear a nice pair of shorts or a skirt instead. Obviously, don't wear any clothing that represents a school or team, something that destroys credibility.

Being a fan doesn't qualify someone to be a sports journalist any more than enjoying "Judge Judy" qualifies someone to be a lawyer. Dress and act professionally and learn your trade if you expect sports information directors, coaches and players to take you seriously.

WHERE DO YOU START?

Glenn Stout was minding his own business, just a fan reading about sports during his gig at the Boston Public Library, when he fell into journalism.

Stout, now editor of *The Best American Sports Writing* series, had stumbled across an old article about a Red Sox manager who committed suicide in 1908. The article cited the pressures of managing as the reason for the suicide.

"If that were the case," Stout says, "I thought there should be a whole cemetery of dead Red Sox managers."

To satisfy his own curiosity, Stout, a 27-year-old librarian, investigated what really happened by reading old newspaper clips on microfilm. He then reviewed an old book on freelance writing to develop a query letter he sent to *The Boston Globe* and *Boston Magazine*. *The Globe* rejected his story idea, but the magazine's editor invited him in.

Stout did not have a single clip, had never tried to write a magazine piece and had majored in creative writing, not journalism. Yet, the editor took a chance, buying the story on the Red Sox manager's suicide for $300 on spec.

"I still had the idea in my head that I wanted to be a writer, but really had no plan on how to become one, but knew I could write," Stout says. "I'd been reading sports stuff for fun forever. So I worked my ass off for a week at a time when you had to write longhand and then go to the typewriter, and turned in the story. He bought it as is, and asked me what I wanted to write about next. I blurted something out, and he gave me a contract for another story for $500. I was their sports columnist for the next three years and have never been without a writing assignment since. I've sold virtually everything I've tried to."

L. Jon Wertheim, now a veteran writer for *Sports Illustrated,* wrote a profile on the New Jersey Nets' Chris Dudley for *Hoop* magazine, an assignment that was a thrill for him when he was a college senior at Yale partly because he could escape a few nights of scraping uneaten food off plates.

"The pay was something like $250, which doesn't sound like much now," Wertheim says, "but it was about 40 hours worth of wages working at the dining hall, so I figured I had pulled a fast one." Today Wertheim is both a lawyer and a full-time writer for *Sports Illustrated* and si.com.

Countless reporters enter the profession at high school basketball courts and football fields in small towns, at minor league ball fields and in hockey rinks. There is no single path to success, although hard work, curiosity and perseverance are excellent guides.

At the same time, there is no such thing as the typical sports story. Cookie-cutter approaches lead to stale, uninteresting stories. Instead, take chances and cultivate a voice as you take readers through sports events.

"You're looking at a game from a point of view," says Bob Ryan, author and award-winning writer for *The Boston Globe.* "That's the key phrase. Why would you send someone to cover a game if you're going to force them into a very rigid box of formality? You could just take the wire story."

Sports writers need be confident, taking chances like a coach or player. "I think more writing is destroyed by an abundance of caution than by risk," Stout says.

CLERKING IS A GREAT WAY TO LEARN

Many small newsrooms have high school or college students working as clerks on the sports desk. They take scores by phone from coaches. They ask questions about key plays and players. And they write. By the end of the night, a clerk may knock out more than 10 short game stories.

And by the end of a month, clerks will have honed their skills and increased their speed, making it much easier to develop a single story on deadline.

Clerking also enables younger reporters to write tight, concise stories. "Cover the game or write a feature, but it's tough to do both at the same time," says Jim Ruppert, longtime sports editor for *The State Journal-Register* in Springfield, Ill.

Typical game stories focus on action at the end of the game first because these later plays are usually most significant or most memorable. Sometimes, writers leap around, focusing on key plays as they relate to trends: a pitcher inducing several double plays or a football team making several defensive stops. Usually, plays are described when they define a trend, spark a rally, address an unusual circumstance, illustrate a storyline or change the momentum in a game. Writers, though, never record the game from beginning to end.

"The game story should tell you a little about the status of each team and the thoughts and emotions of the coaches and key players who made tonight's events happen," says Art Kabelowsky, prep editor for the *Milwaukee Journal-Sentinel*. "Anecdotes and good quotes are better than play by play."

Tell the story through the eyes of those involved. Interview as many athletes as possible. Let the reader see the plays evolve through the athletes' eyes. And complement these descriptions with your own astute observations. Of course, that means taking detailed and copious notes.

Plus, take chances. Be creative. Borrow ideas from other writers.

Ultimately, your success relies on preparation – research and detailed observation – even if you shift gears to a new main theme on deadline. "Have an idea what might be the story," says Rich Chere, hockey beat writer for *The Star-Ledger* in Newark, N.J. "But very often that does not turn out to be the post-game story. Be flexible. You cannot stick with your assumed story if something more interesting or important happens."

ON DRAMA

sports insider

I'm something of an accidental tourist in sports writing. I got bachelor's and master's degrees in print journalism but always envisioned myself as a news reporter or, perhaps, a business reporter. The first job I was offered was in features copy editing. I took it, because it was at a good newspaper where I had interned as a reporter. Within a year, they offered me a reporting position – covering high school sports. For the first couple years, I didn't see myself remaining a sports reporter for long. But over time I realized I enjoyed the inherent drama involved (someone wins, someone loses), the life stories, and the freedom sports reporters have to really develop their own writing style. These are the things that keep me going still today.

Vicki Michaelis,
USA Today

Reporting is essential in new media landscape

The skills you develop clerking and writing will serve you well no matter where technology goes. Reporters now blog at live events, post audio and video and even use social networks like Facebook and MySpace to interact with sources. These new approaches require some savvy and some technical skills, but little else has changed. Instead of printing interview responses, some reporters now post audio clips, editing these responses for length and quality, a common practice for print, TV and radio reporters. Knowing what to ask is at an even higher premium when reporters query sources through Facebook or e-mail. Vague questions will still receive vague responses, except now reporters will have to wait minutes, hours or days to pose a follow-up question. Sports reporters need to understand as much as they can about the teams, players and games they cover so they can ask detailed questions.

Writing a live game blog, or glog, is just another means of covering games that relies on a perceptive writer knowing what to look for during the action. As with anything in sports journalism, preparation is essential. The writing of these entries can be conversational and include commentary, facts and observations – sort of a hybrid that mixes game stories and columns. So, as fans increasingly rely on new media, you'll notice the best Web sites and the blogs where the reporting is the best are locations that offer new information, terrific stories and unique perspectives – not unlike the best sports sections. The technical skills may change but the journalism approaches do not.

BREAKING A LOCKER-ROOM BARRIER FOR WOMEN
(WITH THE HELP OF A LONG NOTEBOOK)

sports insider

All week long at the *Miami Herald*, there had been a tremendous buildup to the big event. There had been meetings, phone calls, more meetings.

The occasion?

I was to go into my first men's locker room that Saturday night.

The Miami Dolphins were playing the Minnesota Vikings in a 1980 preseason football game at the Orange Bowl. I was a 22-year-old summer intern at the *Herald*, between my undergraduate and master's years at Northwestern, and sports editor Paul Anger assigned me to write a sidebar on the visiting team. That required going into the locker room to interview the players after the game. The NFL still had no policy about women reporters being allowed to go into men's locker rooms; some were open, some were not, based on the whim of the team. The Vikings' locker room was going to be open that night.

The significance of the night was twofold: it was not only going to be the first time I had ever been in a men's locker room, it also was to be the first time a woman had ever been in the Vikings' locker room.

Four years earlier, my moving into a coed dorm at Northwestern University had been a bit of an issue in our household. Now I was telling my parents in Toledo about this new development over the phone.

I asked my Dad for advice.

"Just keep eye contact at all times, honey."

My father always made me smile.

The game was Saturday night, August 23, 1980. I dressed conservatively in a simple skirt and blouse. I purposely wore the skirt. It was the closest I could come to a neon sign: Warning! Here comes a woman!

The Vikings beat the Dolphins, 17 – 10. As soon as the game ended, a group of reporters was allowed into a room adjacent to the Vikings' locker room to interview their venerable coach, Bud Grant. As he spoke, male reporters peeled away, one by one, to walk into the locker room. Soon, I was alone with Grant. I asked him a few questions about the game. From watching him on TV for years, I expected him to be gruff. I couldn't have been more wrong. When we were finished, I turned toward the locker room.

"Are you going in there?" Grant asked. He sounded sincere, and not at all menacing.

"Yes."

"You really want to go in there?"

"Well, I don't want to go in, but I have to go in there to do my job."

"All right then," Grant said with a smile and a shrug. "Do whatever you have to do."

And with that, I turned around and walked into a room full of naked men.

It was worse than I thought. Not the naked men. Actually, there were very few naked bodies. The players were in various stages of undress, many still wearing their football pants.

No, I could never have anticipated the problem I was about to confront. It was a preseason game, so there were many extra players on the roster, but no names above the lockers. And even though I was carrying a flip card – the sheet given out in the press box containing all the players' names and numbers – most of the players had taken off their jerseys, so I couldn't tell who anyone was.

To further complicate matters, I also couldn't look around. If I did that, the players could accuse me of being in the locker room for the wrong reason. And that was the one thing I had to avoid.

As it was, as soon as I walked into the steamy, overcrowded room, I heard whoops and hollers from distant corners, from players I could not see:

"We don't go in the women's bathroom!"

"Here for some cheap thrills?"

I took a few tentative steps into the room, then stopped, not knowing what to do. I was stuck. It seemed like a lifetime standing there, but really was only twenty to thirty seconds when, out of the noise and confusion, a player in uniform walked up to me. It was Tom Hannon, the Vikings' fourth-year safety out of Michigan State.

"Who do you need?"

I smiled.

"Tommy Kramer," I said.

Hannon pointed to the quarterback, putting on his necktie.

I mentioned a few other players, and he pointed them out to me.

Then I interviewed Hannon because he had intercepted two Miami passes. I thanked him for his help and beelined to Kramer and the others. Every one of them was dressed except for one lineman who obviously desperately wanted to be interviewed buck naked. He didn't even bother to reach for a towel. As I moved toward him, he walked the rest of the way to me with a smirk on his face, enjoying the discomfort he brought with every step he took. I found this awkward, but not awkward enough not to do my job. I was determined to get the quotes, so I interviewed the naked guy. As luck would have it, the notebook I had brought was not the stenographer size, but an eight-and-a-half-by-eleven. With my height, looking the lineman right in the eye, when I looked down as I was writing, I saw only the notebook.

Forevermore when going into locker rooms, I carried an eight-and-a-half-by-eleven notebook, perfectly positioned.

All this interviewing, which seemed like an eternity to me, took about ten minutes. When I burst out of the locker room, I had just thirty minutes until my deadline, so I ran across the field in the now empty Orange Bowl to catch the elevator back up to the press box. I pulled out my bulky Texas Instruments computer, with its scroll of paper coming out the top. I wrote as quickly as I ever had, sent my story, then sat back and looked at a colleague sitting next to me.

"Oh boy," I said, exhaling and forcing a big smile.

Finally, I could think about what I had just been through. "I just focused on the interviews and tried to ignore all the things that were being said," I told him.

I didn't even think to retell the story of the taunts and jeers, or the naked guy. The end result was the important thing for me.

When I got home that night, I pulled out my diary.

"It was tough – not embarrassing though," I wrote. "Just did my job and got out of the locker room and wrote the story."

Christine Brennan,
is a sports columnist for
USA Today, **commentator for**
ABC News, ESPN and NPR,
best-selling author and a
nationally known speaker.

CHAPTER 2

WRITING
GAME
STORIES

G ood writing comes from solid reporting. That's no secret to anyone who reports for a living. Anybody can knock out a witty one-liner or craft a clever lead once in a while, but only dedicated reporters can deliver captivating stories, compelling insights and breaking news.

"Even the stylists like Gary Smith, Frank Deford and David Foster Wallace report the hell out of a piece," says L. Jon Wertheim, author and reporter for *Sports Illustrated.* "If you have an abundance of material, the writing part is so much easier. In my experience, the pit in the stomach comes when you have 1,000 words of material and a 2,000-word space to fill."

Before each story, reporters need to read, interview and observe as thoroughly as possible.

If there's time for another phone call, make it.

If there's an article worth reading, find it.

If you can get your hands on the rule book, read it.

If a colleague has a good scorekeeping system, steal it.

If there's a practice or event scheduled, attend it.

If there's the tiniest prospect of an interview, grab it.

If you do all this – and then, while the game's going on, you take every note you can – you'll end up with far more information than you can possibly use. That's when you'll know you're becoming a reporter.

"It's a lot of work, frankly," says Bob Ryan, sports columnist for *The Boston Globe.* "And you don't know which 5 percent you're gonna need. But it's all there if I need it."

Sportswriters write all sorts of news and feature stories, blog postings and columns, but most of them spend much of their time covering games. If writing about a game were as simple as showing up and watching, anybody could do it. Journalists, however, realize

digital assist

Create a preview package online. That's what *The Columbus Dispatch* does for the Ohio State football team, something that should be a model for all sports departments. This package includes a cover story, profiles of players from each team, rosters, schedules, updated weather reports – and five keys to winning games. Check out "Buckeyextra" at www.dispatch.com.

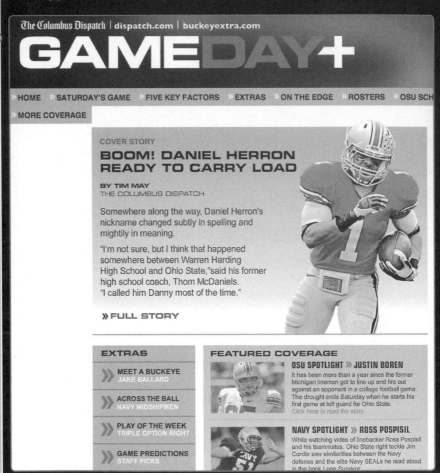

that far more is required. You need to understand the context of the event, know the key participants and have some idea what makes today's game unique – all before you ever arrive. And that's what comes after you've gotten a handle on the basics, like making sure you have press credentials and know how to read the stats.

In the chapters that follow, you'll find practical how-to information on covering every sport to which you're likely to be assigned: what to look for, whom to interview, what to ask. All of the resulting material will go into your notebook or recorder or camera – or some combination of the three. This chapter helps you figure out what to do with the information once you've collected it.

In simplest terms, your job as a sports reporter is to look for angles, leads and story-lines so that even fans who saw the game themselves have reason to revisit it through your eyes. "The goal of a newspaper story, especially in the 24/7 information age of online, is tell people something they couldn't know without reading the story," says Bryce Miller, sports editor for *The Des Moines Register.* "We talk about these key words high in stories – 'first,' 'biggest,' 'only' and 'most.' If you can use any of those words, it means your reporting has identified the uniqueness in the event. Newspapers also have the chance to take you into locker rooms, into interview areas and places quick radio/TV sound bites do not."

Fans have more access to sports information than ever before in newspapers, maga-zines, Web sites, blogs, games and highlights on TV and sports talk radio. As a result, fans' expectations have grown. Readers now expect:

▶ More sophisticated stats.

▶ To know more about trends (why a team is on a winning or a losing streak).

▶ To know what's coming next.

▶ To understand what a loss or a victory means.

▶ A unique angle, something they cannot get elsewhere.

Sports writers need to research teams and players before they even get to the field so they can prepare possible game angles. Then they need to take comprehensive notes. And, finally, sports writers need to ask questions that probe why something happened on, or off, the field.

Crafting a story on deadline is a challenge – whether the deadline is 20 minutes or two days away, and whether you became a sports writer last week or 20 years ago. "You need to keep readers interested by telling a story, whatever the story is that day, in a readable, entertaining way," says Tyler Kepner, baseball writer for *The New York Times.* Kepner cov-ers the New York Yankees, writing 150-plus game stories a season. "It's a grind because you have to churn out so many stories. But I try to make sure, when I sit down to write each one, that they're appealing for more than the dry facts."

There's no trick to meeting a deadline except to start quickly and keep plugging away. After a game, think about the most important thing you want to say – on this day, about this game – and make that point in any words that come to mind. Then, keep writing. You can always change the lead later, when you're done with the first draft; your first goal is simply to get something down.

"I don't worry myself into corners," says Glenn Stout, editor of *The Best American Sports Writing* series and author of more than 20 books on sports. "If you keep working, the words come. Writer's block is a luxury."

LEADS

Start with the most interesting story, not always with the winners or leaders. That story might be a key play, a trend, a significant stat, field conditions, post-game observations or how this game affects the future. All key information about the event should be high in the story, but you don't have to shoehorn it all into the first paragraph.

If a tennis player who's been in a long slump played surprisingly well today, you can lead with that player's story instead of the winner's. If Tiger Woods shoots 77, that's bigger news than Mike Weir leading by two strokes. A player returning from appendicitis or a heart transplant is a better story than simply reporting who leads in the opening rounds.

"Here's a good rule of thumb," says Doug Ferguson, golf beat writer for the Associated Press. "If you were to call a friend who asked you, 'What happened at the golf tournament today?' then your answer is probably the story." Substitute the word game for golf tournament, and you'll have almost foolproof advice for figuring out what's important about any game. What would you tell a friend?

Every story has an infinite number of possible leads and approaches; no self-respecting writer works by formula. To start getting a sense of your options, read as many game stories as you can. Here are some ways to start your game stories:

ON GETTING UNSTUCK ON DEADLINE

I once was stuck as a young writer for a P.M. paper. Agonized over a lead for hours, literally. I took the office electric typewriter home with me. At long last the way out hit me. I wrote a straightforward lead, finished the story, and then went up and revised the lead. I haven't had to do that since – maybe once or twice – but I vowed that day never to agonize over a lead again. Just write, and I have had few problems finding angles since. There's always an angle, it's just which one you pick and how you approach it.

Ed Bouchette,
Pittsburgh Post-Gazette

sports insider

Focus on Significant Facts

Here are a few leads that offer the most significant details simply, in a straightforward approach.

▶ "Natalie Stewart drilled nine aces, Sarah Gisondi recorded eight digs, and Ali Carlson recorded 10 assists to lead Charleston Middle School to the state volleyball championship, a three-set victory over Pekin Junior High in Bloomington on Tuesday."

▶ "Camilo Villegas holed out for an eagle early in his round and made a string of birdies late for a 9-under 63 on the easier North Course at Torrey Pines, giving him a three-shot lead Thursday in the Buick Invitational."[1]

▶ "LaShawn Merritt won a second gold medal at the world championships on Sunday when the United States blew away the field in the 4 × 400-meter relay. Merritt, the 400 champion, ran the anchor leg and took the baton home in 2 minutes, 57.86 seconds. Britain took silver in 3:00.53, and Australia picked up the bronze in 3:00.90."[2]

Describe Something

Watch players and coaches after a game has concluded – on the sideline, on the field or in the locker rooms – to find something that helps define the game just played.

▶ "Shaun Pruitt's head hung lower than anybody's at the Assembly Hall on Thursday night.

"Illinois' senior center had three opportunities from the free-throw line to give Illinois the lead in the final minutes of Illinois' game against Indiana, but the ball couldn't find the bottom of the net. After missing the front end of a one-and-one from the line with four seconds left in regulation, the senior center was unable to convert two more from the line with two seconds left in overtime.

"In a game that saw eight lead changes and nine ties, the No. 14-ranked Hoosiers were able to pull ahead for the final time in the second overtime, outscoring Illinois 14 – 10 in the final period to escape with an 83 – 79 victory."[3]

▶ "As the game clock ticked down to zero, Susie Rowe finally let up, relaxing her shoulders and skipping a bit toward midfield. The senior back flung her stick in the air like a graduation cap and embraced the nearest teammate, fellow senior Danielle Keeley.

"The Terrapin field hockey team had just won the NCAA championship. The Terps defeated Wake Forest 4 – 2 Sunday at Trager Stadium in Louisville.

"For the No. 1 Terps (22 – 2), it is the third title in four years. For Rowe, and the rest of the celebrated senior class, it was the perfect sendoff."[4]

Glogs (game blogs that cover a game as it progresses) enable a reporter to offer key plays along with commentary. Readers can chime in as well, responding to the game or to your commentary. Video, audio or a post-game story can be added as part of the package. Check out 88.3 WCBN Sports, out of the University of Michigan, for their Maize & Blog glog of women's lacrosse at http://maizeandblog .blogspot.com/2009/03/live-blog-michigan-womens-lacrosse.html.

Address Field Conditions

Sometimes field conditions or weather greatly affects a game's outcome. Look at the following example from *The New York Times:*

> PRINCETON, N.J. – The Princeton defense was not the only challenge for Harvard late Saturday afternoon. The Crimson was heading into persistent rain and a gusty wind. A pass did not seem to be such a good idea, especially on a fourth-and-1 late in the game.
>
> Or maybe it was, because Princeton did not expect it. Harvard quarterback Chris Pizzotti floated a pass to tight end Jason Miller for a first down, and the Crimson took the lead four plays later on a 6-yard run by Gino Gordon, then held on for a 24 – 20 victory.[5]

ORGANIZATION

When you have tight deadlines and you're focusing on news, use the inverted-pyramid style of writing. That means starting with the most significant information and then arranging your other points in descending order of importance so that, if the story had to be cut from the bottom, you won't lose anything crucial. In inverted-pyramid structure, you're unlikely to lead with the first quarter in basketball, the first inning in softball, or the first mile during a cross-country meet because the key plays tend to come later, when the game is close. So you would first focus on the final quarter of most football games – unless something extraordinary happened in the opening minutes.

Also, insert the score as early as possible. That could be in the second or third paragraph if you're focusing on a key moment; or that could be the first paragraph if you are filing a straightforward results story on deadline.

CONTEXT AND ANALYSIS

Tell the reader what this game means. Has a team broken an eight-game losing streak? Qualified for sectionals? Lost its fourth straight five-set volleyball match? Earned a berth in a championship?

Break down games into smaller parts, such as scoring runs in basketball, key drives in football or key at-bats in softball or baseball. For example, you might notice that a basketball team played better with a smaller lineup, going on scoring runs of 12 – 2 and 10 – 0 when the starting center was on the bench. You might notice that a soccer team dominated the middle of the field for most of the game, which will allow you to focus on the play of the center midfielders and backs and describe their efforts during these key moments. You might compare the number of running plays with the number of passing plays by each football team during the game or a key series or by each half of the game. Why did the teams run more in the second half? You could also assess how well a team ran power plays in hockey. Why did a team struggle despite having a one-man advantage? For baseball, you should address pitch selection and pitch counts. Did a pitcher rely too heavily on fastballs, especially when he was behind in the count? Or, did a team hit more grounders than fly balls?

Don't forget to convey what happens next. Has the team advanced to the next level of a state playoff? Include this information high in a story. Where does the team play next during the regular season? That detail can wait for later.

Here are some more examples:

▶ "With Kansas' 63 – 21 loss to Texas Tech, MU moved into a first-place tie in the Big 12 North with the Jayhawks by dismantling its second North opponent in as many tries this season. Mizzou previously beat Nebraska 52 – 17."[6]

▶ "Gaudin allowed a leadoff single and walked the next hitter, but escaped the inning with a ground out, a strikeout and a fly out. His sinkers and sliders moved all over, several bouncing in front of catcher Jose Molina. One hit a batter, another was a wild pitch, and three times Oakland moved a runner to third."[7]

▶ "Seattle doesn't game plan for its exhibition opponents, and the Broncos ran a heavy diet of screen plays and short routes. Their longest play of the first half was a 26-yard completion to Eddie Royal on a bubble screen."[8]

▶ "The offense is being helped this year by a couple of things, and maybe they're obvious. One: The inside players have the ability to step away from the basket and be threats unlike the center who clogged the middle in recent years. Although he didn't do it Saturday, center Mike Tisdale has shown great confidence in his mid-range jumper and so has forward Mike Davis. That opens a lot of space to get things done. Two: The Illini start three guards who have played the point at various times. Trent Meacham, Demetri McCamey and Chester Frazier can all pass the ball effectively and their assist numbers reflect the fact that sometimes they have three point guards on the court simultaneously."[9]

Key plays

Describe or cite key plays that change the outcome of a game, highlight key drives, illustrate a trend, describe how a strategy succeeded or failed and show how a player made a difference. Sometimes these events are not obvious – such as a slide into second base that broke up a double play and allowed a run to score in the third inning of a 2 – 1 game. Sometimes the big hit is not really so big, as the following story shows:

> PHILADELPHIA – There could be a lot of empty pews in Philadelphia churches on Sunday morning. The prayers of the Phillies' fans were answered at 1:47 A.M., with a slow chopper up the third-base line that gave the Phillies the victory in Game 3 of the World Series.
>
> Carlos Ruiz, who had homered in the second inning, drove in the game-winning run in the bottom of the ninth with a ball that traveled only about

40 feet. It brought home Eric Bruntlett to lift the Phillies over the Tampa Bay Rays, 5 – 4, at wild and water-logged Citizens Bank Park. The Phillies lead the series, two games to one.

"It was a great night for me," Ruiz said. "I'll remember it for the rest of my life."[10]

The Boston Globe's Fluto Shinzawa focuses on an early goal here that sparked a later rally:

In the second period, Thornton, as the third man high in the offensive zone, winged a shot on goal. Yelle, positioned in front of goalie Johan Hedberg (28 saves), positioned his stick and deflected the puck into the net at 3:37, giving the Bruins the life they needed. Then, at 5:57, Lucic scored the first of his three to tie the score at 2.[11]

In football, teams win and lose based on their ability to both score quickly and produce lengthy drives that keep the other team off the field. Sometimes, a winning drive happens at the end of a big game like the Super Bowl, when the New York Giants rallied to defeat the previously unbeaten New England Patriots during an improbable and bizarre finish. Sometimes a team wins because it put together a drive that did not yield a single point, but did run five or eight minutes off the game clock.

Or maybe the most significant drive is one that put the game out of reach, such as the following one that enabled the Florida Gators to secure a second national championship in three years:

The Sooners couldn't finish. So the Gators finished them off. The joy culminated Thursday with an impeccable 76-yard drive and a 4-yard pass from Tebow to receiver David Nelson in the middle of the end zone with five minutes to go. Tebow created third-down conversion after conversion on that drive to finish with 231 passing yards and two touchdowns to match his 109 yards rushing.[12]

STATISTICS

Cite key stats, but don't rely too heavily on them – especially in the lead. Don't just focus on the fact players scored 30-plus points, ran for more than 100 yards or recorded 20 kills in a match – unless you're writing short briefs for a sports roundup. In more fully developed game stories, stats should support other key ideas. Explain how a softball player drove in seven runs, what enabled a basketball player to grab 15 rebounds or why a miler managed to run the final two laps faster than the opening two. In golf, you might note when players go on cold or hot streaks, something that combines stats and trends. The following passage also explains why a streak ended:

> Marino did much better than that. He made seven birdies in a bogey-free third round, including five in a seven-hole stretch on the back nine. 'I got hot starting on No. 9. I made a couple putts,' Marino said. 'I've been hitting it good all week, but the last two days I didn't make much of anything on the greens. I got on a nice streak the last few holes of today.' The streak ended at No. 17. Eager to finish before dark, Marino nearly hit his tee shot into the group in front of him, a threesome hidden in the sunken fairway.[13]

Stats are essential for understanding all athletic events, but they do not tell the entire story. So be judicious about which ones to insert, and use only those that help illustrate key trends, drives or plays or those that explain how a team won or lost. Readers can easily check box scores and read blog entries to learn more about additional stats from games or events.

QUOTATIONS

Quotations allow your readers to share in the thoughts and emotions of the game's key people. They're a perfect example of why people read sports stories even if they watched the game and know the outcome: Reporters add to readers' understanding by asking questions and finding out things no one could know just by looking.

A good quote takes you inside the speaker's head and helps you see the world through different eyes. The next chapter, about interviewing, provides tips on getting people to talk to you. Once they do, learn to distinguish a good quote from a mediocre one. The fact that someone said something to you and you managed to record the words exactly does not make the quote worth using. A good quote must do more than take up space – it must advance the story. A good quote is either a unique thought or a thought expressed in unique language.

Here's Indians' outfielder Shin-Soo Choo offering insights into Jered Weaver, who pitched a shutout against the Angels: "He was using his fastball early and then throwing his changeup and curveball in hitters' counts. He was hitting the inside corner and the outside corner."[14]

How did Jelena Jankovic blow three match points to nearly lose to Elena Dementieva in the finals of a women's tennis event? "I couldn't believe, you know, that I was able to win this match," Jankovic said. "At 5 – 4 and three match points on my serve, I thought I was going to win right there. And then all of a sudden, she was going for broke on those points and she took her chances. It was tough for me to accept that I lost that game."[15]

Both quotes allow readers to get inside an athlete's head.

West Virginia football coach Bill Stewart relies on clichés in the following quote, which offers no insights into the team's season: "It's going to be a long grind," Stewart said. "It's going to be 12 hard-fought games, but it's going to be great for college football and great for this league."[16] What will be the biggest challenge for the season? How will the team cope with a difficult schedule? Ask questions to solicit quotes that are worth reading.

And, in the following quote, what exactly did Alabama football coach Nick Saban really say about his team's preseason workout? "It was good to get the first scrimmage behind us. It was good to see guys go out there in competitive situations, and see who could step their game up. Obviously, those guys who have a little more experience, have more playing time behind them and a little more confidence usually have a better opportunity to be successful."[17] Saban says very little beyond the obvious.

Don't waste space with quotes unless they offer new information, expert opinion – or are entertaining. At times, you may even want to lead with an entertaining quote:

▶ Miami coach Pat Riley after his team, then 11 – 46, won, to end an 11-game losing streak: "I feel like a mosquito in a nudist colony. I know what to do. I just don't know where to start."[18]

▶ Boston Celtics coach Doc Rivers when asked how many more games Kevin Garnett would miss with a strained abdominal muscle: "You know Doc's a nickname, correct?"[19]

▶ PGA Tour player Rory Sabbatini: "Lick the lollipop of mediocrity once and you'll suck forever."[20]

▶ Bowling Green football coach Gregg Brandon after his team lost 63 – 7 to Tulsa in the GMAC Bowl: "I don't know what happened. We were out of it before we were in it."[21]

LANGUAGE

Paint a picture. Let readers see what happened. Don't write that a tailback scored on a 25-yard run, something anybody can write from reading a box score. Instead, show how the tailback made it into the end zone.

Let readers see key passes: "The key play was Cutler's 38-yard pass to lanky receiver Devin Aromashodu. Cutler perfectly placed the pass as Aromashodu stretched out in front of Giants cornerback Bruce Johnson. It gave the Bears first-and-goal from the 1."[22]

Vivid language also enables readers to visualize key plays like this: "That's when Stroughter, the 233rd pick in April, took over. He took a kickoff at the 5, spun out of some tackles and raced down the sideline until he was pushed out of bounds at the Jaguars 20. Two plays later, McCown fired a 17-yard touchdown to tight end Jerramy Stevens."[23]

Notice the active verbs used in both passages above – "stretched," "raced," "pushed" and "fired." These verbs enable the reader to more clearly imagine what happened. Avoid passive voice – avoid using "was," "were," "is" and "are" – because the resulting wordier constructions often replace, or weaken, more visual verbs.

In addition, vary sentences for style and length. Mix longer sentences with shorter ones. Insert phrases and clauses at the beginning, middle and end of sentences – although not all at once. Don't lull readers to sleep with sentences that all sound the same, sort of like the tide rhythmically slapping against the side of a dock. On the other hand, too many short, rapid-fire sentences can jolt readers. Take chances, try different punctuation: Do whatever it takes to grab readers' attention (and retain it throughout the story.)

STORY SCAN: Breaking down a game story

On deadline, sports writers rarely have time to develop a longer theme-based story. Instead, they address key plays, trends and stats while recording who won and lost. Later versions of the story, something Associated Press calls "write-thrus," may include a feature approach, telling the story behind the final outcome. That's always a good idea. Readers can get the basic information from many sources, so look for stories that reveal something more about the game. Matt Daniels, at the time a senior at Eastern Illinois University, wrote the following story for The Daily Eastern News *after a football game.*

But, first, let's review some elements in all stories – characters, setting, plot and point of view, all driven by conflict. In sports, the larger conflict is clear – one team wants to defeat another. But what about those smaller conflicts? The rookie offensive guard matched up against the all-conference defensive end. The quarterback playing against the team that once cut him, thinking he was too old. The volleyball libero diving for kill shots with a broken left wrist. The golfer with a degenerative leg ailment struggling to play during the final holes. Or, in the story below, a rookie running back forced to play after the star runner gets injured in a key conference game. The stories are endless if you do the research and cover a beat diligently.

HEADLINE: **Adeniji Gives Warrior Effort**

BYLINE: Matt Daniels, Eastern Illinois University

Sweat trickled down Ademola Adeniji's face 30 minutes after Saturday's football game against Eastern Kentucky.

The main character is introduced

The air conditioning in the conference room he sat in at the O'Brien Stadium football offices worked fine.

But the 5-foot-10, 215-pound running back still showed the effects of the best game of his Eastern Illinois football career.

We get a brief physical description and learn he's a football player who far exceeded expectations.

The Springfield native rushed for a career-high 186 yards on 25 carries during the Panthers' 28 – 21 loss to the Colonels.

He broke tackles, used his speed to outrun defenders and used his hands, which Eastern Illinois head coach Bob Spoo said were not the best earlier this season, to catch three passes for 58 yards.

These two sentences serve as nut graf (or thesis), reminding readers the reason a reporter is writing this particular story.

"Oh, I tell you what, he really surprised me," said Eastern Kentucky head coach Danny Hope. "There were two or three times in the game where we had guys hit him in the backfield or hit on the line of scrimmage and he powered his way through."

Lead quote from another character – from an opposing coach offering a different point of view, one readers may not be familiar with through regular beat coverage.

He did this on a day with temperatures in the high-80s, unusual for an early October afternoon in Illinois, and without other healthy running backs to give him a break.

Travorus Bess was limited with a leg injury (two carries for two yards), while Ron Jordan ran once for no gain before he tweaked his right ankle again. Norris Smith didn't dress because of a lingering knee injury and fullback Chip Keys is out for the year with an ankle injury.

"In a sense, it's a running back's dream," Adeniji said of being the only healthy running back. "But certain amount of carries, certain amount of plays, so you can stay fresh to make plays – you need at least two, three running backs."

Context offered, explaining how this player earned the chance to play his best game. First quote from Adeniji offered in eighth paragraph.

But it was all for naught because it was the Panthers' first Ohio Valley Conference loss at O'Brien Stadium since 2004.

"Each week in the OVC, you've got to play game in and game out," Adeniji said. "I mean, individual accomplishment is great, but you need to come out with the 'W.'"

Adeniji's first three carries of the game did not indicate he would have a breakout game. He rushed for 3 yards on his first three rushes, but made it up for it on his fourth rush.

His 17-yard run up the middle on the Panthers third offensive possession moved the offense from their own 5-yard line to the 22.

Adeniji struck next with less than three minutes in the second quarter and the Panthers trailing 9 – 7. Adeniji took a handoff from quarterback Bodie Reeder at Eastern Illinois' own 27. He appeared to be tackled by EKU defensive lineman Andre Soucy at the line of scrimmage, but broke the tackle.

With EKU playing man coverage on the wide receivers on the outside and Colonel free safety Zach Denton the lone defender dropped deep, Adeniji had plenty of room to run.

He used his speed and cut back to the middle, past EKU's linebackers, after breaking Soucy's tackle.

With only Denton to beat, Adeniji ran past him near midfield en route to a career-long 73-yard touchdown run.

"He's a warrior," Reeder said. "He exemplifies what our entire offense needs to be. We all need to fight from the very first snap. He did that and he didn't give up the entire day."

The Panthers employed a formation they hadn't used all season in order to spell Adeniji.

Reeder lined up in the shotgun formation with five wide receivers, three to his left and two to his right.

Key moments for key player – two early runs along with a third described in greater detail. Great observations.

Quote from teammate offers another perspective on Adeniji's performance.

The formation, which Reeder said was installed during practice last week to give Adeniji a break, did not have much success.

The first time the Panthers used it, Reeder threw a backward pass to wide receiver John Gadson and EKU recovered the pass on the Panthers 11.

Eastern Illinois used it eight times and gained a total of four yards. Reeder, not known for his speed, ran two quarterback draws out of the formation and gained a total of one yard on the two draws.

One of the draws, a pre-determined play call, came with the Panthers on EKU's 4 on third-and-goal with EKU ahead, 21 – 14. Reeder was stopped at the 3, and kicker Tyler Wilke missed a 20-yard field goal to end the Panthers drive.

"Maybe I chose the wrong running lane or something like that, but just got to give credit to their defense," Reeder said. "They played well especially when we got down close to the end zone."

The warm weather started to affect Adeniji in the fourth quarter, he said.

It was evident with the Panthers on EKU's 2 with less than two minutes remaining and EKU leading 28 – 14. On first-and-goal, Adeniji's draw up the middle went for no gain. His next rushing attempt went up the middle again, but he was tackled a yard short of the end zone.

"My wind was fine, but it was my legs," Adeniji said. "You try to conserve your energy as best you can each play, but as you can see with the defense, the more you're out there, the more the heat is spreading on you. I want to run 100 percent, if I possibly can, every play."

Spoo said Adeniji's performance the last two games (49 carries for 278 yards) showed Adeniji's true ability.

"You've got to wrap him up or he can break tackles and stay on his feet," he said. "He did that again. Just a hell of an effort on his part."

Analyzes an offensive formation rarely used by the team before this game. Describes two plays and reveals number of times formation used in game.

Quarterback offers insight into previously described play.

Shows another perspective – moments when the running back had trouble running the ball.

Quote reveals more insights into the player's thoughts on these last few rushing attempts.

Concludes with overview of Adeniji's performance with a comment from the head coach.

CHAPTER 3

GETTING THE
MOST OUT OF
AN INTERVIEW

Here's what sports journalists know that sports fans may not: Journalism is not stenography, and an interview is not an ordinary conversation. In a relaxed feature interview – compared with the usual two-minute locker room rush job after the game – sports journalists might like their interview subjects to think they're having a casual conversation. But in fact that's never the case. The interviewee may be answering off the top of his head, but the interviewer must always come prepared, listen closely while simultaneously thinking of follow-up questions, and stay tuned to the computer screen in his mind as it scrolls through the story that's going to be written afterward. Interviewing is a complex, somewhat awkward process that, in the hands of a good interviewer, looks completely smooth and natural.

For sports journalists, interviews serve three main purposes: to acquire new information, to elicit an expert's opinions and to tap into a person's thoughts and feelings. To accomplish all that, the key is preparation: learning enough about the sports, teams and players to ask informed questions. You want to ask questions that yield new information and personal responses that go beyond the basics and help people see the world through the interviewee's eyes. You can't just arrive a few minutes before a game, watch it and then ask a few general questions at the end. Publications and Web sites already contain plenty of hackneyed sports writing without you adding more clichés to the pile.

The 20 chapters in this book that detail how to cover individual sports divide the process into four categories: Prepare – Watch – Ask – Write. Interviewing has its own version of the first three categories, all in the service of having something great to write about. And if there's a fourth category for interviewing, after Ask, it's this: Keep Asking.

PREPARE

A sports fan who goes to an event can simply relax and have a good time. A journalist can't. Being a sports journalist is its own kind of fun, but nobody would call it relaxing. You need preparation to understand what you're seeing in a game, and preparation to do a good interview. Read press guides, evaluate statistics and speak with people familiar with the team and the trainers.

At first, keep your notebook closed and your ears and eyes open. If you are assigned to cover a game at the last minute, you can still try to read some stories and get team stats. Great questions come from sweat and hard work.

Prepare not just yourself but the people you interview. People like to know why they're answering questions. Tell sources right away what you're looking for – for example, "I noticed X during the game, and I wanted to ask about it." This kind of statement eases the person's concerns ("Oh, no problem, I know how to talk about that.") and lets the interviewee start thinking about the topic, which means better responses and more information for your story.

Finally, of course, preparation means anticipating possible story angles, something you can do only by researching people and subjects. Interviewing is like a tennis volley, where the journalist asks questions, the interviewee answers, and the journalist responds to the answers. Without a game plan, you'll be able to hit only soft lobs, superficial questions that yield general responses not worth repeating. Before any interview, learn as much about a person or subject as possible, and prepare a list of specific questions. But remain open to new, surprising responses; be ready to scrap the pregame plan. It's easy to miss something unique that your interviewee has said because you're busy listening for the things you expected to hear.

WATCH

Interviewing is something of an out-of-body experience. On the one hand, you're right there in the room, totally focused on what the person is saying. On the other, you're also standing to the side, assessing the interview as a whole. You're listening and talking and developing new questions all at the same time: "Wait, what does he mean by that?" "How does it connect to what he said before, and to what others have said?" "What might he say if I asked X?" "If I want to use what he's saying in my story, what else might I need to know?"

So you're watching yourself, and of course you're also watching the person you're interviewing. Not all messages come from words. Keep an eye on body language. If the person

digital assist

Host live chats with coaches and players in a location online, where readers can pose questions or follow along. Afterward, post the transcripts of these chats, as *The Dallas Morning News* does. Post headlines from stories and blog entries on Twitter, along with a link, to attract more readers. But you have to tweet regularly about breaking news or readers won't stay signed up. Check out some examples at www.dallasnews.com/sports.

Live chat: Tim Cowlishaw on Dallas-area sports

10:28 AM Tue, Dec 22, 2009 | Permalink | [b] Yahoo! Buzz
Travis Hudson/Producer ✉ E-mail ✉ News tips

Join *DMN* columnist Tim Cowlishaw for a chat about the Dallas-area sports at 1:30 p.m.

Live chat: Tim Cowlishaw on Dallas-area sports	
1:12	**Travis / producer:** Go ahead and leave your questions for Tim and he will begin answering around 1:30 p.m.
1:33	Good to be here after my last pre-Christmas Around the Horn appearance. You won't want to miss it this afternoon. Let's chat.
1:34	[Comment From Tommy C.] After seeing the Giants totally dominate the Redskins last night, am I the only one that has a feeling the Redskins will give the cowboys trouble next week?
1:35	Yes, Tommy, not even anyone in the DC area expects that. Seriously, teams can go up and down rapidly from week to week. But it's hard to imagine the Redskins making a quick recovery from their most embarrassing game in years. There was no reason for them to play that poorly. At point it was 226 to minus-2 in total yards. That fake field goal just before the half a true comedy of errors. So with their injury problems, I don't see how they protect the QB against the Dallas rush Sunday night.
1:35	[Comment From JJ] Cowboys solved the kicking problems for the time being, what else needs to be fixed for the next two games?
1:37	It's kind of silly to complain about the offense but this team hasn't gone past 24 points in a long time. Once it was 24-3, they were done. Of course they should have had 3 more with the chip shot field goal. Really it's just keeping the inexplicable from happening this week to set up the showdown for the NFC East the next week.
1:37	[Comment From Tommy C.]

DRIVEN BY
demand MEDIA   dallasnews

you're interviewing keeps arms tightly crossed or shows nervousness or discomfort in other ways, and if time isn't too short, take a moment to ask easy questions or make small talk and see if you can help the person relax.

During the interview, keep watching body language to help yourself understand what the person feels most passionate, excited or upset about. Those are cues to more questions you can ask and good stories you can elicit. And don't forget your own body language. Leaning back looking uninterested or repeatedly darting glances around the room as if hunting for someone better to talk to shows a lack of respect for your interviewee. Do just what you'd do when talking to a friend: Lean in to show you care.

Ask

This, of course, is the heart of the interview: asking good questions. Every question should have a purpose. Ask questions because you really want the answers, not just to get a quote or to hear yourself speak.

Often, the simplest question is the best, says Steve Goff, soccer beat reporter for *The Washington Post.* What was the difference in the final five minutes? What did you like about your team tonight?

Simple questions encourage clear, lucid answers, even on complex issues.

Here are some more suggestions for drawing out the best information from sources:

▶ Make questions specific. The open-ended questions Goff talks about are a good way to start, to get someone talking. Then target later questions more precisely, to get exactly what you need. Did the quarterback see the lineman rushing in the play? Did the batter notice much movement on that last pitch? "Ask a straight question without beating around the bush," says Ed Bouchette, NFL beat writer for the *Pittsburgh Post-Gazette.* "And do so in a way in which you actually get someone to think and

ON WORKING A BEAT

I have always believed it behooves an editor who has assigned the reporter to walk him through as much of this as possible. The reporter should be sure to introduce himself/herself to the team publicist and, if possible, the coaches and general manager. It's OK to say you're the new person on the beat; sometimes they're new, too. Establishing the relationships, acquiring the various media guides, etc., is also helpful. And don't be afraid to ask questions. That's what you're there for.

Phil Jasner,
Philadelphia Daily News

sports insider

answer, rather than saying yes or no." Of course, you can ask yes-or-no questions but only when you are prepared to ask follow-up questions to acquire additional information.

▶ Ask athletes to summarize their performances. How did the course play? How would you describe the play of their offensive line? What were you thinking when she moved ahead 40 yards on the last lap? Did the opposing team exploit any specific weaknesses at any point during the match? You want your story to convey behind-the-scenes details, the stuff no one can get just from sitting and watching.

▶ Encourage people to tell you stories. Ask about the minute details – sights, sounds and scents as well as thoughts and feelings. Show that you're interested in everything the interviewee can remember about key moments. Listen and take it all down (or record it) because you never know which details you'll need. Then write the story much more concisely in your own words.

▶ Avoid the ultimate cliché question: "How did you feel about (winning, losing, getting hurt, whatever)?" The golfer who sank the winning putt or the batter who drilled the game-winning hit is ecstatic. The running back who fumbled near the goal line in a loss feels miserable. No surprises there. Focus on questions that yield answers your audience doesn't already know.

▶ Keep questions neutral. Your job is to find out what someone thinks, not to persuade the person to agree with you or with some preformed idea of a story. Beware of questions that begin with "Don't you think . . . ?" Most people want to be liked and will agree with you. What does anyone learn from that? The best questions produce answers that surprise you.

▶ Shut up and listen. You are not the focus of the story; nobody cares what you think. "Experts appreciate that you've done your homework and can ask intelligent questions, but they don't want to hear you talk," says Bruce Selcraig of *Sports Illustrated*. "Don't try to impress them. Let them impress you." Resist the temptation to display your expertise. "The worst habit I see in reporters is their need for analyzing the game and forcing a coach or an athlete to respond," says Chuck Gormley, hockey beat reporter for the *Courier-Post* in Camden, N.J. "The role of the journalist is not to show an athlete or coach what he or she knows, but to elicit a response from that athlete or coach."

For most people, it's a rare event to be really, truly listened to by someone who cares about what they're saying. Give the people you interview the respect of listening.

AND KEEP ASKING

Although it's always best to start an interview with a few ideas for questions, the best questions come from listening. What did the person just say? What's interesting about it? What else would you like to know? Get beyond the basic questions and beyond the basic people whom everyone interviews.

▶ Follow up. Let's say a tennis player tells you she served well today. You might ask follow-up questions like these: What about the serves felt particularly good? Had she been concerned about serves before the match? If a player says her opponent played better, ask for details. She played better in what way? With returns, footwork, serves? Whatever answer she gives, follow up by asking for more information on that specific area.

▶ Then follow up some more. Coaches say their pitchers threw perfectly, their runners were fatigued and their team was stale. What do all these adjectives mean? Did the pitcher mix it up better, throwing more off-speed pitches on 1 – 2 counts? Check with the catcher as well. Were the cross-country runners tired because a bus broke down, or because they ran three races in 10 days? Find out the reasons behind the statements. Follow-up questions usually yield more specific information and interesting stories. You won't be far into your sports-writing career before you'll read or see in another journalist's story a great detail missing from yours. If you ask the source why he didn't tell you that, here's the answer you'll almost always get: "Because you didn't ask."

ON CITING INFORMATION

sports insider

Our policy is clear. We strive not to use any material from a source unless it is critical to the story and there is no other way to get it. We do not use any information other than the facts. So a quote like, 'This deal will help reshape his image,' would not be used because it's opinion. But 'the deal is worth $150 million over five years' would be fact.

I had one case where to use source material for a story would endanger a particular source. This was a person I rely on heavily, and I determined the value of the story did not outweigh value of the source. So I sat on that one. I cannot think under any circumstances, or hardly any, that you would do anything to jeopardize a source – because if you are willing to jeopardize a source, you must not think much of him or her to begin with. And if that's the case, there would seem to be some trust missing. And if trust is missing, how reliable is the source in the first place? Sacred ground we're talking about here.

Doug Ferguson,
golf writer, Associated Press

▶ Speak with opposing teams. A forward can discuss the play of a goalie. A midfielder can assess the play of an opposing forward or midfielder. How does the other team's linebacker rate this team's running back? How nasty is your school's softball pitcher's riser? Get these other points of view.

▶ Ask sources to define unfamiliar terms. If you don't know what Fartlek training is, ask the cross-country coach to explain. If you don't know what a nickel package is, ask the football coach. They will appreciate that you want to understand the topic in more detail – and you'll be spared the embarrassment of having an error turn up under your byline. Of course, the more research you do in advance, the less likely you'll have to bother an interviewee with basic questions.

▶ Check and recheck. You're not a robot, mindlessly scribbling down whatever anybody says. Question anything that is unclear, unfamiliar or unverified. Start with the basics, like the spelling of names. John or Jon? Sarah or Sara? Before the game starts, ask team managers or assistant coaches to review the program to ensure names are spelled correctly. Often, particularly at high school and youth sports events, they are not.

▶ Play fair. If someone makes an accusation about another player or coach, go directly to that other person to get a response. People should get the opportunity to defend themselves – immediately, not days later.

▶ Build trust. If someone tells you in advance that a statement is off the record, and you agree, keep your word. Don't report it. Ever. Even if someone doesn't stop to say "off the record," you don't have to report every foul-mouthed comment made by frustrated coaches or players after a game. Allow athletes who've just spent hours competing to have their cathartic moments. Usually these don't have real news value anyway. In time, if you show judgment and discretion, coaches will trust you more, knowing they can speak more candidly about more important issues.

▶ Balance the usual with the unusual. Every team has go-to sources, players or coaches who are always ready with a lively quote or colorful sound bite. When you're pressed for time and desperate for info, it's important to know who these people are. But look too, for the quiet types, the ones who analyze intelligently but need more encouragement to speak. The best players are not always the best talkers.

Sack the clichéd responses

Athletes don't practice speaking in clichés any more than sports writers practice writing them. Yet you'd be hard-pressed to prove that statement by watching or reading a lot of sports coverage. Players frequently state the obvious: "Everyone is working hard to help the team win. You want to do well because you want your team to do well." Gee, really? Press for details. How hard are these players willing to work? Get some information on their training. Show; don't just tell. Then offer these details to readers so they can decide for themselves whether the players are really working hard.

When people use clichés, ask them to explain. Quotes should answer questions, not create them. That means asking the all-important follow-up questions if an athlete or coach offers a statement that is vague or unclear.

▶ "We are extremely eager to get back at them, to avenge our first loss of the season." What specifically has upset this person about the loss? Teams lose all the time, so why does a loss need to be "avenged"?

▶ "We have a lot of chemistry," she said. "One would think it would have been difficult to develop with more new players than returning players on the team. But I actually think it's turned out better. We all get along great and are definitely ready to start the season. We have a lot of confidence." Get some examples that reveal that the team has chemistry. In what ways are the players getting along? Ask for a story or two about specific players or plays.

▶ "My bat isn't as hot as it was a couple weeks ago, but I'm just focusing on staying consistent day in and day out. If I keep bringing energy every day, I think it will only [help] continue my success." How is this baseball player trying to stay focused? Is he doing yoga or reading hitting tips from Yogi? Is this player taking an extra 30 minutes or 100 pitches each day? Get the details.

▶ "I think it's going to give us some good momentum going into conference." This is as clichéd as it gets; the person is saying nothing. How does a victory or good performance help a team in its next game? Is this team now confident it can rally from behind in the fourth quarter? Did a point guard start making some tough passes inside? Ask for particular details so people can understand how this one game might assist the team in the future.

Interviewing the losing team is always challenging. The kicker who missed the field goal in the final minute, the pitcher who allowed the game-winning hit, the volleyball player who served the final point out of bounds – none of them is dying to be interviewed. They're angry, sad and frustrated, and going into the locker room can get you feeling the same way.

It's fine to empathize with the athletes, and – especially in the case of student athletes – to lead up to the tough questions slowly. But do ask for their unique insights into the loss. Can you describe some of the challenges on the eighth hole? What do you think happened in those last few minutes? Frequently, the tone of your voice is as important as the words you use – especially when dealing with high school and college athletes.

Don't use this approach with professional athletes who may believe they're being coddled or pampered. If you have a question, ask it. "Instead of something like, 'Jack, we know you're the greatest major champion of all time, and nothing you do at the Masters will ever change that, but do you wonder if you can still compete at your age?'" says Doug Ferguson of the Associated Press, "I went with this one, 'Is part of you worried you won't break 80?' Jack [Nicklaus] knew what we and everyone else was thinking, and he appreciated the honesty of the question."

CHAPTER 4

HIGH
SCHOOL
SPORTS

Y ou're watching the top-rated running back in your state, someone who has broken every record except one – the career yardage mark. He's eight yards shy with four seconds left to play.

The quarterback takes the snap, turns right and hands the ball to this running back, who somehow eludes a defensive tackle, cuts left, spins past another defender and runs for several more yards before being tackled between the 39- and 40-yard lines. Officially, where does the ball get spotted? Does the runner get an extra yard for going halfway to the next yard marker?

Tough choices. But ultimately, here's the answer: There are no half yards in football. If the ball is closer to the next line, add a yard.

How about this: A basketball player is one assist shy of the school's first-ever triple double. She's scored 20 points, grabbed 11 rebounds and collected 9 assists. Or was that 10? Your notes aren't clear, and no one around you seems to know. But if you're the only media person at the game, you may be the official scorer, so to speak, making these final calls.

Compiling stats for school sports is one of the most daunting tasks in sports writing. In National Football League or college football games, for instance, stats are hand delivered between quarters. Reporters covering high school football have no such help. In many cases, the student managers or parent volunteers who are keeping the stats care little about the visiting team's performance and might not record it accurately.

Know stats, know sports

Covering high school games is the traditional way to break into sports writing, and keeping accurate stats is the way to convince an editor you're worth a tryout. "Most of my young stringers are score takers who have earned a shot," says Art Kabelowsky, prep sports editor for the *Milwaukee Journal-Sentinel*. "It's a meritocracy, though; if you don't pan out, you don't pan out."

Keeping stats is a big deal, echoes Jim Ruppert, sports editor for *The State Journal-Register* in Springfield, Ill. "It is not possible to cover a game without statistics, and in a lot of ways I think it's more important to have a person more proficient in keeping stats than writing on high school coverage."

Once you land a job, remember that part of that job is keeping track of numbers. "We train our reporters and football correspondents to also be official statisticians for games," says Bryan Black, high school sports editor in Norfolk, Va., for *The Virginian-Pilot*. "We have a lot of football coaches who love to inflate their players' numbers. In addition, our deadlines are so severe that there's no way we could get high school football stats from games in the paper unless we kept them ourselves. So our reporters and correspondents are trained to do stats by official NCAA stat procedures as well as to keep a play-by-play. Our staff writers also are adept at making notes for themselves while keeping track of all this."

As you can tell from that description, keeping accurate stats is not the only challenge reporters face in covering prep sports. At games, reporters also need to keep precise notes, track down sources after the game and then file a story – even when there's no press box.

The prep beat is far different from college and pro beats, where sports information directors distribute play-by-play, run to locker rooms and collect quotes, set up post-game interviews and offer official stats, allowing writers to focus more on telling a story.

Prep writers also deal more directly with readers – especially those readers who are the parents of players. Michael Phelps' mom or Derek Jeter's dad is not going to call you to complain about a story. But parents of high school athletes will definitely call if they don't like something you wrote, if you failed to mention their kids' names, or if you simply don't see their child as a star the way the parents do.

"You cannot win covering high school sports, even if you say something nice," says *The Boston Globe* columnist Bob Ryan – who, like many sportswriters, started his career on the school beat. "It's the worst beat. Underline it. Double underline it. It's never enough. Parents will get angry. Even if you say something nice about one kid, another parent will say, 'What about my kid?'"

Yet there's no greater proving ground for a reporter than the prep beat. And on a good day, it can be a lot of fun. "It's an extremely fast-paced and hectic way to work, but

ON OWNING THE PREP BEAT

The best thing a reporter can do on the preps beat is to go out and own it. Get to know the important people at the schools you cover and build relationships with them. The more contact you're in with those people, the better your chances of finding a good feature story or knowing the news of coaching changes or other things like a change in conference affiliations when those breaking news things occur. The worst thing a reporter can do on the prep beat is listen to the parents, most all of whom have their own agenda. If complaints come about coverage (or lack of), it's best for those reporters to let their editor handle those people, many of whom are irrational.

Don O'Brien,
Quincy Herald-Whig (Ill.)

ur very best reporters love it; they get an adrenaline rush out of it," says Black of *The Virginian-Pilot.* "There's nothing like covering high school football, especially when there are talented athletes on the field."

Beginning journalists who view high school coverage as rinky-dink and beneath their dignity are making a big mistake. For one thing, no reporter gets the big assignments until he or she has learned to do a killer job on the smaller ones. For another, these days even large news organizations are putting more emphasis on prep coverage, as local newspapers have done for years. No matter how great a job ESPN and other big outlets do on the national scene, they'll never match local journalists' knowledge of their local leagues and communities – and fans of college and pro sports will never match high school fans for sheer enthusiasm. For most newspapers, high school coverage counts far more in attracting readers than does major college or pro coverage.

PREPARE

- Once you're hired as a prep writer, call coaches and athletic directors in your area to introduce yourself during a short chat.

- Verify spellings of all names. School rosters frequently contain typos, so check with an assistant coach or manager.

- Speak with both coaches before the game begins, to set up a time and place for post-game comments.

- The visiting team often loads onto buses from the field and leaves quickly after a game ends, so speak with players and coaches on that team first.

- ▶ Talk with players first, coaches second. Learn more about the game from those who played it.

- ▶ Check state high school athletics Web sites for scores across the state, determining the next opponent for any school that's advanced in the postseason. Plus, you can learn scores – and, perhaps, stats – of other key games.

WATCH

Stay out of the press box when you can. You'll get a far better perspective by walking the sidelines for many sports, such as football, soccer and track and field, than by sitting in a press box, high above the action. Is the ball at the 39 or 40? Did the hurdler scrape the final bar? You usually can't tell from the press box.

Crowds and commotion might drive you out of the press box anyway, since some schools allow anyone to wander in and out. "More times than I'd like to remember, I have asked school officials why they call it the press box if there's no room for the press,' Ruppert says.

ASK

- ▶ Most prep editors prefer than a reporter speak to at least two to three sources. Deadline drives this, though.

- ▶ Night games can end less than an hour before deadline. That means getting quotes from players may be difficult unless you grab a player before the coach's post-game locker room speech starts.

- ▶ Treat high school athletes far differently from professional players who are paid to perform. Most high school athletes won't play past high school. Most high school athletes play for fun. And most high school athletes aren't as mature or as savvy as older athletes are. So, if a prep player says something that's ridiculous, ignorant or mean-spirited, rephrase the question: "Did you really mean to say that? . . . " If the person strongly restates that opinion, then you can use it, if it's newsworthy. Otherwise, leave it alone.

WRITE

Don't be overly critical of high school athletes. That does not mean you should make excuses for poor plays. You can write that someone fumbled a ball, struck out with the winning run on base or missed a key free throw. But don't say that these kids choked or blew it. That's especially unfair for a teen who's still learning the game.

Each prep game has something unique about it; each has its own story. It's not always easy to see this as you're standing in the sleet on yet another weekend afternoon, missing yet another get-together of family or friends because you have to work. To psych yourself up, remember that teams and fans care passionately about this game and will be checking online as soon as they get home, eager to read your story. Printouts and newspaper clips will earn a place of honor on family refrigerators and in players' scrapbooks.

You'll have the story for your own scrapbook as well, and every story you write paves the way for future stories. "Working for a smaller paper will help you improve your game," says Kabelowsky of the *Milwaukee Journal-Sentinel*. "Even if you are writing for a weekly, find out what the daily paper's deadline is and try to write your story to meet that deadline. It's good practice."

CHAPTER 5

BEYOND GAMES:
DEVELOPING AND
WRITING FEATURES

Residents of a small Texas town are feeling uneasy about the high school girls basketball coach, a woman who turned a marginal program into one of the best teams in the state. She was named coach of the year several times, and teacher of the year once. But the school board fired her. You're a journalist, and you wonder why. People in town had praised her time and again. But, you learn, all that happened before the coach moved in with another woman.

A young girl wants to be a boxer, but her dad fears for her safety. In a dirty, cramped gym in East Los Angeles, you walk near the ring where she's training and notice she's the only girl in the place. You smile at her dad and quietly take it all in. You can't know then, but by hanging around for weeks, you'll find out: Boxing is salvation for this preteen – and also for her father, a former gang member trying to get his own life in order.

A former National Football League superstar has withdrawn from society, skipping Super Bowl festivities (and pretty much everything else). He was among the toughest defensive backs ever to play the game; then, one day, he seemingly vanished. You learn that he lives in the remotest part of a remote Hawaiian island. You decide to spend several days with this former football star, a man whose toughness on and off the field is matched only by his desire for privacy.

As those stories – from *Texas Monthly,* the *Los Angeles Times,* and the *South Florida Sun-Sentinel* – show, sports journalism involves much more than writing about games. Sports reporters also write about individual athletes and coaches, teams and schools and towns. They craft explanatory pieces about equipment and strategy and develop stories about overcoming obstacles. In the stories above, sports writers went beyond game coverage to find stories that extended outside the lines and the ropes.

Features and columns and all the other kinds of writing that go beyond "this happened on the field today"

give writers a chance to explore new territory, develop a voice, and grab readers with the real drama of life. They also give you opportunities to try using multimedia elements to tell stories. (Check out the audio slideshow on boxer Seniesa Estrada, narrated by *Los Angeles Times* writer Kurt Streeter.[1])

Tips on feature writing could, and in fact do, occupy shelves full of books. In this chapter you'll find the basics to get you started pursuing the stories that are all around you. When you're new to journalism, it's tempting to think that writing features must be way easier than covering news or games. Get over that idea. People will read a game story for the information, no matter how you write it. But nobody is required to read a feature. They'll choose to read your stories only if you take them places and show them people and things they couldn't reach on their own. (That's almost literally true in the case of football player Jake Scott, who was tracked down by reporter Dave Hyde.)

There is no set way to write a sports feature, but finding a compelling story is a great way to start. Writing a sports feature is a lot like writing a fictional short story – except, of course, that journalists can't make anything up. The elements, however – scene, setting, character, dialogue, description – are much the same.

Most stories can be boiled down to this: Someone wants something, but someone (or something) stands in the way. Conflict is the key to good storytelling. And the only way to get the facts and emotions and details you need to show people is through good, old-fashioned reporting.

Let's look first at some reporting issues related to developing and writing features. Then we'll address storytelling techniques.

"The most important thing is finding good material. That sounds a little simplistic, but it's true. What makes a good feature? Again, no easy answer. Sometimes it's the person. Sometimes it's the situation. And sometimes you're surprised at what you find. Here's a story: I had been around University of Miami football coach Randy Shannon as a player and an assistant for about 20 years. I didn't know him well. But we'd talk occasionally. When he was named Miami's coach, I heard a story from someone in the school that stunned me: Three of Shannon's siblings had died of AIDS, his father had been murdered and another brother stole his identity. I asked him about this and, reluctantly at first, he talked. We talked some more. I talked with others. He saw I was serious and opened up some. He shared his vision of trying to help kids who came from the streets the way he had. It took several weeks in the summer of 2007, working between other stories. It was a tough feature to do because he was a very private person."

Dave Hyde,
South Florida Sun-Sentinel

REPORTING IS VITAL

Before writing a feature, figure out why you want to do it. Your editor is sure to ask you, and your readers are sure to wonder. What's the news angle, the peg? In other words, why write it now?

For example, if you're pitching a profile, why now? Did a player recently perform well, scoring 40 points or striking out 15 batters? Has a coach recently faced a personal challenge or been hired? Some stories are connected to news events – a coach gets hired or fired, a player gets injured or breaks a record, or players are tampering with bats in order to hit the ball farther and harder.

Perhaps the person you're writing about is connected to an anniversary of an event (like the hockey gold medal game in the 1980 Olympic Games) or an amazing season (like the 1972 Dolphins, the first undefeated NFL team). Perhaps someone just died, so you are writing a more detailed obituary, one that runs days or weeks after the actual death. Or maybe you are writing a story on an issue, like composite bats, connected to a recent event such as when a softball pitcher was hit in the face with a line drive.

Features, especially the longer narratives, are all about rolling up your sleeves and doing some hard work. You can't talk to only one or two people and get enough information to write a fully developed feature. And you can't just sit down and offer your opinions for a column. Reporting is at the heart of any real journalism. Here are a few points to remember as you develop your stories.

Check out venues in your area, such as softball stadiums, basketball gymnasiums, Little League fields, fishing areas or golf courses. *The Boston Globe* assembled a guide to New England's minor league ballparks that blends photos, lists and extended cutlines. You might even add audio with photos of nonathletes such as a peanut vendor or an announcer on the public address system. Check out "Minor League Ballparks of New England" at www.boston.com/travel/explorene/specials/minors/parks_of_new_england/.

Prepare

You'll need to develop new information, not just rehash what others have published or said. To find a fresh angle, you'll have to determine what's already been written about a person, team or topic. Check Web sites set up by the teams themselves, along with those produced by news organizations and by individual players. In addition, read newspaper and magazine stories and check blogs related to these topics. Don't forget to check Twitter feeds and Facebook posts to determine what's new and what's old. Eventually, you'll have several potential angles or story ideas. As always, verify any information you find in blogs or publications or hear in conversations.

Observe

Once you've determined the main characters in your story, look for the main places where significant scenes are likely to happen. To gain a different perspective, visit places away from the playing fields, such as a player's old high school, a river where a rower trains or a coach's home or office. What's on the walls of the coach's office? What does the high school basketball gym smell like? Whom does a player pal around with away from the field? These details may lead to a new, and fresh, angle. Fill your notebook with specific details about places, people and things even though you'll probably never use 10 percent of the information – if you are reporting properly, that is. But you will have the details needed during the writing process.

Ask

You'll also need to talk to a wide range of people, everyone from friends to foes to team-mates to opposing players and family members. One- or two-source feature stories are usually not worth printing. A hulking defensive lineman says he's a lady's man? Ask his mom. A volleyball libero says she can always spot where players are about to spike the ball? Ask opposing players and coaches to verify this. A coach says she's haunted by a childhood event? Call her friends and family to get more details. Don't forget to collect stories that you can piece together in your own narratives. Ultimately, you may not even quote some of these people, but their insights will enable you to find the proper perspective or some compelling angles. If you have time to speak with someone else, do so. Struggling with information? Call a source again. Your job is to collect information and to gain perspective, which means speaking to as many people as possible. So get back on the phone, go to the gym or head to a local hangout, and keep talking. Good writers often say they don't stop reporting until they've heard the same thing three times.

LEARN STORYTELLING TECHNIQUES

Journalists can't make things up. But they can borrow elements used by screenwriters, playwrights and novelists, approaches used in books as varied as *War and Peace* or *The House at Pooh Corner.*

Conflict

Conflict is the key to storytelling. In games, a player or team wants to beat another. Off the field, a player may be working toward getting better despite some physical ailments, or a coach could be trying new approaches to help the team win. Perhaps a young girl wants

---

to be a professional boxer even though females usually don't get that opportunity. Or the story could be about a man who got a lung transplant after a young athlete committed suicide – and how both the girls' father and recipient of the lung received their "second wind" as they learned how to run and breathe again in their own ways. If you cannot find the conflict, you probably don't have a story.

Pamela Colloff, who wrote the story about the fired high school basketball coach and whose work has been featured in *The Best American Sports Writing* series, says the main conflict should be revealed early in any feature. "It's important to establish what the stakes are in the story pretty early on," Colloff says. "I'm not talking about a nut graf. I'm talking about giving the reader a reason to read the story. Who cares about a girls' basketball coach in some small town in Texas? The writer must establish early on why the story's main character is worthy of the reader's time."

Character

Your main character (or protagonist) needs to be a fully developed person, a person literary critics would call dynamic or complex – not flat and simple. Show this person through actions, physical description, dialogue and comments by others. Do not paint this person as all good or all bad. We are all illogical, inconsistent people. There's nothing wrong with revealing this, if these points are relevant. Speak to as many people as possible to learn about this person.

Dave Hyde uses several techniques to define his protagonist, the mysteriously vanishing NFL player, in his story "Where's Jake Scott?" In this passage, Hyde first uses physical

description, and then a mixture of action and dialogue to further introduce the reclusive ex-Super Bowl most valuable player.

At 61, he's still trim. He's completely bald. Oversized glasses cover his face like two storm windows. And he's smiling, thank God. I double-check to be sure.

"Hi, how you doing?" he says.

He shakes hands. He talks in a soft, friendly voice still rooted in Georgia. He says, "I'm not hard to find." He says, "I don't want a story written." He says, "If you'd ask questions, then I'd have to tell the truth." He says, "I live the simplest life you can imagine – wake up every day and decide whether to golf, fish or have a drink."

From this front porch, the Pacific peeks through palm trees across the quiet road. Warm air rides in on a noonday breeze. Scott puts one foot up on the railing and allows the conversation to drift. He tells how his home sat alone on this road when he arrived in 1982. Now the world has joined him. A small place beside him just sold for $1.9 million. A big lot across the road, against the ocean, went for $29 million.

He says, "That's how it goes." He says, "Beautiful here, isn't it?" He says, "Too bad my boat just had its propeller damaged or I'd take you out fishing – just you and me, not for a story."[2]

Setting

Put the person in a place, a physical location, whenever possible. Sometimes you can describe the setting before you describe the profiled person, especially when the setting takes on the role of a character. That's the case in Colloff's story about the woman fired as a high school girls basketball coach. The town whose morals and beliefs clash with those of the coach is introduced in the beginning of the story, which is titled "She's Here. She's Queer. She's Fired" and was selected as one of the best sports stories of 2005.

"I focused on the town as a character, and I started the story by describing the town – for a number of reasons," Colloff said. "The first one was a practical consideration: It wasn't basketball season when I was reporting this story, so my options for an opening scene were more limited than they might have been otherwise. More importantly, though, I thought it was essential to ground the reader in the place where this happened, so that the reader could better understand: (1) the enormous importance that high school sports has in such a tiny and remote place, and (2) the cultural/political landscape that Merry Stephens worked in."

Setting is not always so significant, but putting a person in a place allows the reader to follow more easily. So record as many details as possible.

In Bloomburg there isn't a stop sign, or even a blinking yellow light, at the center of town – just a bend in a winding two-lane road that meanders through the woods toward the Arkansas state line. Every now and then a logging truck piled high with pulpwood rumbles by on its way to the paper mill, scattering twigs and pine needles onto the blacktop below. Otherwise the town is quiet. There is no Dairy Queen, or any diversions to speak of; the closest movie theater is thirty miles away, in Texarkana. Even Bloomburg's 1A high school is too small and too poor to have its own football team. But every November, when teenagers scrawl "Go Wildcats!" in white shoe polish on the back windows of their pickups, the boys' and girls' varsity basketball teams try to make the town proud.

Bloomburg never had much to brag about until six years ago, when the school district hired a young coach out of Arkansas named Merry Stephens. She was the first female coach in Bloomburg history, and also one of its toughest. When just seven girls tried out for the Lady Wildcats during her first year in Bloomburg, Stephens had them practice by playing against the boys. If they were used to making fifty layups at practice, she told them to do twice as many. It wasn't long before the Lady Wildcats started winning. Stephens led the team to the state playoffs three times, and in 2004, when the team had grown to 25 players, the Lady Wildcats made it all the way to the final four. "Half the town went with them," said one parent of the six-hour drive to Georgetown, just north of Austin. "We'd never had a team do so well." The Lady Wildcats didn't win the championship, but they were welcomed back as heroes. When the team's bus pulled into town, people stood on their porches and cheered, and the volunteer fire department led an impromptu parade.

But even after the local Wal-Mart named Stephens Teacher of the Year and the district had chosen her as its Coach of the Year no fewer than three times, many residents felt uneasy about her. Stephens, it was rumored, was a lesbian. And in an area where ministers preach against homosexuality from the pulpit and tracts denouncing the theory of evolution sit next to cash registers in convenience stores, Stephens' sexual orientation was not an issue that most residents of Bloomburg, or its school board, could overlook. In December, just nine months after the Lady Wildcats had gone to the finals, Stephens was abruptly put on leave. The woman she lived with, a teacher's aide and school bus driver named Sheila Dunlap, was dismissed. The board's actions made this otherwise placid town of 374 people erupt in controversy and became the central issue of the school board election in May. "It's divided this town," said history teacher Thresha Jones. "You've got people who feel that Merry and Sheila were done wrong. And then you've got people who think that what the school board did was the only right thing to do."[3]

Voice

Voice is the person behind the page, the reason you and your best friend could write stories on the same subject and they'd sound entirely different. Journalists should have a voice like any other writers. Like a column, feature stories can include commentary and insights from the author. Perhaps the voice of the story is the voice of the person being profiled, where you tell the story through that person's eyes, or it could be in the voice of the person's 10-year-old sister. Do not be afraid to take chances.

"A voice is crucial," says Dave Hyde, whose piece "Where's Jake Scott?" won an Associated Press Sports Editors writing award in 2006. "It makes it easier to write. It also makes it easier on the reader – you tell them what's important through the voice. I typically don't go first person in long features. Off the top of my head, the Jake Scott story is the only one in which I've used the first person. Some people can pull it off well. It just feels forced to me. The reason for using first person in Jake's story was mainly because this is a guy who hadn't been interviewed in decades and was living in this exotic locale, so I thought the first scene had to be me approaching the home and trying to interview him. What was it like? How did he take civilization infringing on his life? And I was nervous before doing it myself, because I didn't know how he'd take it and, let's face it, the paper was spending some good money to send me there in hopes I could pull it off. So that first scene would set up the rest of the story, I figured. I used the first person through the story – trying not to overplay it – because it was easier to tell his story when he was introducing me to his friends: the taro farmer, the poker player. It wasn't that I needed to be in the story. It was just that it was the best vehicle to show who he was and how he was living now."

SPORTS GENRES

Like any writing genre, sports writing can't be easily categorized – especially today when you also have blogs, glogs, slideshows and other multimedia presentations. Then there's also game precedes, sports profiles, columns, Q&A pieces, and all sorts of list and analysis presentations. Sports coverage has always evolved, but the following two categories have remained stalwarts in the sports media lineup.

Sports Profiles

People are complex. So writing about them should not be easy.

Get as much access as possible. Let this person know you would like to hang out at practice, attend meetings and speak with other people in their lives. Be candid. Be honest. (And later, when writing, be fair.)

Every sports feature should include the same elements as a really good feature story. The fact that it is a sports story makes it no different. First and foremost, there must be an attention to detail that quickly convinces the reader that the writer knows what he or she is talking about. A writer should accrue as many specific, revealing details as possible. This helps establish the writer's authority, makes for richer writing, and helps ground the reader in the characters and place where the story is unfolding.

Pamela Colloff,
Texas Monthly

This way, the person profiled will not get worried when you're around so much. You might also get some suggestions for new story angles.

Spend time with the person to be profiled. Hang out – watch practices, attend meetings, follow the person across campus, go to lunch together. Observe and take some notes, even if you can only do so mentally.

If a coach has been vilified in the press or on a Web site's fan forum, address those points, even if they were unfair. You can reveal that these comments were unfair through solid reporting. You also need to address aspects of this person's life that are not favorable. If a person is a known alcoholic, ask her how she deals with that each day. If this is not well known, ask whether she would be willing to share her thoughts on this topic. We do not want to skewer people for their vices and faults, so we need to be empathetic in dealing with them.

The person profiled should be the last person you speak with. Gather stories first from others who are less guarded in offering information and insights. Friends and family are usually more than willing to gab about one another.

"What you can do is show you're a person and try to show you're credible," Dave Hyde says. "Right now, I'm working on a story about Bill Parcells' coaching tree. There are several NFL coaches on it. What I am sure to do in setting up the interview is mention two things: (1) Parcells knows about this story – this happened because one p.r. person called him and asked him (to my surprise). So I learned to get that out of the way first; (2) I mention others I've talked with. Again, that allows the person I'm trying to interview to see others are talking. There's a phrase I heard once: 'The more you know, the more you'll get.' The more you know about a story and can tell the person you're interviewing, the more that person is going to tell you. He or she will see you have some information and so won't be so hesitant to talk."

Sports Columns

Columnists are reporters with an opinion. The best columnists are also keen observers, precise writers and excellent storytellers. Frequently, we forget that readers love stories. But that is difficult to do in 15 – 20 inches or 500 – 800 words.

A good sports columnist should offer meaningful insights, cover sports ignored by others, offer cultural criticism and analyze games in considerably more depth than the average fan. A sports columnist should, at different times, afflict and comfort us. A sports columnist needs to write with style and grace, should have strong opinions (but be willing to sharpen them with facts), and should offer fresh perspectives. Don't forget that sports are intended to entertain, so have some fun while writing columns for fans. Don't write a column if you are only mildly interested in the topic – be as passionate as your readers, the fan(atics) who follow these players and teams.

At the same time, columnists have to know the teams better than fans to avoid making statements that are either implausible or simply laughably wrong.

"Before long, readers lose their faith in the writer's knowledge," says *The Palm Beach Post* sports producer Scott Andera, "and will either actively avoid reading the columnist's work or spread the word to other knowledgeable readers that the columnist doesn't know what he/she is talking about."

Columnists frequently write opinion pieces, offer notes, or playfully address an issue, but they can also tell stories – an approach mastered by sports writer Bill Plaschke.

One more thing: write locally. Focus on teams and events you report on in your town or on your campus, not about the regional pro sports franchise where your information will be secondhand. Give your readers insights into teams and players they cannot get elsewhere, like the volleyball team's top front row player or a field goal kicker on the football team. Readers want commentary on their local teams, and they want good stories, regardless of whether they are about the Los Angeles Lakers, the New York Yankees, or the Cypress Lake High School Panthers.

Writing a column is not easy, as anyone who has written one can attest. You can't claim anonymity or objectivity. The words are your thoughts and beliefs. The words are you. So, before you head out to write your next column, consider some of the points addressed at the start of this piece. But also know: To find great columns, you'll need to put in some time – on a beat, at practices and at games. Coaches and athletes will then see that you are as dedicated as they are, not just some reporter stopping in for a quick peek. You'll get much better insider information this way. Watch intently. Speak (and listen) to not only the athletes but also the trainers and groundskeepers hanging around the fields. And make sure you do the research.

Writing a sports column can be challenging and time-consuming. But your efforts can make a difference in the lives of your readers.

"Like most of us, I became a journalist because I wanted to touch people," Bill Plaschke of the *Los Angeles Times* told young journalists at a national high school convention. "I wanted to make them laugh. I wanted to make them cry. I wanted to leave them angry. I wanted to make them think. In some professions, one might not elicit that range of human emotions from a customer in 20 years. In column writing, it can all happen in the same 20 inches. Such is the beauty of our craft. One cannot just examine and report on a landscape but, however slightly, change it. One can not just touch readers, but embrace them and shake them."

General columnists are losing ground to beat-based columnists and bloggers, which can also create challenges for column writers. Few people know a team better than a beat writer, but how does this beat writer retain personal objectivity after writing blog posts, tweets and columns filled with opinion and jokes?

"In a world filled with blogs and opinion on talk radio and on cable television, there does seem to be a pretty good craving for expert analysis – the real insight of someone who is there," says Tom Jolly, sports editor of *The New York Times.*[4]

But the focus for writing these opinion pieces should not change. Writers still need to offer pieces that are reflective, thoughtful and reported well.

"Once you have the reporting," says Scott Andera, "the rest comes down to good writing ability and a simple mantra: Get in, make your point, back it up and get out."

CHAPTER 6

BLOGGING: FINDING A UNIQUE PERSPECTIVE

J ason Sobel may not have met the Dalai Lama, but he found a sports journalist's version of total consciousness when he was covering the 2007 Masters golf tournament. Unlike Carl Spackler in the movie "Caddyshack," Sobel didn't have to caddy for the 12th son of the lama to gain that clarity.

Instead, as golf editor for ESPN.com, Sobel blogged live from golf's first major event of the year – writing more in one day than he normally would have in four. Along the way, he noticed things he'd never have focused on in traditional stories, and he wrote with a personal perspective and a humorous tone that wouldn't have made it into the print edition of most magazines and newspapers. But that's the point, really. Blogging is supposed to be different.

Here's how Sobel started his blog for Friday's second round at the Masters:

> 8 a.m.: Welcome back to the Masters. I'll be your tour guide for Round 2 today. On our trip through the wild world of Augusta we'll see a few underdogs, some guys playing chicken and one prowling Tiger. Keep an eye out: We may even witness the rarest bird of all – the, uh, birdie. (Don't worry, the puns will get better as the caffeine kicks in.)[1]

Overall, Sobel wrote about 35,000 words in four days, usually posting something every three to five minutes from early morning to early evening.

"That took about ten years off my life," he says.

In blogging, Sobel still covered the basics – player performances on select holes, leaderboards, analysis. But he also described what happened off the course, tested readers with golf trivia, and explained proper course attire for fans. He solicited golf jokes and

"Caddyshack" references, inviting readers to make him laugh out loud if they wanted their comments included on his live game blog, or glog.

The live blog generated thousands of e-mail responses for ESPN.com, far more than the dozen or so he receives during most other tournaments. "It was a lot of work," he says, "but it paid off."

As a blogger, Sobel did the job of at least four people. Besides reporting, he edited, posted and offered commentary usually heard on TV or radio.

He was a reporter and a columnist.

He was an analyst and a stats geek.

He was both solemn and irreverent.

In the end, Sobel bridged the gap between old-school reporting and new media.

"I wanted to tell the story informally," Sobel says, "and not be so insider-ish. I wanted to offer some quick thoughts."

Here's a little-known secret about blogging, something the talented but humble bloggers rarely mention. To live-blog well, one must have considerable knowledge of the subject at hand. A fan who has watched a few golf events and read a little about the players on the PGA Tour wouldn't have a clue how to blend stats, anecdotes and analysis the way an experienced journalist like Sobel does.

Consider the knowledge it took to write these two posts during the Masters. Someone posting comments online every few minutes can't take time to look this stuff up. Experience matters.

By the way, Wetterich's rise through professional golf is akin to if Gary Coleman had won that California gubernatorial race . . . and was named President of the United States a year later.

Eighteen months ago, Wetterich was toiling away at Q-school. He made it through, got hot during a six-week span last season during which he won the Byron Nelson, made the Ryder Cup team and now he's giving interviews in Butler Cabin. Even Tiger can't say he did all of that.

2:04 p.m.: Staring at the leaders, it finally hit me: This is the Masters, it's playing like the U.S. Open . . . and we have a PGA Championship leaderboard.

It really is, with a bunch of guys who aren't necessarily household names, but aren't bad players, either. Sort of like what we usually see at the year's final major, where it's just an eclectic, unpredictable leaderboard. A leaderboard only a diehard could love.[2]

But not every blog has to come from experience. FanNation.com, for example, has an eclectic mix of blogs from both veteran journalists and fans who address issues ranging from college basketball to ultimate fighting. *Sports Illustrated* bought a stake in this blogging Web site, which gets about four million unique visitors each month.

SB Nation, which partners with Yahoo.com, is another portal for sports blogs that offers regular beat coverage of every major professional sports league – and coverage of more niche sports as well.

Will Leitch, a novelist and sports journalist, turned Deadspin.com into one of the most popular sports blogs, attracting more than 700,000 readers a month with its mix of news, gossip, commentary and smart-ass remarks. Here's another lesser-known fact about bloggers: The best of them are erudite, something they don't always want others to know. They're just as likely to mix in references to farts as to Shakespeare, politics or sports history, all in one paragraph. Even people who don't immediately understand every reference can still follow along.

BLOGS ARE HERE TO STAY

Some bloggers rant, rave and rip into teams, leagues and players. Other bloggers act more like devout fans, rationalizing mishaps on the field and making excuses for misdeeds off the field. Bloggers can no more be stereotyped than the average sports fan.

Critics argue that many sports blogs are widely read but not worth reading, that blogs stream mostly sports-centric nonsense, allowing anyone with a computer to air grievances and spout opinions. Of course, views depend on whom you're asking – those who believe sports should be covered in a more traditional manner or the millions of fans who read these blogs each day.

ON STARTING OUT

sports insider

New media literally landed me this job with USAHockey.com. I was a print reporter and moved into online because that's where a better paying job was. I work solely online now and do some random freelancing for print, but for the most part its all online. Magazines and newspapers are going to have to work hard to catch up because I feel there are a lot of managers out there wanting to stick to a print formula in a digital world. If you're just entering the field, diversify as much as possible.

Cameron Eickmeyer,
USAHockey.com

One thing is certain, though: Blogs are not going away any time soon. These days, fans watch sports on TV while following along online – maybe simultaneously visiting some of their other favorite sports sites. Fans are used to interactivity in all things, and they expect the same from sports journalism.

ESPN and CBSSports.com regularly glog major league baseball, National Football League, National Basketball Association and National Hockey League games. The NHL was among the first of the pro sports leagues to embrace bloggers, realizing that any kind of coverage could only increase interest – and attendance – for its pro hockey franchises. Bloggers regularly report on nearly every NHL franchise

College papers have started to live-blog football and basketball games. Elsewhere on the Web, you'll find live blogs for auto racing and tennis. Pick a sport, and at least several people are blogging it. Blogging is another way to convey information for readers – and a way to help writers see more.

"Your powers of observation are doubled and tripled when you live-blog," Associated Press baseball beat writer Ben Walker told The Poynter Institute. "You see things and look for things that you would not look for in a story. You might look at a situation in a different way."[3]

CARVING A NICHE

Blogging today resembles sports writing in the 1920s, when that genre started to evolve. In some ways, blogs emulate those pre-1920s stories in that both of them are running narratives that begin with the first pitch, drive or kickoff and conclude on the final play of the event. Game stories in those days read more like short stories with a beginning, middle and end – and they were sometimes told in first person. Like those older stories, blogs include personal opinion. And like more modern game stories, blogs address trends, key plays and analysis.

Live game blogs are only one way to cover sports events. Sometimes several beat writers contribute to an overarching theme, like *The New York Times'* Bats blog where the paper's four baseball beat writers offer analyses and updates primarily on the Mets and Yankees. Experienced journalists like Jason Sobel and Bruce Feldman blog golf and college football, respectively, offering insiders' viewpoints in a style that average fans can understand. In some ways, these blogs are hybrids of the news stories and columns you see in the newspaper.

Each of these blogs is narrowly focused. Niche is essential to blogging. Nobody's covering Little League in your town? Volleyball coverage at your school is nearly nonexistent? Start a blog. Even if you have a small staff, you can start a blog that covers sports in general at your university, although it might be better to break out blogs for your most

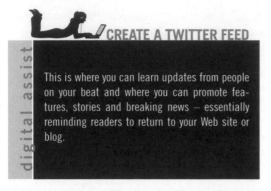

popular sports – usually football and basketball.

Dan Woike, who covers Southern Cal for Rivals.com, says his readers don't care so much what's happening in the rest of the college football world. They want info on their team, USC. He doesn't focus on national or league issues unless he can localize how those issues affect Southern Cal athletics.

If a softball pitcher from Arizona State gets arrested, Woike would blog about how the arrest might affect the Trojans' chances in a scheduled game. He wouldn't write a straight news story saying that a top-rated team had lost its top player; plenty of other media outlets exist to do that.

Though blogs don't have stringent deadlines, most professional journalists try to post something as soon as an event concludes, adding newer details after speaking with coaches and players in the locker room. This resembles an old process in which reporters used to file quick game stories for a newspaper's first edition and then keep revising the story for later editions through the night.

"You have to bring the latest information as soon as you get it," says Greg Bedard, Green Bay Packers beat writer for the *Milwaukee Journal-Sentinel.* "If a reader knows you have everything first, why would they go anywhere else?"

The Associated Press still uses this process for all breaking news, which means the wire service may send out more than a dozen write-thrus (revised versions of one story) before an editor selects the latest possible one for newspaper publication. Readers see only that final choice. With blogs, in contrast, Internet surfers can watch as a story develops and changes.

TIPS FOR BLOGGING SPORTS

Individual blog posts can range from one paragraph for notes and quick updates to 1,000-plus words for features and game stories. "Not being tied to a budgeted length allows for the story to grow more organically," Woike says. "There are temptations to get wordy at times, but really, if there's good information, there's always room for it."

Here are some other suggestions for blogging sports:

▶ Be balanced, mixing positive with negative. Blogs won't thrive when they're filled with mostly negative commentary and news.

- In a quick post, such as an item on a player's status or a reaction to a recent game or issue, it's acceptable to use just one source. Blogs don't always have to follow traditional journalism guidelines.

- Build a relationship with readers, as Sobel did with the Masters blog. Respond to e-mail, and post some readers' comments on the blog. That, after all, is the point of interactivity. For most writers it's a novel rush to get instant feedback, to find out how people perceive your words and what else they'd like to read.

- Edit closely. Few things are more precious to a writer than an editor. But with blogging, in most cases, you'll be your own editor. Before you spell-check and post something, read it aloud so you can hear errors in syntax or structure. You may also want to read the story backwards, a paragraph at a time.

- Give yourself the freedom to develop a voice. Readers don't want straight news all the time. On blogs, readers connect as much to personalities as they do to the postings themselves. If you think the receiver ran a horrible route, say so. Pleased that the Netherlands lost in the World Baseball Classic? Then let it out, like Deadspin's Tommy Craggs: "The cuddly Dutch honkballers lost to Venezuela, 3-1, in this afternoon's edition of the World Small Sample Size Bingo Tournament, which means the Netherlands' Cinderella run may soon come to a close. Dank God."[4] Readers usually can tell where bloggers stand on any issue.

- Keep your writing style much more conversational than in a traditional sports story.

- Report. Blogs may allow more room for style, but style without substance means nothing. You want to break news before others – but be sure to credit others when they get the story first. Deliver quality information that's relevant, that packs a journalistic punch.

- In blogs, nothing's too insignificant to post. Not every post needs to be a journalistic gem. USC's third-string quarterback is lifting weights in the off-season? Wisconsin's second-string point guard scored five points during a summer league? A goalie's getting a new uniform assigned? Fans want to know.

- Link to others. Link to players' names in first reference so readers can easily access their statistics and biography. For colleges, this means inserting a link to the athletic department Web site. For professional sports, you'll usually link to a league site. At the high school level, you may need to link to your own stats pages unless another site also has this information.

▶ Credit others when they do a terrific job, and link to great resources that offer more information on points addressed in the blog.

▶ Offer alternative opinions. Don't repeat the same arguments everyone else is making. And don't attack other writers or bloggers. That's too easy. Instead, focus on angles or arguments that have not been addressed.

In some ways, a blog is like a sidebar, a place where sports writers can expand on game stories and offer additional quotes, stats and facts that could not fit. "A blog is also a very good place to analyze more in depth the implications of what was written," says Bedard.

There are no hard and fast rules for blogging – except that words alone are not enough. Add audio clips, photos and many links to your posts, elements that will give your reporting more depth and keep readers coming back for more.

AUTO RACING

T he Super Bowl is the most watched sports event in the United States, attracting about 100 million TV viewers nationally. But even the Super Bowl can't compare to auto racing when it comes to getting fans to show up and cheer.

Each February, NASCAR draws just over 200,000 fans to the Daytona 500 stock-car race, a two-week event often called racing's Super Bowl. That makes the crowd at the Daytona International Speedway about the same size as the population of Madison, Wis., or Orlando, Fla. Another NASCAR event, the Brickyard 400, attracts about 300,000 fans to Indianapolis Motor Speedway, home to the Indianapolis 500, an open-wheel race that grows to the size of Cincinnati or Pittsburgh each Memorial Day weekend.

Auto racing is the fastest-growing sport in the United States, regularly drawing more than 6 million fans to 30-plus major stock-car races across the country. That figure doesn't include tracks that host races by the Indy Racing League or the National Hot Rod Association, or the nearly 100 short tracks where small-town drivers compete.

NASCAR also attracts a sizable TV audience, averaging about 10 million viewers for its 20-plus races, making it about the fourth most popular sport on TV. And NASCAR is far from the only motor sports league in the United States.

The Indy Racing League averages slightly fewer than 1 million TV viewers, and another million also attend its races across the country. This circuit features open-wheel racing, meaning the wheels are outside the car's main body.

The circuit for Formula One, another form of open-wheel racing, does not feature a single Grand Prix event in North America, preferring more exotic places such as Monte Carlo, Kuala Lumpur and Singapore. Formula One races go through both city streets and self-contained courses.

Drag racing is also popular in the United States, attracting more than 100,000 fans to larger events, like the Gatornationals in the National Hot Rod Association's 20-plus race series. Hundreds of drag races and stock-car races take place at small tracks across the country, while additional motor leagues race trucks, motorcycles and midget cars. Although NASCAR may be the most widely recognized, Americans love all kinds of motor sports.

PREPARE

Learn the Basics

▶ Know the scoring system for any series you cover. In NASCAR, all races are worth the same, meaning a driver earns 185 point for a victory (to 34 points for 43rd place) in the Daytona 500 and for the Dickies 500 at Texas Motor Speedway. Drivers compete in the first 26 races to earn a berth in The Chase, where the top 12 drivers compete in 10 races to determine the points champion. Entering these final races, drivers have their points readjusted to 5,000. Drivers get an additional 10 points for each victory in the first 26 races. Races in The Chase are scored the same as during the regular season. Drivers earn 50 points for winning IRL races, the points gradually decreasing to 10 for 25th to 33rd places.

▶ Qualifying determines where a driver will start in a race based upon speed for a single lap. Usually, 33 drivers start in each NASCAR race and are lined up three abreast for 11 rows. About 20 to 25 drivers start in IRL races.

▶ Drafting, a practice that enables two or more cars to drive faster than they could alone, is an important part of stock-car racing. Cars that travel in a line, nose to tail, take advantage of an aerodynamic effect. The lead car pulls the second car along by displacing the air in front of it, something that also creates a vacuum between the lead car's rear end and the nose of the following car.

▶ Drivers don't always agree on the proper approach to drafting, especially during the final laps of a race when a second-place driver can use a turn like a slingshot and vault into the lead. "Personally, I'd love to be in second knowing I had a friend behind me," three-time Daytona 500 winner Dale Jarrett told *USA Today*'s Seth Livingstone. "But I'm not going to make that move until we're headed down the backstretch. You actually lay back a little bit going through Turn 1. That's where you have to start picking up speed and gaining that momentum and getting the car behind you on your bumper. That's the key to making a pass – having the guy on your bumper to help push you. Then you can dictate what's going to happen from there."[1]

sports insider

The best time to speak with drivers is right after practice or qualifying once they are out of their cars. Once they confer with their crew chief, you can sometimes catch drivers walking back to their haulers. Team owner and crew chiefs, it just depends. It's just sort of understood that you don't approach a driver, crew chief or crew member when they are in their garage stall, which they view as their personal workspace.

Jared Turner,
SceneDaily.com

Bumping is another significant practice during races. Drivers in trailing cars intentionally tap the car in front of them, causing the lead car's rear tires to float, or momentarily lose traction. As the lead driver corrects the steering and regains traction, the trailing car will usually shoot through the gap before the next corner. Bumping is usually done after corners, not entering them, because cars are more likely to spin out of control on turns. Bumping is a legal practice when executed properly, but these taps can lead to cars spinning out and wrecks, something that invokes fights on the track and catcalls from fans.

Race cars do not have air conditioning, although teams may hook a hose to pump cooler air into a driver's helmet. Most race cars also do not have doors, speedometers, windows, anti-lock brakes, air bags, gas gauges and brake lights. Drivers use tachometers to determine speed.

Team engineers calculate how far a driver can go before running out of gas, although a bouncy needle for a fuel gauge indicates a driver had better return to pit row to avoid getting stuck out on the track. Teams, knowing a pit stop would end a chance to win a race, will sometimes gamble they have enough gas if they have the lead with only a few laps left to go.

Cars are inspected before and after NASCAR races, sometimes several times during a race weekend. Post-race inspectors ensure that cars are not cheating by altering anything – from the engine's size, the number of tires used, the size of the gas tank to the design of the body. Post-race inspectors also check ignition, rear-end gears, power train and fuel for additives.

▶ Teams have tried to gain a competitive advantage by soaking tires so they grip the track better and by putting bumps and ruts into the body to make it more aerodynamic, among other things. If caught, though, teams get penalized.

▶ Drivers are part of a team. Here are a few other team positions:

▶▶ **owners:** May own more than one team, which is disallowed in all other team sports. Drivers from the same team may assist one another during the race by drafting off one another or by blocking other drivers.

▶▶ **crew chief:** Oversees everything from checking a car's specifications and determining how a car gets built to assigning tasks to other team members. In some ways, the crew chief is like a manager or coach. Like a coach, a crew chief is lauded when a team wins and can be fired when a team does poorly.

▶▶ **engine specialist:** Helps build and fine-tune engines before and during races.

▶▶ **tire specialist:** Much more significant than some might assume. Makes adjustments to tire pressure that can be critical to the car's performance and finish.

▶▶ Teams may also have several engineers and mechanics, but only seven team members are allowed over the wall to help in the pit during races.

▶ Flags are waved several times during a race by someone, aptly called the flag man, on a stand near the start/finish line. Here's what each colored flag signifies:

▶▶ **green:** Go. Used to start, and restart, races.

▶▶ **yellow:** Caution. Used to essentially stop the race because drivers may not pass one another during caution laps. Their positions are set. And cars tend to bunch together, meaning lengthy leads are eliminated. Drivers can take pit stops and retain their positions unless the caution ends before they can return to the track. The yellow flag is used when track conditions become unsafe because of weather, accidents or debris.

▶▶ **green and white checkered:** Restart races for final two laps only.

▶▶ **red:** Stops races when weather (hard rain, fog) or track conditions (badly damaged wall) have made it unsafe to race – and changes are not likely soon. Cars must stop and line up straight behind a pace car, in order.

▶▶ **black:** Penalty for a driver who has broken a rule or whose car is unsafe. This driver must immediately leave the track.

▶ ▶ **white:** Lead driver is on the final lap.

▶ ▶ **black and white checkered:** Winner has just crossed the finish line.

▶ ▶ **blue flag with diagonal stripes:** Tells drivers who are a lap behind to yield to those on the lead lap.

▶ Learn important racing terms:

▶ ▶ **air foil:** a stabilizer used to create a downforce, keeping drag racing cars from destabilizing and going airborne down the track.

▶ ▶ **AMA:** American Motorcyclist Association

▶ ▶ **ARCA:** Automobile Racing Club of America

▶ ▶ **chicane:** A sequence of tight serpentine (s-shaped) curves used to slow cars in a road race. The curves are sometimes located after long straightaways, making them good spots to pass other drivers.

▶ ▶ **Christmas tree:** the electronic device between lanes at the starting line that displays the calibrated light countdown for each driver, starting with three amber lights to green, which denotes start. The bottom red light signifies a foul start, which disqualifies a driver for starting too early.

▶ ▶ **drag racing:** where cars take off from a dead start, racing down a straight line – usually in head-to-head matchups. NHRA features three classes – Funny Car, Top Fuel, Pro Stock.

▶ ▶ **funny cars:** drag racing cars with forward-mounted engines that compete in the following categories – Top Fuel, Pro Stock, Pro Stock Motorcycle.

▶ ▶ **loose:** a term used to describe a car whose rear end starts to fishtail, or overtake the front end, when it enters or exits a turn. A loose car may not be getting enough traction.

▶ ▶ **"lucky dog" rule:** on cautions, the first driver who's one lap behind gets placed at the end of the lead lap with the leaders. Drivers don't move up like this on the final 10 laps.

▶ ▶ **NASCAR:** National Association for Stock Car Auto Racing

▶ ▶ **NHRA:** National Hot Rod Association

▶ ▶ **pole position:** the top position on the front row earned by the driver who records the fastest lap during qualifying. All other drivers are positioned according to these qualifying times.

▶ ▶ **pro stock:** drag racing cars that cannot use anything such as nitrous oxide to turbocharge a car. Few modifications are allowed to engines.

▶ ▶ **restrictor plates:** aluminum plates placed on NASCAR autos designed to reduce a car's speed. The plate is put between the carburetor and the engine's intake manifold with four holes drilled in it. This reduces the flow of air and fuel into the engine's combustion chamber, decreasing horsepower and speed.

▶ ▶ **short track:** stock-car tracks that are less than a mile in length.

▶ ▶ **sixty-foot time:** time a hot rod takes to cover the first 60 feet of the track, the most accurate means of measuring a car's speed.

▶ ▶ **spoiler:** Creates downforce on the rear of a vehicle, which increases traction. The spoiler stretches across the width of a race car's rear end, creating aerodynamic drag that slows cars. So teams try to put the spoiler as low as possible to allow for more speed on straightaways.

▶ ▶ **Sprint Cup:** the name for NASCAR's racing season that was called the Winston Cup Series from 1971 to 2003. The season's racing champion is determined by a system in which drivers earn points based on how they finished in each of the 20-plus races. They can also earn points for leading laps. The top 12 drivers compete in an additional 10 races called the Chase for the Champions.

▶ ▶ **straightaway:** long, straight stretches on a race track.

▶ ▶ **superspeedways:** tracks that are more than two miles long.

▶ ▶ **tight:** a term used to describe a car whose front wheels lose traction before the rear tires do, meaning the car won't be able to steer sharply through turns.

▶ ▶ **top fuel:** drag racing cars that are long and narrow with thin front tires, resembling open wheel cars in some ways. These cars do not use gasoline, relying instead on nitromethane and methanol.

▶ ▶ **trioval:** A racetrack that is shaped sort of like a triangle with smoother edges and less distinct edges. In some ways, the track is outlined like an oval with a slight fifth turn, sometimes called a "hump."

▶ ▶ **victory lane:** spot on racetrack's infield where the winning drivers park to celebrate.

Get Ready

▶ Contact a track's media relations person as soon as possible – a few months early if you know you'll be assigned to cover a big race. For some races, you may need to request credentials at least a month in advance. If you request early enough, you can get a pretty decent parking spot, usually reserved for established media outlets.

▶ During race weekends, drivers have tight schedules. Get to know the public relations contacts so they can carve out a 10- to 15-minute interview during the weekend. The team's PR representatives manage and chaperone drivers throughout the weekend. "Work with them prior to the event and find the cracks in the driver's busy schedules," says Erik Arneson, vice president for media relations for SpeedTV. Many PR contacts prefer receiving e-mail they can retrieve off their BlackBerrys to getting phone calls.

▶ At Formula One events, individual time with drivers is nearly impossible. But reporters covering NHRA drag racing may be able to get unlimited access throughout the weekend since fewer media cover this circuit.

▶ Study the schedule for an event – practices and qualifying may last up to four days – to determine opportune moments to interview team members. "If you show up on race day expecting to be able to speak with drivers, you will be disappointed for the most part," Arneson says. "Get there a day or two earlier before the tension of race day builds for the participants." If you are covering a local race, where drivers show up that day, arrive earlier in the afternoon to introduce yourself to drivers and to set up interviews.

▶ Research each driver's performance – at this specific track, at tracks similar in size, during the season, in recent races. Read published stories and interview drivers and crew members to determine how each driver is preparing for this race. Information gained this way could prove essential when writing a story on deadline. "During the race, have primary, secondary storylines – and, maybe more – that you track, but be open to the unexpected," Arneson says. "Don't stay so focused on the planned storyline that you miss something bigger."

▶ Bring an Ethernet cord for the laptop and a tape recorder. Most of those interviewed won't have time to wait for you to scribble quotes and information into a notebook. The Ethernet cord helps when the wireless network in the track's media center slows to a crawl, which can happen when people log on at once.

▶ Attend practices and qualifying to find angles for race day. Storylines may evolve over several days leading to the main event. A team's performance may also reveal who's set for a big weekend or who's in for a big struggle.

▶ Two important things to record during a race: (1) When cars pit, which can help you understand the team's strategy, or cycle, for the race, and (2) What drivers and crews are saying to each other on their radio channels, which is usually accessible in the press box. Most everything else will be provided by post-race box score, usually within a half hour.

▶ During pit stops, note the various pit strategies – who took two or four tires, who took gas only, and who didn't pit at all down the stretch. At times, several drivers may be gambling that their final tank lasts them across the finish line. Always note the lap when drivers head to pit row. Readers will want to know how far the drivers traveled on the final tank and when others were forced to pit, taking them out of contention.

▶ At the start of each flagged caution, write down the running order for all lead-lap cars, along with any other notable drivers who are not on the lead lap. Drivers typically pit during cautions, so recording this order enables you to determine how many positions a driver gained or lost during these stops, something that is not readily available from a box score. "I also try to keep track of what the running order is every 20 to 40 laps," says Nate Ryan, *USA Today*'s auto racing writer. "At the end of the race, I try to transcribe as many quotes off the radio and TV interviews that I can." Note reasons for cautions as well.

▶ Record lead changes – the drivers involved, the lap, location on track (back straight-away, far turn) and a brief description (bumped right bumper, went low).

▶ Look beyond the drivers for stories – crew members, former drivers in attendance, NASCAR officials, business leaders associated with the sport.

▶ Look for anything that appears unusual, such as a long pit stop, a top driver in the back of the back, a car making bold moves to pass several drives in a short span.

▶ Races play out depending on the type of track. At short tracks, drivers are more packed together so you'll notice more action toward the start of a race. At superspeedways, you'll notice more action toward the end of the race.

Here are some notes from a writer who covered the Checker O'Reilly Auto Parts 500:

221 – 48 retakes lead quickly after restart

235 – 48 clinches in bonus points

261 – Debris caution

262 – Pit stops

264 – Order: 48 2 26 99 29 88 11 16 5 18 20 31 42 10 9 47 6 70 / 07

Small puncture in RR [right rear] tire, didn't build up quite as much in RF [right front]. Pound and half low

269 – 24 blows up

273 – Red flag, 84 jacks up 38 after 5 spun . . . order: 45 19 5 66 43 38 77 84

Over the radio: How'd it feel there, Jimmie, was it better?

Yeah, OK.

OK.

Roger Penske came down and said the Indy guys trying to keep you honest with the 2, said you'd know what he'd mean.

10 – 4, tell him thanks.

10 – 4, he's laughing up here.

Red flag: 17:52

278 – Restart

283 – Caution, 41 and 18

285 – 16 20 07 pit

289 – Restart with 24 to go

291 – Debris yellow, 41 bumper fell off

(Over the radio) Knaus: You are doing a great job

292 – No one pits

296 – Restart

Seventh victory, started from the pole, first guy to win three in a row at Phoenix

305 – caution, 20, 17, 10

37th or better?

10th caution . . . 307 – 311, 55 laps

312 – restart

Lights are on for finish . . .

(over radio) Johnson: Screaming on the radio . . .

(over radio) Knaus: Awesome, awesome, awesome job.

JJ: That's right!

(over radio) Knaus: Spectacular performance

Led 217 laps

Over radio: Jimmie you got a copy?

10 – 4 boss.

Have I told you lately you are the man?

Appreciate it, buddy.

▶ Determine how fast a team pits from the moment the car leaves the track to the time a team returns. Compare these times with other leading contenders. Can also clock the time it takes a team to make changes once the car has stopped. In addition, determine the reason for pits during the later stages of races.

▶ Speed on opening laps compared with later laps.

▶ Brake usage on smaller tracks with far more turns.

▶ Determine who and when drivers draft off one another.

ASK

▶ Ask about pit stop strategies during the race. Did a team change two tires instead of four during the final 25 laps? A few seconds can prove the difference between first and fourth place in tight races. Yet, this gamble could cost a driver speed on the track. Crew chiefs may wait until the last minute to decide on several things, including the number of tires. You can also ask whether these tires were scuffs, tires previously used for a few practice laps or sticker tires that were never used before and that are more dependable.

▶ For most events, the leaders are brought to a media center. You'll have to chase all others down on pit row or in their garages. NASCAR offers access to the top 12 drivers each weekend for press conferences, but this usually yields quicker, shorter responses. You'll be lucky to get one to two questions answered and few follow-up questions. If you plan to write a longer story, contact the team's PR person at least several weeks before the event. You probably won't get any individual time with the top drivers during the weekend unless you are a major media player.

▶ For strategy, ask the crew chiefs. Drivers can supply additional information for strategy, and they can also offer detailed observations and explanations for actions on the track. Owners can offer commentary on their drivers: "There's going to be a lot of coaching, but he's got the mental capability to do it," driver and owner Kevin Harvick said.

▶ Interview track officials only when a controversy arises.

▶ Speak with drivers after they complete practice and qualifying, usually right after they confer with their crew chiefs. You can sometimes catch drivers walking back to their trailers on the track.

▶ Don't approach owners or crew chiefs when they are in the garage stalls; this is something many consider a violation of their personal work space.

▶ Sometimes a car returns to the track after a crash or a collision. Speak with team members to find out what was needed to put the auto back on the track.

WRITE

▶ Some writers use very little race description beyond who leads on certain laps; they focus instead on trends or issues in a race – unless the race has a defining moment such as a huge pileup or one driver passing another to win. "For the most part, I think it's to be avoided because most readers have seen the race and are seeking forward-looking analysis," says Ryan. Race description may be more important when a driver wins for the third time in a row or the sixth time in 10 races. By this time, readers know a great deal about this driver and the reasons for his success. At this point, many writers consider adding more race description.

▶ Write mph. You do not need to spell out miles per hour.

▶ For drag racing, note the miles per hour and the seconds drivers took to complete their drag races. For example: "Cory McClenathan clocked 308.57 mph (3.847 seconds) to defeat Morgan Lucas in the final."

▶ The winner is not always the story. Perhaps a driver led for all except the final five or 10 laps. That driver may be the focus for the main story. A wreck that eliminates a significant portion of the field could also be a main focal point. Another possible lead: a driver who wins in his hometown or at a track where he has traditionally struggled.

▶ Focus on drivers who are new or who have changed teams, even if they do not finish with the lead pack. Ricky Carmichael, a legendary motocross rider, fared poorly in his first effort at Daytona as he tried driving a truck in an ARCA race at the speedway. Here's how *USA Today*'s Nate Ryan led his story:

DAYTONA BEACH, Fla. – The all-time winningest motocross rider's crash course in stock cars continued recently with a crash.

Caught in an ARCA pileup at Daytona International Speedway, Ricky Carmichael climbed from a battered Chevrolet figuring his race was over. Then his crew scrambled to cut off the front fenders and hood.

"I said, 'You're going to drive it wrecked now,'" car owner Kevin Harvick said. "He was like, 'Is this safe?' I said, 'It's fine, like taking one fork off the front of a bike.' He said, 'Dude, that's impossible.'"

Without complaint, though, Carmichael hopped back into the car, its radiator now fully exposed, and drove to a 21st-place finish, 28 laps down. He showed as much deference during practice a few days earlier when Harvick delivered some sharp-tongued advice on the radio.[2]

BASEBALL

More than any other sport, baseball is about numbers that measure a player's success during a career, a season, a game and even an at bat. Baseball is quantified like no other sport. Certain numbers hold particular significance – .367 (Ty Cobb's lifetime batting average), 56 (Joe DiMaggio's hitting streak in 1941), 74 (Barry Bonds' single-season home run record), 511 (Cy Young's career wins record).

Numbers also define a player's season – .300 is an excellent effort by hitters while 3.00 is an equally impressive season for pitchers.

Even specific plays can be reduced to a numerical equation, of sorts. A double play, where the shortstop catches a ball and throws it to the second baseman, who, in turn, relays the throw to first base is expressed as 6 – 4 – 3. A fly ball caught by the center-fielder is F8. Numbers quantify and explain games.

The best players get hits about 30 percent of the time. Batters have a few thousandths of a second to decide whether to swing a bat 2¾ inches in diameter and hit a ball that is about the same diameter – and that is thrown as fast as 100 mph from 60 feet, 6 inches. The pitch may go straight, curve, dive down, veer left, cut right or appear to rise.

"To imagine baseball without statistics would be a Zen exercise, I would think akin to contemplating the sound of one hand clapping," writes baseball historian Bill James, whose abstracts have elevated stats into the mainstream. "If a baseball game is played in the forest and nobody keeps stats, does it count in the standings? No."

Practice keeping score while watching games on TV or at the local ball fields. And take exhaustive notes in a notebook as well. That's how baseball writers manage to succeed even when games throw them a curve.

Learn the Basics

▶ Playing positions are assigned numbers that correspond with their positions, something that makes keeping score easier and more streamlined.

▶ Here are the assigned position numbers:
1 – pitcher
2 – catcher
3 – first baseman
4 – second baseman
5 – third baseman
6 – shortstop
7 – left fielder
8 – center fielder
9 – right fielder

▶ Next, familiarize yourself with abbreviations used for recording plays. A strikeout can be recorded two ways: A regular notation of K can mean the batter struck out swinging. A backwards K can denote a player looked as the third strike landed in the catcher's mitt.

▶ Here are the key abbreviations:
1B – single
2B – double
3B – triple
HR – home run
RBI – runs batted in
BB – base on balls (walk)
HBP – hit by pitch (awarded first base)
PB – passed ball
WP – wild pitch
SF – sacrifice fly
Sac – sacrifice bunt
SB – stolen base
FC – fielder's choice
E – error (batter reaches base on fielder's mistake)
BK – balk

Chart a player's performance through a season, career – or even a game. *The Boston Globe* developed an amazing interactive graphic citing each of Manny Ramirez's 500 career home runs, everything from the locations he hit to the most (left field), to the ballparks where he had the most success (Fenway, of course) to the pitchers who were victimized for the most homers (Jamie Moyer). You might want to start smaller, charting where a tailback ran the most (left, center, right) and the number of carries for loss, 0 – 4 yards, 5 – 10 yards, etc. You could also chart locations for baskets for a game or season. Check out "Tracking Manny Ramirez's Hunt for 500 Homers" at www.boston.com/sports/baseball/redsox/extras/manny_500_homeruns/.

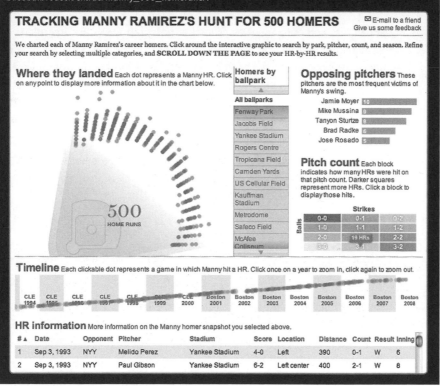

CS – caught stealing (for any base)

DP – double play (although you probably record this as 6 – 4 – 3, for example)

DH – designated hitter

IW – intentional walk (when a batter is purposefully issued a base on balls)

Balls are cited first in pitch counts, meaning a 1 – 2 count reflects one ball and two strikes on the batter. With two strikes, a batter can foul off as many pitches as he desires without striking out. A batter strikes out by swinging and missing on a third strike, taking a called third strike or bunting a third strike into foul territory. In addition, a ball tipped into the catcher's mitt is also counted as a third strike.

▶ A batter can reach base on a third strike, though, if the catcher fails to hold onto the pitch – unless a runner is on first base with fewer than two outs.

▶ A batter can reach base eight ways: hit, walk, hit by pitch, fielder's choice, error, dropped third strike, catcher's interference, fielder's obstruction.

▶ Next, familiarize yourself with these terms:

▶ ▶ **at bat:** hits and outs count as official at bats, but walks and sacrifices do not. So a batter who walked twice is officially 0-for-0, but a batter who singled and struck out would be 1-for-2. (An official at bat is one where a batter has recorded either a hit or an out, something that is recorded for calculating batting averages.) Because walks do not count as either an out or a hit, they are not used – neither are sacrifice flies, sacrifice bunts or when a batter is hit by a pitch.

▶ ▶ **balk:** when a pitcher stutters, fails to stop properly in the stretch or touches his mouth while on the mound, among other things. All runners get to advance one base, and a ball is added to the batter's count.

▶ ▶ **batting average:** measure a player's ability to collect hits. This is calculated by dividing total hits by total official at bats.

　● Someone with 28 hits in 100 at bats would have the following average:

$$28 \div 100 = .280$$

▶ ▶ **catcher's interference:** when a batter hits the glove of a catcher during a swing, usually because a catcher is trying to sneak forward to throw out a base runner attempting to steal. Play is called dead and the batter is awarded first base. All other runners advance one base.

▶ ▶ **earned run average:** measures a pitcher's ability to prevent runs. To calculate this, divide total number of earned runs by total innings. Then, multiply this number by nine, which represents a full game.

$$\text{earned runs} \div \text{total innings} \times 9 = ERA$$
$$91 \div 194 \times 9 = 4.22$$

▶ ▶ **earned runs:** Runs a team scores without the aid of errors or passed balls.

▶ ▶ **fielder's choice:** the batter reaches base but a force out is recorded. This counts as on official at bat but not a hit, meaning this batter would be 0-for-1.

▶ ▶ **infield fly rule:** This applies to pop ups hit in the infield when there are fewer than two outs and a potential force out at third base or home. The umpire has to exclaim "infield fly" if a ball hit in fair territory can easily be caught. The batter is out regardless of whether the fielder drops the ball. Base runners can advance at their own risk, but they are not required to do so even if the fielder drops the ball.

▶ ▶ **on-base percentage:** measures a player's ability to reach base. Add each time a player reaches base for any reason except by error or fielder's choice. Divide this by total plate appearances.

$$(H + BB + HBP) / (AB + BB + HBP + SF)$$
$$(28 + 12 + 2) \div (100 + 12 + 2 + 8)$$
$$42 \div 122 = .344$$

▶ ▶ **on-base plus slugging percentage:** measures a player's overall offensive value by combining on-base percentage and slugging percentage. The best players will average around 1.000. To calculate, add on-base percentage and slugging averages.

$$OBP + SLG = average$$
$$.344 + .535 = .879$$

▶ ▶ **passed ball:** a thrown pitch that the catcher misplays, allowing any runner to advance at least one base.

▶ ▶ **sacrifice fly:** a fly ball hit by a batter that enables a base runner to advance at least one base. A sacrifice bunt also enables a runner to advance an extra base.

▶ ▶ **slugging percentage:** measures a batter's power. To calculate this, add all official at bats, but do not include walks, sacrifices or hit by pitch. Next add total bases. Next, divide total bases by official at bats.

$$Total\ bases \div at\ bats = slugging\ percentage$$
$$221 \div 400 = .552$$

▶ ▶ **total bases:** This is used to calculate slugging percentage. To add total bases, multiply singles by one, doubles by two, triples by three and home runs by four. Then add the sums together to get this total.

Singles	$42 \times 1 =$	42
Doubles	$28 \times 2 =$	56
Home runs	$29 \times 4 =$	96

▶ ▶ **value over replacement player:** evaluates the number of runs a player contributes to a team beyond what a replacement player at the same position would contribute if given the same number of plate appearances. Albert Pujols' +98.1 score led the majors in 2009. Players can also earn negative scores.

▶ ▶ **wild pitch:** an errant pitch that allows runners to advance at least one base.

Get Ready

▶ Bring a scorebook to all baseball games. Get lineups from both teams along with potential substitutions. Keep score. But also write notes about each inning on either an extra notebook or a computer.

▶ What's the big picture? What does this game mean to the teams involved? How does it affect them? Why is the game important?

WATCH

▶ Be observant; record the tiny details that bring a play to life, such as the number of bounces a ball took before it was caught, where a tag was applied, and where a fielder stood when he threw the ball. Some baseball writers like Tyler Kepner, who covers the Yankees for *The New York Times,* type these notes onto a laptop for reference on deadline because they know fans watching at home will have had a chance to view key plays repeatedly with instant replay. "In my ideal world," he says, "every seat in the press box would have TiVo so we could replay and pause whenever we want."

▶ Look for the less obvious factors that helped a team win – the middle reliever who pitched three shutout innings to keep the game close, a double play that held off a rally, or the batter who fought a pitcher for a 10-pitch walk before scoring. The big inning or the three-run homer does not happen unless the smaller things happen along the way.

▶ Write a few sentences at the end of each inning describing how each team scored so you will have this when you write the gamer later. (Make sure you also keep a good account in a scorebook.)

▶ Determine how many runners each team leaves on base. You will see the stat, LOB, in many box scores. This number can be perceived at least two ways. On the one hand, a team with many runners left on base (say, 10 or 12) must have hit pretty well to get so many players on base. Even teams that score eight or 10 runs will leave higher numbers of runners on base. On the other hand, a team may have hit poorly in clutch situations. You'll notice this when a team has left many runners on base but has scored far fewer runs (perhaps two or three). In addition, look for specific examples from the game to illustrate this, perhaps by focusing on an at bat where a hitter failed to drive in runners already in scoring position (second or third base) with fewer than two outs.

▶ Determine when (and how often) a team uses the sacrifice bunt in a game. Some managers rely on this much more often than others. For example, one coach (or manager) might bunt a runner over to third when the team has no outs to set up a sacrifice fly while others might prefer to give his batters two opportunities to drive the runner in with a hit. (Look for trends during the season, if this is your beat.)

▶ Determine how often a batter hits a ball to the right side of the field to advance a runner. A good right-handed hitter will often try to hit balls toward right field (or to second or first base) in order to send a runner from second to third, especially if there are no outs. This is really an unofficial sacrifice, where the batter has given himself up to help the team. As a result, the team would only need a long fly ball to get the runner across the plate. This is not considered a sacrifice, though, because the batter might also punch the ball through the infield for a hit. Still, take note of times when batters do something unselfish like this.

▶ Learn to spot the less obvious plays. Key plays are not always as obvious as a game-winning single in the bottom of the ninth or a grand slam in the sixth inning. Look for the plays that do not stand out quite so clearly, such as a hard slide in the fourth where a runner broke up a double play that, in turn, allowed the inning to continue and a run to score in a game determined by a single run. Or look for a batter who fought off a tough pitcher for a 10-pitch walk late in the game that forced the starting pitcher out of a game and allowed his team to score against the reliever. Or look for a successful hit-and-run that confused the defense and allowed an easy grounder to short to roll into left field, sending a runner in for the decisive score.

▶ Learn the game by speaking with veteran coaches and players, by reading reports on games by regular baseball beat writers, by listening to baseball announcers and by reading the rules book, among other things.

▶ Determine how many outs a pitcher records from fly balls compared with ground outs. Pitchers and managers prefer ground outs. They can lead to more double plays and are less likely to go for home runs. You'll also find these outs reflect the types of pitches thrown. A sinker-ball pitcher is more likely to get many more ground outs than a pitcher who relies on a fastball. Of course, any pitcher can hang a curveball that floats to the plate softly with nary a break. That's a nightmare for all pitchers.

▶ Isolate a moment or turning point in a game. "I will say that I try to isolate on a moment or turning point in the game," says Dejan Kovacevic, baseball beat writer for the *Pittsburgh Post-Gazette.* "Or, to give the game a face or personality that might make it memorable. I want the reader, even the one who attended in person, to feel it important to pick up the paper the next day to have a definition of that game."

▶ Look for ministreaks during games. Did a pitcher retire nine batters in a row across four middle innings, or retire the final eight batters? Did a team score a run in five straight innings, or connect for eight straight hits? Look for these ministreaks as well. They might not be the lead, but they are interesting to note elsewhere in the story, especially if you can connect the streak to the bigger story.

▶ Focus on hits that help a team increase its lead during late innings, especially those that put the game out of reach. Some baseball teams track these hits that allow a team to go for an opponent's jugular, earning this stat the moniker "jug runs."

▶ Focus on plays that sustain rallies, which can include a hitter who hustled to beat out the back end of a potential double play, a runner going from first to third, RBI hits with two outs.

▶ Note how umpires differ and can affect the game. Umpires have slightly different strike zones, but don't focus on a zone that is slightly wider, higher or tighter than normal. Instead, focus on how pitchers and batters adjust to these calls. Find a play that helps illustrate how players changed their approach.

Record pitch counts. Batters hit far better – and far worse – during certain counts. For example, batters who hit a first pitch hit about .340, about 120 points higher than batters who try to hit with the pitch count at 0 – 1. Pitchers tend to dominate when the count is at 0 – 1, 0 – 2 and 1 – 2. Batters are more in control when the count is 3 – 0, 3 – 1 and 2 – 0 because they can be more selective in the pitches they decide to swing. See how frequently a pitcher goes to certain counts – and then evaluate the results. In addition, count total pitches for each inning and overall. Unlike softball, baseball pitchers usually start to tire at around 80 or 90 pitches, depending on the level of play. A high pitch count (more than 20) in a single inning can also tire a pitcher.

Sit behind home plate for an inning, if allowed, so you can track the location of pitches, see where the catcher sits and observe where the pitches land. This will show whether the pitcher hit the spots where the catcher tried framing, or positioning, his mitt.

Focus on body language. Do players hunch shoulders after a controversial play or costly error? Do players stand on the top steps of the dugout, watching the game, even when they trail? This says much about a team's character.

Be a stats geek. Go through box scores to analyze stats. Look for trends in hitting and pitching stats for individuals and teams. For example, you might find that a team has left more than 10 runners on base over the past six games, or that the team has averaged 2.1 runs per game during the past two weeks. (Ask high school coaches, or their team managers, if you can review their scorebooks before games. That means arriving to the game much earlier, when the teams are warming up.) You might also notice that a pitcher has not walked a batter in his past three games or that a hitter has gone 9-for-12 in his past four games. Some other team stats to consider: errors, stolen bases, and number of times a team has grounded into a double play (that's GIDP in most box scores).

Check for hitting streaks such as those listed above, so afterward you can ask questions that focus on why players are doing so well. Also, check for streaks where players are struggling. Check to see if a player has gone hitless in his last nine at bats or if he has managed just two hits in his last 19 at bats. It is particularly interesting when excellent players struggle (in a long season, every hitter struggles at some point). Hitting is a difficult thing to do, perhaps one of the most difficult things in any sport. Do not be unfairly harsh on players when this happens, but citing stats that reveal a hitting drought is not a problem.

▶ Check to see how a pitcher has performed during the past several games or weeks. Has this pitcher won or lost a number of games in a row? Has this pitcher struck out 10-plus hitters per game or walked four-plus a game? Also, see how many unearned runs this pitcher has allowed recently (or for the season). Errors cause pitchers to work harder, and, as a result, to often allow more runs to score. You can also check for other stats, such as ERA and number of pitches per game. You can also check into how many runs this pitcher typically allows in the first few innings against the last few innings, or how a pitcher does after 80 or 90 pitches. These are more detailed stats that will be harder to get at the Little League or high school levels unless you are charting every game. But as you get to the higher levels, these stats are out there – usually compiled by sports information offices or the major league clubs. Make sure you speak to pitching coaches, catchers and managers to get more insights into these stats. Stats alone do not always tell the story. A pitcher might be throwing through injuries or may have lost his mechanics. Ask these questions to determine the reasons for pitchers' performances.

ASK

▶ As you review the following questions, make sure you realize your approach is as important as the questions you ask. "Every human being is different, so my approach is different with each individual," says Kovacevic. "Some respond best to a joke or even a jab. Some prefer it serious."

▶ Ask players to explain a key at bat, pitch or defensive play. What pitch were you expecting at 2 – 2 in the seventh inning? What did you throw with two outs and the bases loaded in the sixth? Can you walk me through the pitches during the entire at bat? On the double-play attempt, what happened on that throw to first that bounced in the dirt and into the dugout?

▶ Ask coaches or the manager to explain their strategy or to comment on key moments in the game. Why did the manager pinch-hit for someone? Did they notice anything different about a batter who fared well or a pitcher who struggled?

▶ Ask managers and coaches to explain reasons for recent trends. Do you know what's caused your pitcher to struggle recently? Do you know what has caused your shortstop to go on a hitting streak lately?

▶ Ask catchers to describe how their pitcher fared? Did they locate pitchers especially well or poorly? Did they notice any changes in velocity or trajectory compared with past games with this pitcher? Did batters chase pitches or lock in more than usual?

▶ Stick to questions about the game. "The code after the game is you ask only about the game," says Bob Dutton, baseball writer for *The Kansas City Star.* "If you're working on feature stories or takeouts, that stuff gets asked before the games. Afterward, players are looking to get out and go home or back to the hotel. Nearly all are good about talking about the game, but they don't like being cornered for a 20-minute session."

WRITE

▶ Try something new each time you write; otherwise you will fall into a rut. There is no best way to write a lead, but the points above might help you to develop your own creative leads to game stories. "As soon as a lead starts working for you, you get formulaic, and I try very, very hard to avoid that," says Kovacevic. "Especially in baseball, where your annual byline count is easily 800 or more, it is important to avoid predictability."

▶ Look for a story. Do not automatically focus on a scoring play or some key stat.

▶ Address the game's significance. Does the game clinch a playoff berth or eliminate the team from the postseason? Is this a conference or district victory? Does this advance the team in a tournament?

▶ For preview stories, do not lead with the fact two teams are going to play one another; instead, find an angle that is more interesting. What's the history between the teams? What's the significance of this game; for instance, does it impact the conference or district standings? Find something about the upcoming game to introduce the fact that the two teams will be playing. Perhaps, this is the first game of a conference schedule.

▶ Use RBI in first reference. Still, find other ways to cite them. For example, you can also write that a player "drove in three runs," not just that "he had three RBIs."

▶ Write earned run average in first reference, reserving ERA for subsequent references.

▶ Batters go 2-for-3, not two for three.

(continued on page 82)

① Record pitch counts for each batter to find trends. Review scorecard between every inning. This batter grounded out on a count (1 – 2) that does not favor batters.

② Put an "X" in the box right below the final out for an inning as a reminder to use the next column for the ensuing inning.

③ A backwards "K" denotes that the batter took a called third strike. A regular "K" means the batter swung and missed for strike three. Other letters used on this scorecard are:

F: flyout
L: lineout
P: popout
U: groundout (unassisted)

④ This batter walked on four pitches after the previous batter worked the count to three balls.

⑤ This is the 10th batter in a row who made an out, a trend worth noting – as is the fact that six outs were on grounders. Is the pitcher throwing more sinkers? What are the pitch counts? Talk with players afterward.

⑥ Fill in diamond boxes when someone scores so you can more easily track runs. Also, draw a line to the location where a ball is hit.

⑦ Denote when a batter drives in a run.

⑧ This batter hit into a double play where the ball was caught by the shortstop, who threw to the second baseman, who relayed it to first before the batter reached that base. The nu 6 – 4 – 3 correspond to the positions in the "Field Positions" box in the lower-right-hand of the scorecard.

⑨ Batter hit a fly ball to left field.

⑩ Batter grounded out to shortstop, who threw to first base.

⑪ Sacrifice bunts, like sac flies and base on balls, do not count toward official at-bats.

Team Name	VISITOR Team Name	Date:	Place:
		Time:	

PLAYERS	POS	1	2	3	4	5	6	7	8	9	10	AB	R	H	RBI
1 Jeter	6		3U			4-3		6-3				4	1	1	0
2 Damon	7	L-4				5-3			rbi			2	1	1	1
3 Teixeira	3			F9		K						4	1	2	1
4 Rodriguez	5	rbi	6-4-3			4y		6-4				4	0	1	1
5 Posada	2	6-3					F7		K			4	1	1	1
6 Matsui	dh	L4			4y		4-3		5-3			4	0	0	0
7 Swisher	9							F8				2	0	1	0
8 Cano	4		P6		5-4			3U				3	0	0	0
9 Cabrera	8		K		4-3							3	0	1	0
10															
11															
12															

| Total | RUNS | 2 | 0 | 0 | 1 | 0 | 0 | 0 | 1 | 0 | 0 | 30 | 4 | 8 | 4 |
| Total | H/E/LOB | 2/0/1 | 0/0/0 | 1/0/0 | 1/0/1 | 0/0/0 | 0/0/0 | 0/0/0 | 1/0/1 | 2/0/1 | X/X/X | / / | | | |

PITCHERS	TOTALS	W	L	IP	AB	R	ER	H	SO	BB	FINAL SCORE	RUNS	HITS	ERRORS
Pettitte				8	30	3	2	8	6	1	Visitor			
Rivera				1	3	0	0	0	2	0	Home			
											Umpires Luciano			
											Scorer Raff			

Field Positions

▶ Avoid clichés in all writing. For baseball, this includes jargon for home runs such as "dingers," "jacks," and "taters" that are hit and not "tattooed" or "rocketed." In addition, runs are scored, not "plated"; line drives are not "frozen ropes," and games are not "contests." In addition, bases are loaded, not "juiced"; runs are not "manufactured" like widgets and the third game of a series is most definitely not a "rubber game."

▶ Baseball may have more commonly used terms than most other sports. Here are the correct spellings for the most used terms: ballpark, baseline, center field, designated hitter, doubleheader, double play, fastball, first baseman, ground-rule double, home plate, home run, left-hander, line drive, lineup (n.), passed ball, pinch-hitter, pinch-hit single, pitchout, playoffs, sacrifice fly, shut out (v.), shutout (n.), squeeze play, strike zone, wild pitch.

BASKETBALL

F eel like putting on your dancing shoes, baby? Then, it must be time for the Big Dance, where Cinderella always makes an appearance. And it's also when clichés slip into copy as seamlessly as the feet of that young maiden. (See?)

Basketball inspires a great deal of vague lingo spewed by TV broadcasters and writers trying to add "color," instead of clarity, to their reports.

Clichés are most rampant during the NCAA Basketball Tournament. The Big Dance. March Madness. A time when small basketball schools "punch their dance card so they can go dancing." Bubble teams burst. And so does sanity.

Clichés are not just reserved for March, unfortunately. You'll find some of the following misused terms in stories any time of the year.

Long-range shots are taken from "downtown."

Players dribbling the entire court to score after a rebound go "coast to coast."

Shots that fall through the net are "drained" or "find the bottom of the net." And 3-pointers, or "treys," are frequently "buried."

On drives to the basket, players "take it to the hole." Free-throw attempts are taken from the "charity stripe," poor shots are called "bricks," and outside shooters "light it up from the outside."

"Clichés are a touchy subject at the AP," says Jim O'Connell, national college basketball editor for the Associated Press. "Our previous sports editor, Darrell Christian, had a fungo bat at the ready to use on anybody who wrote them and especially on any editor who let them through. He instilled in us that clichés weren't just crutches, they were the sign of a lazy writer. If that was the best you could come up, was including that thought really necessary? His pet peeves were 'Cinderella' and 'back to the wall.' God help anybody who couldn't come up with something better than that to describe an underdog's victory or a tough situation."

In addition, games are unfortunately called "tilts," teams fight back when their "backs are against the wall," victories are "hard-fought," and players assert their will until it all converges in March during the Big Cliché. Please, delete them all. These overly worn phrases are neither hip nor clever. They define an uncreative writer with a poor vocabulary.

"Description beats out clichés any time," says Doug Ferguson, AP's national golf writer. "I would imagine a lot of aspiring writers are trying to dress up their copy with a cute phrase, instead of relying on their powers of observation. Some of the best pieces are so simple – short sentences, common words. It's the order in which they're presented, and the detail, that makes them so appealing."

So be more creative by finding unique angles, by focusing on an otherwise overlooked but decisive play, and by writing precisely. Your writing will improve, editors will stop gnashing their teeth and readers won't scratch their heads when reading your copy any more – which is really a slam dunk for everybody, right?

PREPARE

Learn the Basics

▶ College basketball games, if they don't go into overtime, last 40 minutes in two 20-minute halves. High school games last 32 minutes over four eight-minute quarters.

▶ Basketball courts are 84 feet by 50 feet at the high school level and 94 by 50 in college and the National Basketball Association. Some other numbers: rims are 10 feet above the ground, the free-throw line is 13 feet from the rim, and the 3-point line is 19 feet, 9 inches in high school, 20 feet, 9 inches in the National Collegiate Athletic Association, and 23 feet, 9 inches for the NBA.

▶ Check stats for trends such as team and individual scoring, rebounding, assists, fouls. You might also check for a team's shooting percentage in the fourth quarter or second half, and compare it with the first half. Checking stats and box scores may also reveal that a bench player's presence usually results in a higher plus-minus percentage, meaning the team scores more points than the opponent when this player is on the court. Study and have fun with numbers; they can yield great stories and insights.

▶ In basketball, the key individual stats include assists, blocked shots, field-goal percentage, free-throw percentage, rebounding, scoring average, steals, 3-pointers made and total points. These stats are also important for evaluating a team. Plus, check

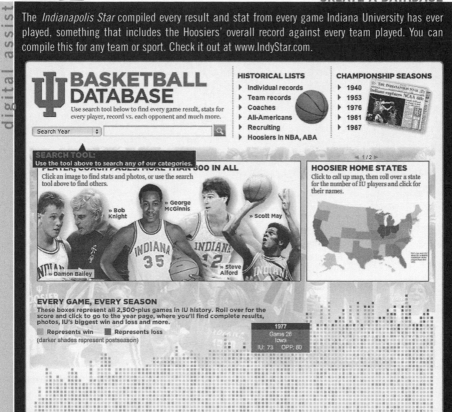

The *Indianapolis Star* compiled every result and stat from every game Indiana University has ever played, something that includes the Hoosiers' overall record against every team played. You can compile this for any team or sport. Check it out at www.IndyStar.com.

digital assist

into the teams' averages for points scored and allowed. Which teams have the largest disparities between the two?

▶ As in baseball, basketball positions are denoted by the following numbers.

▶▶ **1** – point guard, a player who's usually the best ball handler and playmaker and is a good shooter. Runs the offense like a quarterback.

▶▶ **2** – shooting guard, a player who's usually the best shooter on the team, an excellent ball handler, and a tough defender on the perimeter.

sports insider

1. Watch for runs. Basketball is a game of runs, and the team with the most usually wins.
2. Watch for tempo and know which team is comfortable playing in which tempo.
3. Take the time to understand game plans (learned through pregame interviews) and what goes into executing those plans.
4. Watch for which team is getting to the free-throw line the most. Games are won at the free-throw line.
5. Take time to watch practices. This will give you incredible insight into what a team does, or doesn't do, in games

Brady Sallee,
women's basketball coach, Eastern Illinois University

▶▶ **3** – small forward, the most versatile player on the court, who can handle the ball and shoot like a guard, play low under the basket like a power forward, and defend both big forwards and quick guards.

▶▶ **4** – power forward, a more physical player who is a good rebounder, can move quickly in the low post to create shots, and can block shots.

▶▶ **5** – center, usually the tallest player who is an excellent shot blocker and rebounder and has some good low-post moves.

▶ Violations are penalties that cause a team to lose possession. Here are the main court violations:

▶▶ **10 seconds:** teams must move the ball across the midcourt line before this time elapses.

▶▶ **double dribble:** players may not dribble once they have stopped; neither can they dribble with two hands.

▶▶ **five seconds (to inbound):** teams must inbound the ball within this time, although players can call time out to reset before the time elapses.

▶▶ **lane violation:** players may not step over the lane on free throws until the ball hits the rim, otherwise the shot is either retaken or waved off, depending on which team steps over the line.

▶▶ **line violation:** players may not step on the line as they inbound the ball.

▶ ▶ **over and back:** players may not go over the centerline and return to the back-court unless a defender has last knocked the ball into this area.

▶ ▶ **palming:** players may not put their palm under the ball, carrying the ball instead of dribbling it.

▶ ▶ **traveling:** players may not take more than 1½ steps between dribbles, although players sometimes walk with the ball with two or more steps without getting called for this violation.

▶ Personal fouls are violations called on individual players for illegal physical contact – and they're usually called on defenders. Players who receive five personal fouls at the high school and college levels are no longer eligible to play in the game. NBA players get an extra foul, needing six to foul out. Here are the main types of foul infractions:

▶ ▶ **block:** players may not step directly in front of a moving ball handler, impeding an opponent's progress through physical contact.

▶ ▶ **charge:** the ball handler may not run into or through defenders who have established a set position, one of the few offensive fouls. Defenders will often fold their arms over their chests and brace for contact when they get to a spot on the floor before the ball handler. But these defenders may not be moving at the time of contact. In the NBA, players cannot be called for a charge within four feet of the basket.

▶ ▶ **hand check:** players may not slap a ball handler, something that usually happens while trying to steal the ball.

▶ ▶ **hold:** players may not grab jerseys or hold another player in any manner.

▶ ▶ **illegal use of elbow:** players may not extend, or throw, an elbow at any time to back off a defender, something that can cause great injury.

▶ ▶ **illegal use of hands:** players may not slap a ball handler, something that usually happens while trying to steal the ball, or hit the arm of a shooter.

▶ More serious fouls – technical, intentional and flagrant – merit tougher penalties, usually uncontested free throws and possession awarded to the team suffering them. These also count as personal fouls. Players called for two of these are immediately sent from the game. Here are some clearer definitions of each:

▶ ▶ **flagrant foul:** excessive contact that may be perceived as an attempt to harm an opposing player. The opposing team gets two free throws and possession of the ball.

► ► **intentional foul:** a deliberate, physical foul committed on a ball handler, usually late in the game to stop the clock by the team that's trailing. The opposing team gets two free throws and possession of the ball.

► ► **technical foul:** called for unsportsmanlike behavior such arguing a call and using inappropriate language. The opposing team earns either one or two free throws and possession of the ball. Teams can also be called for calling a time out when they've already been exhausted or when a player entering the game did not have his name properly entered into the playbook.

► Familiarize yourself with the following terms:

► ► **3-point play:** a basket followed by a converted free throw.

► ► **assist:** passes that directly lead to baskets. Players with 10-plus a game are excellent playmakers.

► ► **backcourt:** the area where the ball is inbounded before going across the mid-court line.

► ► **bank shot:** score that bounced off the backboard and into the basket.

► ► **baseline:** the line that runs under the basket, outlining the court's end boundary and the location where balls are inbounded after baskets.

► ► **boxing out:** players block out opponents under the basket, battling for the best position to grab a rebound.

► ► **crossover dribble:** player transfers control from one hand to the other while dribbling.

► ► **double double:** when a player records 10-plus in two of the following – assists, rebounds and points.

► ► **fadeaway:** jump shot where a player jumps or steps backward during the attempt, perhaps the toughest shot to defend.

► ► **goaltending:** when players interfere with shots on their downward flight, which results in the basket counting regardless where it lands.

► ► **jump ball:** method of starting a game and any overtime periods. Jump balls have essentially been replaced by the alternating possession rule to settle situations where the ball is held by two players or possession is unclear when the ball is knocked out of bounds. Teams take turns getting possession on these plays, indicated by the possession arrow lit up at the scorer's table.

▶ ▶ **lanes:** rectangular, painted area extending out from the basket where players line up for free-throw attempts.

▶ ▶ **low post:** area on either side of the basket, where players try to set up to receive passes and score.

▶ ▶ **man-to-man defense:** defensive style where players are responsible for covering a specific opposing player, regardless of where this player moves.

▶ ▶ **perimeter:** area beyond the foul circle where players take longer shots to eventually draw the defense from the basket, opening up more lanes for layups and cuts to the basket.

▶ ▶ **pick and roll:** offensive play where a player sets a screen for a teammate with the ball, slides past or behind a defender, and receives a pass, usually taking a short jumper or layup.

▶ ▶ **post up:** when an offensive player battles for the best position near the basket to catch a pass and score, usually backing into a defender and dribbling after receiving the ball.

▶ ▶ **screen:** where players stand between the ball handler and defender, allowing this player to take a more open shot, pass or drive to the basket.

▶ ▶ **shot clock:** teams must attempt a shot every 24 seconds, defined by the ball hitting the rim. Shot clocks are reset for personal fouls, illegal defensive violations and balls that are knocked away by a defender's foot or hand. Teams must attempt shots every 30 seconds at the collegiate level, while state high school associations are split in their use of shot clocks.

▶ ▶ **sixth man:** player who comes off the bench first and – usually – most frequently.

▶ ▶ **squaring up:** where players set their shoulders square to the basket for a shot.

▶ ▶ **swing man:** a player capable of playing both forward and guard positions.

▶ ▶ **trap:** an attempt to prompt a turnover by suddenly sending two players at a ball handler at the same time.

▶ ▶ **triple double:** when a player records 10-plus assists, rebounds and points.

▶ ▶ **turnovers:** when the offense loses control of the ball for violations, fouls and errors such as poor passes, steals or having the ball bounce off a foot and roll out of bounds.

▶ ▶ **weak side:** the side of the court on the other side of the ball.

▶ ▶ **zone defense:** defensive style where players are responsible for areas on the court, guarding anyone who enters these zones.

Get Ready

▶ Show up early for the game to record the lineups in your own scoring book. Check with the official statistician, managers and coaches that the players and the numbers match up. At high school games especially, verify the class standing and any team and individual stats for players on both teams. Record full names, numbers and class standings of all players before the game

▶ Record the names of the game officials in case anything unusual happens in the game. Also, interview them afterward in such instances. I covered a state high school basketball game where a coach chased the officials off the floor and into their dressing room.

▶ Establish relationships. If you're new on a beat, introduce yourself to the team's publicist or sports information director – and, if possible, to the coaches and general managers. Read various media guides. "And don't be afraid to ask questions," says Phil Jasner, basketball beat writer for the *Philadelphia Daily News.* "That's what you're there for."

▶ Check to see what the team's all-time series record is against this team. See if you can find anything interesting in the numbers.

WATCH

▶ Basketball is a game of runs. The team that runs off the most streaks of points usually wins. Record them while taking notes through the game. So take note of those 6 – 0, 8 – 0, 10 – 2 and 12 – 4 runs during a game. Later, analyze what prompted these scoring streaks.

▶ Games can also include scoring droughts, periods where a team fails to score – or even to take a shot. Did a team fail to score over a six- or eight-minute stretch? You can go back and check your notes to determine the exact time lapses. But compare the time against the official play-by-play, which is available at college and professional games. For high school games, you'll have to trust your notes.

▶ What team goes to the free-throw line most frequently? Games are often won at the free-throw line. Did one team get more free-throw attempts in the final five to 10 minutes? Is there a great discrepancy? In stories, you can focus on one team's proficiency or failings at the line down the stretch.

▶ Look for things that don't show up in box scores but that helped a team to win, or remain close, in the game. These include picks, hustle, blocking out for rebounds and screens set. Coaches love when players do these perceived little things that can yield big rewards, so make sure you get their insights and commentary after the game.

▶ Focus on shot selection. Did the team tend to make more shots inside or outside? From the left or right side of the court? Did this change between halves or in specific quarters? Note locations for shots in your notes, and then verify this afterward when possible. Most statisticians, though, won't have this at high school games.

▶ Focus on a coach's or player's reactions during the game – and also right after the game concludes – something that can reveal a great deal about attitude and effort. That's what an Associated Press sports writer did in the following lead.

> When the buzzer sounded, Dirk Nowitzki walked off the court gently touching his bloodied mouth.
> Although his front right tooth was missing, Nowitzki and the Dallas Mavericks hadn't felt this good in more than a week.
> Nowitzki led a team-wide break from a series-long shooting slump, scoring 30 points as the Mavericks beat the San Antonio Spurs 112 – 108 Saturday to avoid being swept from the second-round series. Game 5 is Monday night in San Antonio.[1]

▶ Break down rebounds right after a game. How many were offensive, which are more difficult to collect since the defending team is usually in better position with more people close to the basket? Offensive rebounds give teams second-chance shots and can help a team overcome a poor shooting performance. Describe a key rebound during the game and ask questions after the game to illustrate a team's prowess under the basket.

- How does a coach make adjustments? Rarely does a game plan have legs for the entire game. Coaches usually have plans B, C and D. How do coaches adjust to minor and major changes in their original game plans? For example, did a coach have to adjust to how to defend against a trap on a ball screen, or to a defensive alignment by the opposing team? Try to see if a team changes its defense, from a man-to-man to a zone, for example.

- Compare playing styles and tempos. How does a team that presses fare against a team that plays zone? Does a team look more comfortable playing a faster-paced game, taking off on fast-breaks? Or does the team play better in a slower half-court offense, methodically moving the ball around? Or does a team do well adapting to both tempos? Coaches want to assert their playing style, forcing the other team to adapt to one where they don't play as well.

- Assess individual match-ups – guards against guards, centers against centers, forwards against forwards. What enables players to win these man-to-man battles? And how do these smaller victories lead to larger team wins?

- Focus on points scored in the paint, the area under the basket. This can reveal a great deal – that a team did not play as tightly on defense, that a skilled dribbler was able to sneak through defenders, that a team grabbed a large number of offensive rebounds that were put back in, and that a team dominated physically near the basket, among other things.

- Focus on fouls. Did a player have to sit out for an extended period because of foul trouble? Do players in foul trouble remain in the game? If so, carefully watch their defensive efforts, determining whether the opposing team drove more toward them on the way to the basket, hoping for a reach-in or bump that would result in a final foul that would send them to the basket for the remainder of the game. Or do players in foul trouble continue to play aggressively? How did the team respond when a player fouled out – by playing more relaxed, thinking the game would be easier once this opposing player left the game, or by giving up when this teammate departed?

- Here are few other things that can generate questions and story angles:

  - Fast-break points.

  - Points scored off turnovers.

  - Points scored by bench players.

  - Second-chance points.

► ► Number of ties, especially if many occur in the second half. Nobody really cares that a team traded leads in the opening 10 minutes, but they will if these quick changes happened during the final 10.

► ► Pivotal moments in the game; game-changing moments.

► ► Assists: Who fed the scorers the most? Describe the types of passes.

► ► Offensive and defensive alignments.

► ► Trends either in team results or within the game. The team might have won or lost its last four games by a single point or two. Or, the team may have lost the ball countless times at midfield or been called for penalties near their own basket.

► ► Determine how a coach recognizes match-ups. Ask them, along with some players, afterward.

► ► Locations of shots. Keep a chart to see where the team took (and made) most of its shots in a quarter, half or game.

► ► Look for streaks in a game, such as those 8 – 0 or 12 – 2 runs. Cite the key plays and performers during the streaks.

► ► Divide stats by half (or by quarters). Did a team do much better statistically in one period than the other?

► ► Look for stat trends. For example, tell the reader if one team has averaged 20 3-point attempts during the past six games. Find out the reason for this as well. Reading archive stories will help find such trends.

ASK

► Ask players to describe a key play. Was the shot set up with a screen? Did you have a good look at the basket? How did you anticipate the pass on that steal? How were you able to get under the basket for that rebound? What were you thinking at the time?

► Ask coaches what went right and wrong during the game? Did the team play well near the basket, blocking out to gain better position? Did the team hustle? Did the team pass well?

- Ask players to describe their opponents, particularly those matched directly against them. How did one team's guard think of the play of the opposing two guards?

- Ask how teams adapted to the other team's tempo or approach.

- Ask coaches about their tactics. How did they adjust their game plan during the game? What worked and did not?

- Why did a coach keep a player in the game despite having four fouls down the stretch of a college game? Ask coaches about anything related to foul trouble. Did the coach stay with a player, believing the previous fouls were not merited? Could this coach not afford to pull out this player despite the foul problems? To understand their approach, ask coaches why they either kept or pulled players in foul trouble.

WRITE

- Break down a key run. Why did a team go on so many runs of points in a game? Did one team go on an 8 – 0 run to take a four-point lead only to see the other team regain the advantage on a 12 – 4 run. How did these teams string together the scoring streaks? Did they start off turnovers and lead to fast breaks? Did the team rely on a slower game, feeding the ball inside to its bigger players? What was the score before and after this run? How did this run prove decisive?

- Too often, stories begin with the leading scorer, when this is not the most significant stat or reason for a team's success. Instead, focus on a play, or series of plays, that illustrates how a team performed. That could be an offensive rebound and put-in that shows a team's aggressive play, or a missed shot down the stretch that shows a team's poor shot selection or poor skill in shooting.

- Don't rely on adjectives and adverbs to describe impressive plays. Instead, break them down so someone can visualize, or follow, the play. *Sports Illustrated*'s Grant Wahl focused on a single pass to begin a preview piece on the NCAA Final Four:

  > Four seconds. That's all it took. Four seconds for UCLA freshman forward Kevin Love to bury Xavier for good after the Musketeers had mounted a comeback with an 11 – 2 run in the second half of last Saturday's West Regional final. Four seconds for Love to snatch the ball out of the net,

take one step out-of-bounds – his right foot planted, his left foot inches above the floor – and snap an immaculate, 70-foot chest pass to teammate Russell Westbrook for a layup and a 14-point lead. Four seconds to crush Xavier with basketball's answer to a 60-yard touchdown throw. For one glorious, fleeting moment the old-school chest pass was as sexy as a Dwight Howard slam dunk. "I love hearing the oohs and aahs you get from the crowd," Love says, "because you rarely ever hear them for a pass. You usually just hear them for a dunk."[2]

▶ Is this the team's worst loss, or biggest margin of victory? Cite the last time the team lost by such a margin. Then, determine reasons for such a great victory or terrible loss. If the game is a blowout, focus on how and why one team dominated.

▶ Focus on reserves and bench players who contributed significantly, helping a team during a key run or in a particular area such as rebounding or making 3-pointers. Or, perhaps, this player's hustle inspired the rest of the team to play harder.

▶ Cite how teams scored most of their points during runs. Did they make a series of layups, make several mid-range jumpers or convert a number of free throws?

▶ Focus on key plays down the stretch, even when players miss shots.

With less than a minute remaining, the Sixers had two chances to take the lead: Thaddeus Young missed a tough baseline layup with 42.9 seconds to play, and Andre Iguodala, who finished with 22 points, missed a 15-foot jump shot with 22.9 seconds left.[3]

▶ Did a player dominate in one aspect of the game, scoring 30-plus points, grabbing 15-plus rebounds or assisting on 10-plus baskets. If so, cite the reasons for this player's success, which will be a mix of your observations and responses during post-game interviews.

▶ Put summaries of key scorers near the end of the story. List only the top stat leaders, if significant, since the agate will already list these in the summaries.

▶ Cite who the next opponent will be, including the location of the game and the opponent's record, somewhere in the story. Unless the game is pivotal, such as a playoff match-up or a game that can determine a conference champion, you can cite the next game near the end of the story. You might also create a fact box that lists the next opponent as part of all game precede stories.

(continued on page 98)

To reveal trends or to track key plays in a game, it is important to track as much information as possible, such as the time period between baskets, when a player earned a fourth foul, or how frequently a team turns over the ball. You'll also notice many ministreaks, like a 10 – 2 scoring run, and trends during shorter stretches, such as a team turning over the ball five times during a two-minute period. These lead to wider analysis and more specific (and illuminating) questions after the game for coaches and players.

1 *Team names with records.*

2 *Scoring averages for both teams entering this game are cited for easy reference.*

3 *Field-goal shooting percentages.*

4 *3-point shooting percentages.*

5 *Free-throw shooting percentages.*

6 *Average turnovers per game.*

7 *Average total rebounds per game.*

8 *TO is shorthand for turnover by Burke.*

9 *Periodically, cite time remaining for each half down the left side of the page so you can better cite elapsed time for rallies or scoring droughts.*

10 *0/3pter is shorthand for missed 3-point attempts.*

11 *T/A is shorthand for turnaround jumper.*

12 *10j or 12j is shorthand for midrange jumpers. Obviously, this is an estimated distance. Walk off 10 or 12 steps from the basket before games to get a better sense of distances like this.*

13 *Put scores down the middle of page to separate teams.*

14 *Denotes player made one of two free throws. You can add circles to note which shot was converted – in this case, the second one.*

15 *FT is short for free throw.*

16 *The circled 3 denotes that a player converted a 3-point shot.*

17 *l-u is shorthand for layup.*

18 *Circle or put a square around scoring runs. In this case, Cypress Lake scored 8 points in a row.*

HOME — Zephyrhills (17-9) ① **VISITOR** — Cypress Lake (18-4)

Time	Player	Action ⑩	Score	Player	Action ⑧
20:00 ⑨	Anderson	0/3pter ⑩	-	Burke	TO ⑧
			-	Matthews	0/3pter
			-	McNeal	T/A ⑪
18:51	Cunningham	10j ⑫	2-0 ⑬	Sutton	(3 pt)
	Walton	TO	2-3		
17:24			2-5	Hansbrough	12j
17:10	Anderson	1-2FT ⑭	3-5	Matthews	1 FT ⑮
		O●	-	Hansbrough	(3) ⑯
	Thompson	TO	3-8		
			-	Ellington	1-u ⑰
15:09	Walton	miss 10j	3-10		
14:42			3-10	Hansbrough ⑱	(3)
			3-13 ⑱ →	Sutton	
14:10	Anderson	2-2	-		
13:57	Cunningham	0/3pter	5-13	Ellington	5j
			5-15		
	Matthews		5-15	Matthews	12j
			5-17		

Time	Player	Action	Score	Player	Action

PTS avg: 77.3/66.7	FG%: 46.1/40.5 ③	3pt%: 36.9/33.1 ④
FT avg: 79.0/69.2 ⑤	TO: 11.8/15.5 ⑥	Reb avg: 24.1/22.9 ⑦

② ④

▶ Game's significance. Does the game clinch a playoff berth or eliminate the team from the postseason? Is this a conference or district victory? Does this advance the team in a tournament?

▶ Focus on a coach's decision or strategy.

▶ Focus on a stat leader if the stat is truly worth addressing, such as 30 points or a triple double. (Typical sports roundups, which are a series of two- or three-paragraph game stories, lead with a stats leader.)

▶ Here are the common spellings for several other basketball terms: backboard, back-court, fast-break offense, field goal, field-goal attempt, foul line, foul shot, free throw, free-throw line, full-court press, half-court press, halftime, hook shot, jump shot, layup, midcourt, and slow-down defense.

BOWLING

Just as golfers need to read contours on a green for the best line to a hole, bowlers need to determine the oil patterns that funnel balls into the pocket on a bowling lane.

Bowlers look for the best line to the pins, trying to hook the ball at the right spot so it rotates back at the right time and the right spot so it hits in the pocket and sends pins ricocheting off one another for a strike.

In bowling's early days, oil was spread over 60-foot lanes to protect the wooden planks from the constant pounding of balls dropping and rolling toward the pins. Oil not only protects lanes, it significantly changes the playing conditions, forcing bowlers to adjust on their approaches.

Today, lanes are oiled in a manner that helps the ball catch, hook back away from the gutter and into the sweet spot down the middle of the lane. In heavy oil, the ball slides more and doesn't hook as well. In light oil, the ball runs more over the lane, the friction allowing the ball to hook better.

For example, is the oil thicker at the end of the lane, requiring a more direct line to the pocket? Is the oil farther down the lane, meaning the ball will not hook back in if the ball strays too far outside? Does the oil widen out down the lane, preventing bowlers from using the same angles on each shot?

Leagues use more than a dozen patterns whose descriptions and explanations would require an entire chapter.

Lane conditions deteriorate through constant play, especially during professional tournaments where more than 100 bowlers will roll at least nine games apiece during early rounds, wearing down the oil and the best paths to the pins.

Bowlers try to combat changing conditions by changing balls, using different weights and textures, by changing the placement of their feet as they approach and release the ball, and by changing where they aim the ball.

But this does not always work. That's why even the best bowlers can struggle at times, shooting games 50 to 75 pins below their averages.

The Professional Bowlers Association sends staff to determine the best way to pattern oil at each venue.

Left-handed bowlers may appear to gain slight advantages during tournaments since fewer bowlers are wearing down their patterns. But they have to react to lane conditions in other ways.

In addition, conditions frequently change during games. See a player suddenly miss the pocket or face a few tough spares after a string of strikes? Odds are, the lane conditions changed, which is something worth investigating afterward.

PREPARE

Learn the Basics

▶ Balls have changed a great deal through the decades, going from oak wooden balls to urethane, plastic and reactive resin – or even a combination of all three materials. Balls are designed in varying weights and density alignments. Balls, 8½ inches in diameter, range from about 6 to 16 pounds. Older competitive bowlers usually use balls that are 14 to 16 pounds because the extra weight allows the ball to drive better through the pins.

▶ The 10 pins are aligned in a triangle over four rows, with one in the front row, followed by 2 – 3 – 4 in the next rows. Pins are 15 inches tall and reach 4.75 inches at their widest point; they weigh 3 pounds, 6 ounces.

▶ 300 is a perfect score in bowling, when someone throws 12 strikes in a row.

▶ Bowlers are allowed nine balls per PBA competition during qualifying but unlimited during match play.

▶ Like golf, bowling is a controlled-motion sport, so the top players bowl 100 games a week to improve their techniques and skills. Like golfers, bowlers also fall into slumps and need coaches to diagnose problems in their techniques.

▶ Bowling takes a toll on a body. So, during bigger tournaments, bowlers won't hurt themselves trying to throw every ball hard. Instead, they try to grind it out, preserving their energy and bodies for games during later rounds.

▶ Some professional bowlers work with psychologists to improve their games.

▶ Scoring: A game consists of 10 frames, and a bowler can throw the ball a second time in any frame where pins remain. Strikes and spares are rewarded. After strikes, the next two throws are added to that frame's score. For spares, the next throw is added. Bowlers can throw up to three times in the 10th frame – once after a spare and twice more after a strike.

▶ Scores are recorded for games, blocks and total pinball. A block is typically a qualifying round of nine games.

▶ Technological advancements in balls and oil patterns have helped increase scores during the past several decades. League bowlers regularly average 200. The top professional bowlers average 220-plus.

▶ Format for National Collegiate Athletic Association championships: Teams are seeded based upon a qualifying round where five-bowler squads will roll four team games and four five-game Baker matches. (The Baker format allows five team members to follow each other in order, each bowling a complete frame until a complete, 10-frame game is bowled.) The fourth Baker set of games will serve as the position round, meaning the pinball in this round will serve as the tiebreaker. Next, teams are placed in a double-elimination bracket, where they compete against one another in a best-of-seven Baker-style bowling competition. Ties within Baker games are decided by a ninth and 10th frame roll-off.

▶ Tournament events are set up in the following format. First round: Bowlers roll nine straight games to determine which 64 bowlers will advance to the next round, where they bowl another nine games over nine different lanes. Totals for both rounds are counted to determine the 32 who will be seeded in a bracket. This is similar to the system used in tennis, where the No. 1 player competes against No. 32, No. 2 plays

No. 31 and so on. The winners of these match-play games keep playing until only four remain for the championship finals.

▶ The PBA's four major events are the Masters, U.S. Open, World Championship, and Tournament of Champions. The league, which typically has 20-plus events scheduled across the country, retains a strong fan base, attracting about 1 million TV viewers for its finals. The season runs from April through October.

▶ Familiarize yourself with some key terms:

> ▶ ▶ **7 – 10 split:** if the ball does not travel tightly to the pocket, the two corner pins will be left, a spare attempt that is extremely difficult to convert.

> ▶ ▶ **ABC:** American Bowling Congress, formerly the sport's official rule maker.

> ▶ ▶ **anchor:** the last person to bowl in team competitions each frame, typically the best bowler.

> ▶ ▶ **approach:** this refers to both the 15-foot area right before the foul line and to the manner in which bowlers go to the line before releasing the ball down the lane.

> ▶ ▶ **baby split:** when the 2 – 7 – 8 or 3 – 9 – 10 pins are left after the first throw.

> ▶ ▶ **foul line:** if a bowler goes over this line, the throw does not count and a 0 is recorded for the throw. If this is the first throw of the frame, the pins are reset. If all pins are subsequently knocked down, the player earns a spare. Most lanes have automatic detectors that use a light beam.

> ▶ ▶ **gutter:** a depressed area about 9½ inches wide on each side of a lane; it collects balls that fall off the lanes, sending them down past the pins to the pit area to be returned. A gutter ball results in a 0.

> ▶ ▶ **head pin:** the first pin, front and center.

> ▶ ▶ **lanes:** made of either real or synthetic wood and 60 feet in length and 41 to 42 inches wide with 39 boards running between gutters that run down each side.

> ▶ ▶ **mark:** term for when a player records a strike or spare, denoted by marks of X or /; numerals are not used.

> ▶ ▶ **open frame:** frame having neither a spare nor strike.

> ▶ ▶ **PBA:** Professional Bowlers Association.

▶ ▶ **perfect game:** 12 consecutive strikes for a score of 300.

▶ ▶ **pit:** area where pins go after they're hit to be swept, collected and reset.

▶ ▶ **pocket:** area between the first and third pins where the ball can drive through and ricochet more pins to gain a strike. The pocket is between the first and second pins for left-handers.

▶ ▶ **spare:** when a player knocks down any remaining pins on the second throw in a frame.

▶ ▶ **strike:** when a player knocks down all 10 pins on a single throw.

▶ ▶ **USBC:** United States Bowling Congress, a relatively new organization formed after a merger of the American Bowling Congress, Women's International Bowling Congress, Young American Bowling Alliance and USA Bowling.

▶ ▶ **WIBC:** Women's International Bowling Congress, the governing body for women players.

Get Ready

▶ Arrive early to speak with league officials to determine where scores from qualifying rounds will be posted for tournaments. For information about team matchups, speak with coaches to determine who is keeping the official statistics. Ask whether league officials can e-mail all qualifying, match-play and final scores to you, saving you and your editors from typing them in yourself. At tournaments, these scores may also be printed and distributed to all sports journalists.

▶ For tournaments, call either the bowling pro or the general manager of the lanes to verify the times and format for all rounds from qualifying to the finals. In addition, secure press credentials. If you can, go to the bowling lanes in person, an extra effort that may yield more cooperation during the event. Bowling gets very little coverage, so a little enthusiasm can go a long way, allowing you to connect better with the people who can offer some terrific story angles.

▶ For college matches, contact each school's sports information director to get team and individual stats. In all likelihood, these stats may be on the university's athletics page, but the SID may have additional information not cited.

▶ Speak with coaches, bowlers or league officials to chat about any upcoming event. In these informal conversations, you will likely learn several story angles and discern at least a few trends not cited on any stats sheets.

WATCH

▶ Focus on the leaders. Did any bowlers do something dramatic to remain among the leaders? Did they pick up any difficult spares?

▶ Move around the bowling alley to watch the best matches and to find something interesting or unusual. Perhaps the two top bowlers are competing against one another in an early round or in a team competition. Maybe a bowler is rolling an unusually high score or a player has a distinct throwing style. Or, perhaps, a bowler inexplicably rushes off the lanes, as Mark Baker did after throwing eight consecutive strikes during a tournament in Miami. Dick Evans, a Hall of Fame bowling writer, followed Baker to the paddock where bowlers kept their equipment and street clothes. Baker had split his pants. "Like most young Californians, he did not wear underwear," says Evans, "so he had to use his street pants for the final two frames." After returning, he finished for a 279 game before winning the tournament the next day and prompting Evans to write his famous story, "Moon Over Miami."

ASK

▶ Talk to bowlers who either leaped into the leaderboard or who fell out of contention. What happened in the later rounds? Did the balls not stick on the lanes as well? Did a player bowl poorly, or exceptionally well, on certain lanes in the alley? Did a player fail to convert spares down the stretch?

▶ Ask players to comment on opponents who are red-hot. What did you notice about their games during the final frames, or rounds? What did they appear to be doing differently?

▶ As in golf, it's impossible to catch every frame during tournaments or even team matchups, so ask bowlers to describe their rounds. Did they have any trouble in any games? Did they have problems on any lanes? Did any lanes feel easier to read?

▶ Ask bowlers about the conditions of the lanes. Was it tough to read the lanes? How did they roll? Toward the end of the tournament, how were lane conditions compared with earlier rounds?

- Be friendly and be enthusiastic. Bowlers, especially at lower-level competitions, receive little coverage except having some scores posted in the newspaper once in a while. By showing enthusiasm, you can usually get some terrific insights and nearly anything else you want from the local proprietors.

- Bowling is as much about strategy as posting high scores, especially in championship rounds where a player competes against another to advance or to win a title. If another bowler missed a spare, what was your plan for the ninth frame? Did you do any research on the lane conditions? What was your strategy against this opponent?

- Professional bowlers know how to read the lanes, seeing where the oil is placed down to the pins. Ask bowlers to describe the oil on the lanes, particularly on those used for championships or head-to-head team competition. Where did the ball catch the oil? How did the oil work with your game? Did your hook catch it at the right spot?

- Ask bowlers about their approaches. Did you have to change anything today? Did you have to change speeds? Angles? Directions?

- Ask bowlers to describe a decisive shot.

- Cite the leaders after each round of bigger tournaments, explaining the performance that vaulted someone into the lead; for example,

> Roth put together a nine-game block of 1,997, a 221.8 average, to take a 29-pin lead through the second round. His overall pin total is 4,141, a 230 average for 18 games.

- Briefly explain the format for each tournament, especially what happens in the round coming up:

> The 154-player field has been cut to the top 50, who will bowl nine more games Thursday before the field is further reduced to the top 32, who will compete in match play on Friday.

WRITE

- In tournaments, note leaders who fell out of contention during the later rounds.

- Offer some background for tournament winners. Has this bowler been a consistent winner? Is this the first victory for this bowler? If you're covering high school or college matchups, offer each bowler's record.

(continued on page 108)

1. *"/" denotes a spare, which is when a bowler knocks down all 10 pins on two throws in a single frame.*

2. *"X" denotes a strike, which is when a bowler knocks down all 10 pins on a single throw. Spares and strikes are called marks.*

3. *Open frame, when a bowler fails to knock down 10 pins in a frame. Make sure to note which pin(s) were left standing.*

4. *A game consists of 10 frames.*

5. *After strikes, the next two throws are added to that frame's score. If three strikes in a row are thrown, for example, a bowler earns 30 pins for the initial strike.*

6. *After spares, the next throw is added to that frame's total score. In this case, six pins are added, resulting in 123 for the fifth frame.*

7. *Bowlers can take three throws in the 10th frame if they earn a mark on the first two throws.*

Name	1 	2	3	4	5	6	7	8	9	10	Total
Roth	9 /	X	X	7 2	8 /	X	X	9	8 /	X X 8	
	20	47	66	75	95	124	144	162	182	210	210
Anthony	X	X	X	X	7 /	6 3	8 /	X	X X X		
	30	60	87	107	123	132	152	182	212	242	242

▶ Try to find something out of the ordinary. A lucky strike at a key moment. A cough that upsets a bowler on the way to the foul line. Then explain and describe these moments.

▶ Record the number of strikes and spares, but open frames are what usually cost the top bowlers. Describe the frames where bowlers fail to mark.

▶ Mention any bowler who rolls a perfect game, or even has one going into the 10th frame.

▶ Look to see who moves up the most during qualifying rounds. Did a player move from 45th to 22nd? 24th to 10th? Obviously, the closer they are to the top, the more interesting it is to readers, but even large jumps in the middle are worth noting.

▶ Bowling has a great deal of jargon, but avoid using terms such as "Cincinnati" for an 8 – 10 split, "dime store" for a 5 – 10 split, "kegler" for bowlers, "five-bagger" for five strikes in a row, "garbage hit" for a strike made without hitting the pocket, "turkey" for three straight strikes, or "snake eyes" for a 7 – 10 split.

CROSS COUNTRY

O dd things can happen at a cross-country race. Runners get speared by other runners' spikes. Mud sucks the shoes off their feet. They plow through snow and splash through standing water, trip over rocks and roots, streak past moose and deer. Cross-country runners race one another, not the clock; overcoming obstacles is an integral part of the sport. Courses are plotted around high schools, through county parks, on golf courses, and in any accessible open area. So most of what the runners do, they do far from the eyes of journalists or coaches. In addition, poor weather and course conditions can slow top-rated runners. "Sometimes," says Oklahoma State coach Dave Smith, "weather can be an equalizer."

Although cross country is both a team and an individual competition, team accomplishments usually trump individual successes. The main goal is to place your top five runners ahead of your opponents' top five. "It's better to go home in the van full of seven happy guys rather than one happy guy," University of Oregon runner Galen Rupp said after the 2007 nationals, where the Ducks won their first team title in 30 years. He was a happy guy despite losing the individual title, which he went on to win the following year.

While cross country is not as popular as football or baseball, it's far from obscure. Hundreds of thousands of high school students compete each fall, and the sport has many enthusiastic followers at every level. In 2007, thousands of fans filled Oregon's football stadium to watch the nationals on a giant screen. That same year, cross country was the most viewed sport on the Web site of the National Collegiate Athletic Association.

PREPARE

Learn the Basics

▶ Five kilometers is the most common distance for high school runners. At college, men typically run 8K and women 5K during the season; however, they run 10K and 6K, respectively, at nationals. To convert kilometers to miles, divide by 1.6. But you can avoid tough math simply by remembering that a 5K race is 3.1 miles, a 10K race is 6.2 miles, and then estimate the other distances accordingly.

▶ Cross-country teams enter seven runners in meets. Only the top five finishers count in the overall scores, with one exception: If two teams are tied, the sixth-place runner becomes the tiebreaker. In addition, these sixth and seventh runners push back scores for competing teams, so their overall finish can be significant.

▶ Cross country is scored by adding the finish (1 point for first, 2 for second, and so on) of a team's top five runners. The lowest score wins. The lowest possible score is 15, when a team takes the first five spots $(1 + 2 + 3 + 4 + 5)$.

▶ Calculate pace. Pace is the average time per mile, so someone who raced three miles in 15 minutes ran at a pace of 5 minutes per mile. You can calculate this by dividing time by miles. You will have to change minutes to seconds for most calculations. Thus, you would multiply 15 minutes by 60 seconds before dividing by three miles.

▶ Determine splits. These are a runner's times for segments of a longer race, typically set up at mile or kilometer marks. Thus, in a three-mile race, splits are usually kept at the 1- and 2-mile marks. In a 10K race, times are often kept at the 2-, 4-, 6- and 8-kilometer marks. By getting these, you can determine where, and when, a runner either faltered or took off. Coaches usually record their own splits during the race. After the race, you can ask the coaches or the team managers for records of the splits if the final results do not include them.

▶ Individual runners can advance to state and national championship races even when the team does not. That means some runners will advance from conference and regional meets unattached to a team. As a result, these runners are eligible to win individual titles and earn All-America status, but their finish is extracted when calculating team scores. Thus, an unattached runner who finished fourth would not be included in the list used for scoring purposes. Instead, the runner who finished fifth would be moved up to fourth, sixth would move to fifth, and so on.

sports insider

> "The notes I take during a race usually involve who is in the lead at various stages. I figure the first fifth or so of a race – up to say, 5,000 meters, is sort of a feeling out process for everyone involved. Unless there is something earth-shatteringly fast or slow going on with the pace, I'll wait a bit to see how things are progressing. If an announcer happens to be giving splits, say for the first mile, I'll write that down. If there's a small group running in the lead, I'll try to keep track of their order at various stages, and try to note at what point in the race the eventual winner took the lead. . . . Post-race interviews are really when you pick up about 75 percent of the information you need to write a story. . . . The competitors can tell you how the race unfolded usually better than your notes can. Coaches, if they are available, are the best source for runners you may want to know about but weren't paying close attention to."

Doug Binder,
The Oregonian **(Portland, Ore.)**

In college, the conference championship is the primary race for teams. Previous performances mean little. Most all-conference teams and coach of the year honors are based on results in the conference championships. At the high school level, runners typically advance from district and regional meets to reach the state championships.

Training methods vary for teams, but Fartlek training is very popular. This is a speed workout that requires runners to pick up the pace for short periods during longer training runs. Runners may run hard for 15 – 20 seconds, then slow down for a minute or so, before repeating this faster pace. Coaches sometimes apply this training during races, asking team members to pick up the pace during short bursts to pass runners and to play mind games with other runners.

Coaches use a variety of strategies. Sometimes, they will ask their top runners to slow down just enough to allow teammates to pick up their pace and follow them, at least for the first half of a race. In a sense, team members draft off their top runner. Running together, or in a pack, is a major psychological boost. Conversely, this deflates runners whom they pass as a group. Coaches use a variety of psychological ploys like this during races.

Get Ready

Walk the course before the race to determine which mile or kilometer markers you can readily reach. Depending on your own physical abilities, map out one or two places to view the runners. Only direct observation lets you describe the runners and help your readers visualize the race: "Steve Jones breathed hard at the four-mile marker. His legs seemed to slow down and his body swayed to the side, unlike the six runners who ran effortlessly past him." But make sure you can reach the finish line before the leaders. Races are often won or lost in the final stretch.

▶ In addition, check the terrain. Where are the hills? A hill late in the race can have a big impact on runners. What's the elevation? Teams that train at higher elevations usually have an edge because their bodies are more accustomed to working with less oxygen. Colorado State, for example, would probably do much better running a race in Indiana than an Indiana team would do running more than 5,000 feet high in Boulder.

▶ Research the best times in the conference or the region, listing the top 10 runners. For college, you can do this by checking Web sites; for high school, you'll probably need to call coaches. Knowing recent leaders won't just help you write a preview story if assigned; it will also give you a pretty good idea about who should win. "Seldom in a sport like cross country are there major surprises from someone rising up from the back of the pack," says Doug Binder, who regularly covers cross country for *The Oregonian* in Portland, Ore. "The leaders are generally the same because they have more ability, and prove that week after week."

▶ Determine the last time a runner from a team or a school has reached a state or national meet: "Cypress Lake High School returned to the state meet for the first time in eight years, placing fifth."

▶ Speak with key runners and coaches off the record before the meet; ask them about strategies, plans and injuries so you can better find story ideas. Usually you need to develop rapport with the coaches before they will reveal these details, even off the record. Make sure you do not report anything that is told to you under this reporting condition. Instead, use this information to plan your coverage and to find your story angles.

▶ Determine what's at stake in this meet. A conference title? A chance to compete at the state meet? An undefeated dual-meet record? A chance for a runner to test herself against a top-rated runner?

▶ Know the credentials of top runners. Reporters covering the 2008 NCAA Division I Cross Country Championships knew that Galen Rupp had finished second the previous year when another runner used a strong kick to beat him during the final stretch. Rupp subsequently used a final kick to win in 2008. That information enabled sports journalists to address a significant storyline.

▶ Do not expect coaches to reveal their team strategies before a race, especially a major meet. "I'm no more likely to answer that question than a football coach will tell you his first 10 plays," says Colorado's Mark Wetmore, whose teams have won both men's and women's team and individual titles.

digital assist

The Roanoke (Va.) *Times* used elevation maps, panoramic views along the course, audio, text and photos to guide readers through a 100K ultramarathon that includes 13,000 feet of climbing through the Jefferson National Forest in western Virginia. The newspaper also focused on a local runner to further attract readers. Check out "Running on Empty" at www.roanoke.com/multimedia/hellgate/interactive.html.

Running on empty

Hellgate, 110 runners, 100 kilometers, 18 hours

WATCH

Calculate the elapsed time between each of the first five runners on the top teams to determine what strategy worked best or, at least, to note interesting gaps for the reader. A 20-second gap between the top five runners would be worth noting, as would a minute gap between the fourth and fifth runners. "In most meets that we run, our five scoring runners should all be in the top 10 to 15 percent of the total field by the time they finish," says Donald Fritsch, whose University of Wisconsin – Lacrosse team has won two NCAA Division II titles. "They should be within striking distance of these spots at 5K and they should have these spots secured by 7K."

▶ Consider the weather. Some runners do better in muddy, rainy conditions; others do better when the weather is hot. "The steps are much more difficult in mud," say Stanford's Chris Derrick. "That extra effort – that sloppiness on the course – can tire you out on each and every step."

▶ Watch for pack running. Runners may stay together for most of the race, often to pull each other along. In some ways, pack running works like the drafting methods used by cyclists and race car drivers. It also eases the psychological burden of running alone.

▶ Track strategy by observing. Some teams like to go out hard, daring others to keep up. Some teams start slow, then push hard in the second half. Some teams stay steady, throwing in occasional surges.

▶ Track strategy by recording split times. The opening mile can give a sense of a team's strategy. After the race, check splits to compare the pace for the first mile and the last mile. Most colleges supply this information, but high schools rarely offer much beyond final time and overall place. Get split times from coaches or team managers.

▶ Look for the coach. Unlike other sports, cross country makes few demands on coaches during an event. Before the starting gun explodes, the coach has already outlined team and individual race plans and trained the runners physically and mentally. After that, "They [his runners] would run as well if I sat in the van listening to the radio," says Colorado coach Mark Wetmore, who has coached NCAA teams and individual titlists for both men and women. Still, you may want to observe how a coach watches the race – running to mile markers, riding in an all-terrain vehicle or sitting at the finish line to record times.

ASK

▶ Talk with as many coaches and runners as possible to get a clearer picture of the race. Unlike football and baseball, cross country's main action does not evolve in front of fans and writers. You'll need to gain these valuable perspectives to better understand, and explain, the race for readers.

Choose questions that encourage runners to talk you through the race. "Post-race interviews are really when you pick up about 75 percent of the information you need," says Binder. "The competitors can tell you how the race unfolded usually better than your notes can." Specific questions can coax runners' thoughts and fill in the narrative of the race. Where was the course easy or hard? What were the conditions like? What surprised you? Were you keeping an eye on any particular runners? When did you know you had won (or lost)?

Ask coaches about pre-race workouts and race strategies. Questions coaches wouldn't answer before the race, they usually will after. Here's an example of something a coach might say after a race: "Our strategy was to go a little conservative because there's a hill on the first mile," Eastern Illinois University coach Geoff Masanet says. "Then, we wanted to get rolling on miles two and three before throwing in a surge at the fourth mile."

Ask if anybody set a personal best time, also referred to as a personal record. Do not use the acronym PR, because these are not actual records. Write "personal best" instead: "Jay Daniels clocked in at 18:03, 27 seconds faster than his previous best time."

WRITE

Include the name of the event, the distance and location of the race.

Include a paragraph that names team and individual winners. Example: "Pioneer took the Class 1 title with 82 points, 63 better than runner-up Saginaw."

Focus more on the top runners from your primary readership area. Your readers will be more interested in a local girl who finished 18th at a regional meet than a winner who lives more than two hours away. Cite the overall winners in the story, but lead with local angles.

Spell out times in first reference, writing 15 minutes, 37 seconds. You may abbreviate times in second reference: "Aaron Smith won the 5K race in 15 minutes, 20 seconds, followed by Matt McElwee in 15:32."

If this is a postseason race, state how many teams will advance to the next level. And also state the time and date of the next race.

Cite course records set during any meet.

▶ You might want to cite the top freshman or sophomore finishes, especially if these runners are from your readership area.

▶ Describe performances among the leaders:

> Bridgewater's Betsy Hennessey won her third consecutive state title, pulling away in the final mile to become the winningest girls cross country runner in New Jersey history. Hennessey clocked in at 17 minutes, 29 seconds, over the 5K course. Susan Tomko of Raritan stayed within striking distance until midway through the race when Hennessey slowly extended her lead.

> Rupp, an Oregon senior with a history of placing second in national championship races, let loose with a burst over the final 200 meters, shedding challenger Samuel Chelanga of Liberty University and winning the individual title at the NCAA Cross Country Championships in raw, windy weather.[1]

> The Rupp-Chelanga matchup lived up to its billing as a classic battle. Chelanga, a third-year sophomore from Kenya who won the pre-national meet in Terre Haute in October that did not include Oregon, went out hard again. This time it was 4:21 for the first mile. By 3K, Rupp had closed to within three seconds, and they were even by 5K.

> "I knew he could come back," Chelanga said. "I was just trying to pull away and make him work hard to make it more competitive."

> The ploy did not take Rupp by surprise. He and [Oregon coach Vin] Lananna had discussed the scenario. "Coach just told me to sit back and not panic," Rupp said. "I knew I was going to have to run smart and stay focused on what was going to give me the best plan to be successful. It was something I was prepared for and I kept chipping away."

> In the final 800 meters, both runners surged, taking turns with the lead until Rupp, outkicked last year for two NCAA titles, made his decisive move.[2]

▶ Address course or weather conditions at the race if they are significant.

> Seventeen degrees, 21-mile-per-hour winds and a negative five degree wind chill – not the most ideal running conditions.

> Yet, that was the weather Monday in Ames, Iowa, the site of the NCAA cross-country meet. Despite the harsh conditions, 505 runners, nine of whom were Ducks, lined up for two chilly races.[3]

FIELD HOCKEY

Penalty corners are a vital part of field hockey, frequently proving the difference between winning and losing. The Netherlands women's national team scored 12 of its 16 goals on penalty corners to win the 2008 Olympic gold.

Penalty corners are awarded for infractions inside the shooting area, the 16-yard semi-circle extending out from a back line where the goal sits, or for deliberate fouls committed outside the circle.

Penalty corners combine similar scoring advantages found in two other sports. As in soccer, these shots are similar to direct free kicks on goal. Also, as in a power play opportunity in ice hockey, teams compete with players-up advantage.

To start after the penalty corner, a player sets up on the back line, about ten yards to the right or left of the goal, before passing the ball to a teammate standing just outside at the top of the shooting circle. This stopper can then either stop and roll the ball inside the circle for a shot or can pass to another player.

Meanwhile, four defenders and the goalie stand behind the baseline, either all inside the goal or just outside, until the ball is first passed out. The rest of the defender team remains behind the center line.

Players can score only when they are inside the shooting circle. Initial straight shots, which can travel more than 100 mph, must cross the goal line below 18 inches, unless they're tipped up either by another attacker or one of the defenders. Drag flicks, which travel slightly slower, can be flicked at any height because they're classified more like a hands-apart push.

Teams usually have several penalty corner plays prepared. The most skilled teams convert 40 to 50 percent of these plays. Teams also usually place a player near the corner of the net, where they can get a rebound off a blocked shot or receive a pass to score.

"An effective penalty corner unit is a very important asset," says Richard Sutton, assistant coach for Kent State University. "It is possible to be outplayed for the majority of the game and then through winning corners create easy goal-scoring opportunities against the run of play. Also, the reputation of a strong attacking corner unit will also mean more open play goals as opponents are keen not to give away corners."

PREPARE

Learn the Basics

▶ Teams play 11 to a side, including a goalie. Substitutes can be inserted an unlimited number of times throughout the game except during penalty corners.

▶ Sticks are made of hardwood, curved at the head, rounded on one side and flat on the other. They are much shorter and lighter than ice hockey sticks, forcing players to bend over most of the time. Players must use the flat, or face, side of their sticks to pass or shoot. Left-handed sticks are not allowed, so players must adjust to the right side as needed.

▶ The ball is very hard – solid plastic, weighing between 5½ ounces and 5¾ ounces with a circumference of $8^{13}/_{16}$ inches to 9¼ inches.

▶ A continuously running clock is used to track halves, just as in soccer and rugby.

▶ Two 35-minute halves constitute a full game.

▶ The playing field is roughly the same size as a football field – seven yards wider and the same length – at 100 yards by 60 yards.

▶ Goals are seven feet high and 12 feet wide.

▶ Players with the ball, called attackers, try to score against those without the ball, called defenders. The best players almost always play in the middle of field where most of the action takes place.

▶ College games are played on synthetic turf. Turf emerged as the norm for college and international surfaces after it was first used in the 1976 Olympic Games. Fields are soaked before games so the wet synthetic turf can hold the ball better.

▶ The ball can't be lifted above knee level.

▶ Players are not permitted to play balls off their feet, ankles or lower legs. Umpires won't call this infraction, however, if the other team has already gained possession of the ball.

- Officials are referred to as umpires.

- Players need to touch the ball inside the offensive circle before scoring. Shots taken outside the circle do not count unless the ball touches a player inside the circle, even on a deflection. Shots taken outside this area don't count as a shot on goal since they would not have counted.

- Players cannot double-team opponents, which is called a third-party infraction in field hockey; however, not every umpire chooses to enforce the rule, so players may take advantage of this the same way basketball players tempt the three-second rule by staying within the free-throw lane longer than allowed.

- Retaining possession of the ball is essential to everything a team does – it creates scoring opportunities and it prevents the opposing team from setting up its own scores. In this way, field hockey is more like soccer or basketball than football.

- Players may not use their bodies to move opponents. Physical play is not allowed, prompting a progressively rigorous series of penalties. Green cards are essentially cautions, while yellow cards result in a five-minute suspension, giving one team a one-player advantage while the penalty is being served. A red card results in a player being suspended from the rest of the game, and probably for the next game as well.

- Restarts are similar to those in soccer, where a player can quickly put the ball down and pass it off.

- Goalies may use any part of their bodies to deflect or block balls shot on goal. They must also carry a stick, like an ice hockey goalie. In addition, goalies typically wear helmets, a different-colored shirt as well as padding to their legs or arms. Goalies must use their sticks to play balls outside the defensive circle.

ON KEEPING NOTES

sports insider

I use a regular 8 x 11.5 legal pad. In the top right, covering the first five lines, I have "shot with save" and "shot with no save" for each team. During the game, I keep track of all goals, penalty corners and timeouts. I also keep track of any noteworthy plays, like a defensive save, a spectacular save by the goalie or a shot hitting the post. For penalty corners, I use just the minutes (not the seconds) for the time. I also keep track of how many shots teams are getting on their penalty corners, because it's a good way to show how well teams are taking advantage of their opportunities.

Matt DiFilippo,
Kennebec (Maine) *Journal*

- Goalies focus on three main things during games – themselves, the player with th ball and the back (or weak) side that is usually not as strongly defended and that i more open when the goalie slides to protect the side where the ball is being played Teams try to pass to the weak side to get a more open shot at the net, forcing th goalie to dive toward the far post to knock the ball away.

- Unlike ice hockey goalies, field hockey goalies don't use gloves.

- Games are more open and much faster in overtimes because teams field six player plus a goalie, four fewer than during regulation. The first team to score wins durin the five-minute overtimes.

- Tackling in field hockey does not allow physical contact. Instead, tackling describe players' attempts to steal the ball from an opponent who is dribbling or passing similar to the way soccer players attempt to steal.

Get Ready

- Read about the players and teams in order to find storylines and better analyze th game. Who are each team's top scorers? What happened the last time these team played each other? How well do these teams convert penalty corners – or preven them? Check their percentages.

- Find out the conference, records and other stats of teams involved, including whethe this is a conference game.

- Check with team managers or coaches to see whether either team plans to recor stats. Then determine if this person seems trustworthy. Otherwise keep your own. A college games, this won't be a factor because sports information offices keep accu rate stats and can produce them quickly.

WATCH

- At high schools, you may want to walk along the sidelines to follow the action. Goal can be scored quickly amid a flurry of bodies, making it difficult to discern the scor ing play. Being closer enables you to see through some of this interference. At colleg games, you can usually watch the game unfold much better from a press box.

- On the sidelines, you can also hear the players and coaches talking, which can inform your descriptions, interviews and game analysis.

Unsure who scored the most recent goal? Traditionally, players retrieve their own shots from the goal after they score. You can verify this afterward.

Keep track of the major actions on the field – goals, penalty corners and timeouts. Record the times for each play along with a brief description of the play. Did the shooter slap it? Take a pass down the right side and then move to center? Did a defender fall down? On the penalty corner, who took the pass, what angle did they use and how did the defender cover the attackers?

Also, keep track of all shots on goal. Record where on the field they were taken and the reason they did not go into the net. Did a team take far more shots from the right side? Did a defender deflect the shot? Did the goalie use her stick to deflect a low, hard shot? Later you'll need these details for the box score, such as the one shown below.

Goal	Time	Team	Goal scorer	Assists	Description
1	1:48	Iowa	Hennessey	Nicholson	long pass in front to 14 who shot it in
2	8:12	Florida	Duffy	Raft	22 crossed wide to open 12 (Raft) in front of net
3	21:02	Florida	Costanzo	Tatman	20 passed to 12 who was alone on right side
4	43:09	Iowa	Esposito	Poulter	6 scored on diagonal pass from 17
5	65:51	Florida	Ryan	Turner	scramble in front of net, 19 poked it in

Record the number of shots a team takes on its penalty corners to determine how well they've used these scoring opportunities. This can lead to questions and further analysis after the game.

Describe noteworthy plays – a spectacular save by a goalie, a shot hitting the post in a close game or an acrobatic play by an attacker to score a goal. As always, note the time and the field location of these plays.

Record physical plays to illustrate the tone of the game. If you see few aggressive or physical displays, that can also be an angle for the story, something that can also lead to questions after the game.

▶ Walk the sidelines to catch the conversations among players and coaches. Record some of these conversations for reference after the game. "If I hear a coach say, 'Hustle back on defense!' a few times," says Matt DiFilippo, who has covered countless field hockey games for more than a decade at Maine's *Kennebec Journal,* "I may ask after the game, 'It sounded like you wanted your players to get back quicker on defense. Has this been a problem all season or just something happening today?' "

▶ As with most sports, coaches appreciate writers who can see beyond who scored. Take note of who set up goals or who played well defensively, stopping a potential goal. Afterward, ask coaches to describe or comment on these plays.

▶ Ask coaches about strategy, such as adjustments made to counter the opposing team's tactics. What was your team's game plan entering this game? What adjustments did you make later in the game?

▶ Ask coaches whether they altered their strategy in overtime, when teams use fewer players on the field, going six on six plus a goalie. This creates much more open space during the extra period. The first team to score in the 15-minute overtime period wins. Disqualified players may not return during these periods. During the regular season, ties are recorded. At the college level, overtime is played only during championship events. "Tactically, from a global picture, you need to stay under the ball. Everyone needs to stay under the ball," says University of Maryland coach Missy Meharg, who has won six national titles and has been named national coach of the year seven times. "So even when you play defense in the front third of the field, what you're trying to do is get everybody under every line of three players so you don't put yourself in a situation where it's a two-on-one behind the forwards. You want to recognize getting penalty corners is the way to win or lose the game. You don't take any gamble – there is no gamble in terms of your possession. Defensively, you just drop back awhile."

▶ Ask about field conditions. Colder conditions create conditions that are slicker, meaning the ball will roll much more quickly, bounce, or even skid, across the field. This makes passing and receiving more difficult. How did the slick surface affect teams' game plans? Did coaches or players notice plays where the slicker surface caused problems for either team?

▶ For postseason games, ask players and coaches to describe the team they play next: After playing them twice this season, do you expect anything different tomorrow?

Defenders, or sweeps, need to be mobile, quick and good stick handlers, knocking balls away from potential attackers. They also need to communicate and pick up open players. Interview a defender to get perspective on the opposing team's offensive attack or to gain insights into any goals scored. They can see plays develop in front of them much better than anybody else on the field. Ask them to describe goals the other team scored.

Look for obvious mismatches, such as defenders who cannot keep up with attackers.

Take note of whistles. Did it appear many were blown throughout the game? Ask both coaches whether they felt that too many, or too few, penalties were called during the game.

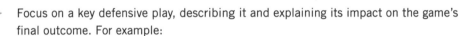

WRITE

Focus on game-winning goals and on players who've scored several goals or recorded several assists.

Focus on a key defensive play, describing it and explaining its impact on the game's final outcome. For example:

> Suzie Rowe dived in front of a shot on goal, deflecting it to teammate Nicole Muracco who raced downfield and fired a shot into the left corner of the net to lift Maryland to a 2 – 1 victory in overtime.

> On Iowa's next possession, the Hawkeyes had a chance to tie the score on a penalty corner. Roz Ellis fired a shot to the left corner, but Wake Forest back Liz Fries knocked the ball out of bounds, giving Iowa another penalty corner attempt.

Note when a team scores a series of goals in a row: "North Carolina scored four straight goals after falling behind 2 – 0 midway through the first half."

Describe the play of the goalie, recording key stats and exceptional plays. "Wake Forest's Crystal Duffield slid left, using her stick to deflect Maryland's first shot, sending the ball to Rowe. On the ground, Duffield lifted her leg to block Rowe's slap shot, knocking the ball out of bounds and leaving the score 2 – 2."

Go through your notes to note when a team failed to take a shot for a prolonged period or to mention when a team has taken several shots over an abbreviated time period.

Iowa's Caitlin McCurdy took a shot two minutes into the second half. The Hawkeyes did not take another one for the next 14 minutes thanks, in part, to Maryland's tight defense up the middle.

Maryland's Katie O'Donnell fired a shot into the right corner to make it 1 – 0, starting a six-shot barrage from the Terrapins during the next four minutes that left North Carolina shaken and trailing 3 – 0.

▶ Describe great performances by either goalie.

Maryland's Alicia Grater did not allow a goal, making an acrobatic move to knock away a shot on a breakaway and saving six other shots on goal.

Alicia Grater finished with six saves, none more important than three diving saves early in the second overtime period. The Hawkeyes had three open looks at the cage – the latter two coming off penalty corners, but Grater thwarted each of their attempts. Iowa outshot the Terps 11 – 10.[1]

▶ Focus on key goals – describing, analyzing and offering perspective on how the goals were scored.

Senior forward Jackie Ciconte scored the game's lone goal eight minutes in to end Duke's season in the national title game for the third consecutive year.

Ciconte calmed a bouncing ball at the Blue Devils' 25-yard line, dribbled around goalkeeper Christy Morgan and shot it into the back of the cage.

"It went to the left side of the goal, I popped it around the goalie, prayed and I hit it in," Ciconte said. "I just got lucky."[2]

After AU's had a wide shot on a penalty corner with about 20 minutes remaining in the half, Maryland countered on the restart and broke down field about. Freshman Katie O'Donnell (Blue Bell, Pa.) sprinted down the sideline and took a running shot from the top of the circle to the opposite post, finding the back of the net, giving Maryland a 1 – 0 lead. It was the Terps' first shot of the game.[3]

▶ Describe penalty corners.

The corner went to Minke Smabers. As her short pass reached Paumen a defender was closing in. So Paumen rolled the ball back to Swabers, who unleashed a shot. Zhang dived and saved, pushing the ball to her right but not to safety. Van As was positioned by the post for just such a rebound and ripped the ball into the goal.[4]

FOOTBALL

Football locker rooms are pretty frenzied – especially after National Football League games when more than 60 players are changing clothes, showering and answering questions.

After games, players expected to get the most questions are brought out to a podium for interviews in a press conference format, and they answer questions addressed from any media in the room. This is where you'll find the player who made the decisive play down the stretch, ran or threw for a great deal of yardage, or recorded several sacks. The head coach will field questions first in this room, which usually adjoins the lockers.

At the same time, the locker room is opened, allowing reporters to wander until they find a player to interview. More often than not, journalists are huddled around a few players, packed in tightly trying to hear what is said. In these scenarios, etiquette is minimal. Call out questions loudly, especially if you're in the back. And record any responses, regardless of who posed the questions.

"Any more, it's how to get close enough in a scrum to a player to ask the question and whether to interview the quarterback in the interview room while you miss everything else in the locker room," says Ed Bouchette, NFL beat writer for the *Pittsburgh Post-Gazette,* "or whether to stay in the locker room and miss the quarterback."

Keep in mind: These are not times for lengthy conversations. Decide whom you want to speak with and ask one to two quick questions and move on – or hang around if you feel these questions were not properly addressed. Perhaps a better explanation will be offered.

Better yet, go find another player who is not being mobbed. What is this person's perspective on the key plays? What did this player notice during the game? You may get a whole new angle, one that all those packing around the same players may not get.

One other suggestion: First, speak to the players least likely to get mobbed and then talk to those everybody else has spoken with after the pack has thinned or evaporated. But keep an eye on these players. There's no guarantee they'll be around.

At the college level, players remain in the locker room with their coaches for a cooling off period, instituted so players wouldn't make inflammatory comments when their emotions were highest right after games. After five to 15 minutes, players are brought out for press conferences, and the lockers are opened to media.

The NCAA's contracts sometimes obligate players and coaches to speak with TV reporters first, but this doesn't take much time, perhaps four to five minutes.

At the high school level, the school's athletic director determines entry into the locker room. Frequently, coaches will allow reporters inside. But some coaches prefer to have players brought outside to speak with reporters.

Before games, introduce yourself to both coaches, asking about the best time to talk. Visiting teams tend to depart rather quickly, so it's usually best to speak first with this head coach, going onto the field after he shakes hands with the opposing coach. Ask a few quick questions. If possible, speak with at least one visiting player for some insights.

Then head to the home team's lockers, where you'll ask a few more questions before racing off to write the story on a tight deadline. That's the nature of most high school football, except in the few areas where games are played on Saturday afternoons, a much more relaxed atmosphere where you won't have to abbreviate your interview sessions.

PREPARE

Learn the Basics

▶ Learn something about the teams before the game. AP football columnist Jim Litke reads everything he can, calls general managers and coaches, and gets transcripts of press conferences. "For example, if the winless Detroit Lions were to play the defending Super Bowl champion Giants," Litke says, "everybody would be predicting a disaster. I would prepare by knowing why Detroit has been a miserable franchise for years. Was it lousy management, bad draft picks? Bad coaching? And how the Giants got so good." He then files the information under specific headings for history, key figures and trends.

▶ Football teams have more specialized coaches than any other sport, assistants who focus on linebackers, defensive backs, offensive linemen, running backs, quarterbacks, special teams, and coordinators who oversee the offense and defense. So don't just go to the head coach, who'll probably defer to these assistants for more detailed responses.

Add 17 yards behind the line of scrimmage to determine the length of field goals. A team that has the ball on the 20-yard line will be attempting a 37-yarder because the goal posts are 10 yards behind the line of scrimmage and because teams place their holder seven yards behind the line of scrimmage to set up the kick.

Games tied at the end of regulation are determined differently in professional and in amateur leagues. In the NFL, the first team to score during a 15-minute fifth (or overtime) period wins the game, giving the team that first receives the ball an added incentive – although this team can fumble, lose the ball on an interception or fail to earn a first down, giving the opponent much better field position following a punt. If neither team scores during a regular-season game, the game is recorded as a tie. In college games, teams each get a chance to score from the 25-yard line. If the score is tied after each team gets a single possession, the process is repeated until one team scores more points during a subsequent possession. In most high school games, teams each start from 10 yards out.

Several referees are charged with watching the game. These officials are back judge, referee, replay officials.

Know your penalties, which can halt or extend a drive – and which create angry debate among fans. Here are some infractions that officials call frequently:

- **blocking below the waist:** pretty self-explanatory, punishable by a 15-yard penalty.

- **clipping:** hitting or blocking a player below the waist from behind, punishable by a 15-yard penalty.

USA Today assembled a bowl calendar, charting every single postseason game and adding bowl logos that readers could click on to get more detailed information and features about each matchup, such as "Who has the edge?" Afterward, the newspaper added related stories and notes. Check it out at www.usatoday.com.

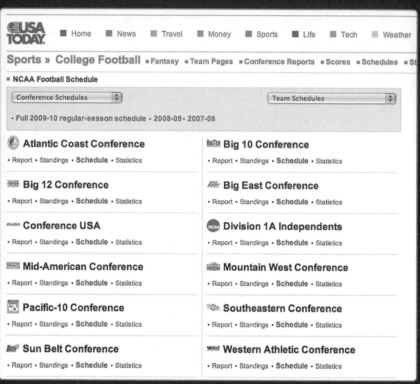

▶▶ **delay of game:** failing to snap the ball before the play clock expires, punishable by a five-yard penalty.

▶▶ **encroachment:** when players make contact beyond the line of scrimmage prior to the snap, punishable by a five-yard penalty.

▶▶ **face mask:** when players grab the mask of an opponent, punishable by a 15-yard penalty and an automatic first down unless it can be determined to be unintentional, which merits a five-yard penalty.

- ▶▶ **false start:** when a player crosses line of scrimmage prior to the snap without making contact, punishable by five yards.

- ▶▶ **holding:** grabbing or holding any part of an opponent's body or uniform, punishable by a 10-yard penalty.

- ▶▶ **illegal motion:** when two or more players move at the same time, or even one player moves toward the line of scrimmage, prior to a snap, punishable by a five-yard penalty.

- ▶▶ **illegal player downfield:** when a lineman goes downfield on a passing play, usually when the quarterback is scrambling, punishable by a 10-yard penalty.

- ▶▶ **intentional grounding:** when a quarterback intentionally throws the ball away to avoid a sack, punishable by a loss of that down and a 10-yard penalty. If this happens in the end zone, the defensive team earns a safety.

- ▶▶ **offensive interference:** when an offensive player, usually a receiver, interferes with a defensive player trying to catch, or intercept, the ball, punishable by a 15-yard penalty.

- ▶▶ **pass interference:** when a defensive player interferes with anyone trying to catch the ball; penalties for this infraction vary. In the NFL, the ball is placed at the spot of the infraction and a first down is awarded. If the foul is committed in the end zone, the ball is placed on the 1-yard line. In National Collegiate Athletic Association games, teams are awarded 15 yards for defensive pass interference.

- ▶▶ **unsportsmanlike conduct:** when players make contact with an opponent after the ball is out of bounds or the play is completed.

▶ Familiarize yourself with the following terms:

- ▶▶ **audible:** when quarterbacks call out a new play at the line of scrimmage, usually when they suspect the defense is trying something new or when they see a mismatch in coverage.

- ▶▶ **blitz:** defensive strategy employed to disrupt and pressure the offense by rushing additional linebackers or defensive backs.

- ▶▶ **bootleg:** misdirection play where the quarterback fakes a handoff to a running back going in one direction before running in the opposite direction to either pass or run the ball.

- ▶ ▶ **bump and run:** technique intended to disrupt a receiver's pass pattern at the line of scrimmage, usually by a defensive back. No contact is allowed beyond five yards, something that will prompt a penalty.

- ▶ ▶ **fair catch:** players returning punts may wave their hand in the air right before catching the ball, indicating they won't return the ball and making it illegal for opponents to make any contact during this attempt. A 15-yard penalty is called for any contact. If the ball is dropped or fumbled by the punt returner, either team can attempt to recover it.

- ▶ ▶ **forward progress:** spot where a ball carrier's momentum halted. This is where officials spot the ball even if a ball carrier has been pushed back several yards.

- ▶ ▶ **Hail Mary pass:** term use for a desperation pass thrown far downfield in hopes that someone will find a way to catch it, usually in the final moments of a game. Avoid using this popular term whenever possible; use desperation pass or some other term instead.

- ▶ ▶ **neutral zone:** area between the defensive and offensive lines of scrimmage where the ball is placed to start each play.

- ▶ ▶ **nickel package:** defensive alignment where a fifth defensive back replaces a linebacker on downs where the offense is more likely to pass.

- ▶ ▶ **play-action:** when a quarterback fakes a handoff to a running back in an attempt to draw in defensive backs and linebackers before throwing a pass.

- ▶ ▶ **pylon:** orange foam marker that marks each side of a goal line at the two side-lines. These pylons are in bounds, meaning a player who brushes across it before being knocked into the sidelines has officially crossed the goal line for a score.

- ▶ ▶ **PAT:** point after touchdown attempt that earns one point following touchdowns. The ball is placed at the two-yard line in the NFL and the three-yard line for college and high school games.

- ▶ ▶ **red shirt:** players gain an additional year of college eligibility if they did not play in a single game during a season even though they practiced and traveled with the team. Red-shirts are an option in all sports, but are used more frequently in football.

- ▶ ▶ **red zone:** area inside the 20-yard line where teams are most likely to score.

- ▶ ▶ **roll out:** when a quarterback runs parallel with the line of scrimmage, surveying the field for a pass receiver. Teams use this when the defensive unit has pressured the quarterback, forcing quicker throws and recording sacks, and when the quarterback is fast.

- ▶ ▶ **safety:** the only way a defensive unit can score, usually by tackling the ball carrier in the end zone. Safeties can also be recorded when the person holding the ball steps out of bounds in the end zone, when a snap or fumble rolls out of the back of the end zone, or when someone intentionally kneels down for a safety. Penalties, such as holding or intentional grounding, in the end zone also result in a safety.

- ▶ ▶ **turnovers:** when teams lose possession of the ball on offense through fumbles and interceptions.

- ▶ ▶ **two-point conversion:** instead of kicking a PAT, teams can attempt to score two points from the two-yard line, using a single play to get into the end zone. For college, teams start from three yards out.

Get Ready

▶ Arrive early for games. Give yourself time to find the field if you have never been there. Plus, you want time to get rosters, speak with team managers and statisticians and find a place to cover the game. I'd recommend getting to get games at least 30 minutes early, but would strongly encourage you to get there an hour beforehand. That way, you can also scout the locations for the locker rooms and find a suitable parking spot. You'll also want to check with the official statistician, managers and coaches to ensure the players and numbers match up on the program. At high school games especially, verify the class standing and any team and individual stats for players on both teams. Record full names, numbers and class standings of all players before these games. Also, make sure you have read past stories on both teams to find potential angles leading into this game.

▶ Verify names in programs, especially at high school games, before adding them to your stats sheets.

▶ Devise a system for keeping score. During the game, keep a running play-by-play that includes basic information, such as the person running the ball, the number of yards gained, down and yardage needed, and time of the game. In addition, add a few quick descriptors such as running back cutting left and eluding two defensive backs before being tackled down the sideline. Here's how veteran Associated Press football columnist Jim Litke tracks the game.

1 – 10/Bears 35	Forte runs right for 6
2 – 4 – 41	incomplete pass to Olsen
3 – 4 – 41	Olsen, slant pass for 6 (1st down)
1 – 10 – 47	Forte, run up middle for 1

Litke adds notes in the margin about anything unusual. "Say Olsen's first-down catch was a tipped ball, or the opposing defensive coordinator threw down his clipboard when the catch was made," he says.

▶ Check for individual and team trends entering this game. Does a team have a poor takeaway margin? Does a running back have a series of 100-yard rushing games? Has a defense limited the opposing team to a low scoring average or few rushing yards? At the same time, has this team allowed many yards passing? You can use this information to better assess a team's success during the game – and to ask more informed questions after the game.

WATCH

▶ Focus on a team's performance inside the opponents' 20-yard line, something now regularly referred to as the red zone. Did a team change its approach inside the 20-yard line, running more when passing moved them there? Or did a team pass more frequently near the goal line after a sustained drive of running plays? Did a team forsake the two-minute drill once near the goal line? Assess these changes in a team's offense. Afterward, ask the offensive coordinator to walk you through a series to learn why they ran these plays.

▶ Compare teams' total yardage, addressing any major differences or a team's particular prowess (400-plus yards) or inadequacy (100 total yards).

▶ Focus on the passing game. Did a team attempt mostly shorter, slanting passes? Did the quarterback usually complete passes to receivers over the middle or down the sidelines? Did a team attempt more passes in any one quarter, half or series? Assess the running game in the same manner, looking for trends.

▶ Focus on turnovers. The best teams recover more turnovers (fumbles, interceptions) than they relinquish. Focus more on decisive turnovers – the fumble near the goal line, the interception that ends a lengthy drive – than on those caused by desperation, such as a long pass as time expires or when a quarterback is forced to throw on every down to overcome a 21-point deficit. Some turnovers are more crucial than others.

▶ Review tackles. A team that has more tackles either played a much better game or was forced to play longer on defense because its offense played poorly. Determine the reason for the number of tackles. You can also focus on players who have more than 10 individual tackles in a game, describing a few key tackles and offering reasons for this player's prowess. Perhaps an inside linebacker kept plugging holes up the middle to stop the opposing team's running backs – or, perhaps, a cornerback had to tackle running backs who kept slipping past linebackers for longer gains. Remember, stats can show both success and failure, so don't assume a high number is always a good thing. Clearly, a cornerback with more than 10 tackles is usually something coaches fret over.

► Break down key drives. How did the team move the ball 80 yards on 12 plays: by running, throwing or converting several third-downs? Did penalties help? Did the team even go to third down on the drive? Assess the drive so you can properly address it in the story and so you can ask questions after the game.

► Determine one-on-one and team matchups. For example, determine how one team's defensive backs fared against the other team's receiver? Did this defensive back limit the receiver to a fewer receptions than he normally gets?

► Record time of possession. Quarters in high school and college games are almost always 12 minutes, while the NFL plays 15-minute quarters. Teams that control the ball win the game for many reasons. That means a team kept driving the ball. That also means the other team had the ball less frequently and wasn't able to do the same. This could also result in one team's defense getting worn down, especially in the fourth quarter. So a team that controls the ball for 39 minutes in a 60-minute NFL game is usually going to win. The same is true for a high school team that holds the ball for 30 of 48 minutes. If the ball-controlling team does not win, focus on the reasons for this. For example, the other team may have capitalized on some turnovers or made some quick, lengthy scoring plays. Either way, this is an interesting aspect of the game. Did a team that's ahead assemble a time-consuming drive in the final quarter, one that left the other team with little time to rally for a score? Scoring is not the most essential part of these late-game drives. Taking time off the clock can be the main focus.

► Write a narrative after each period, a mini game story that focuses on key plays and trends. After each period, write another narrative that should be placed above the previous one, meaning the running for the third period would be inserted first, followed by summaries for the second and first periods, respectively. At the conclusion of the game, write three to five paragraphs that include a lead and a general overview that can be filed immediately for early print editions and for the Web site. After interviewing players and coaches, work on a version that may be revised a little, with a few updates and quotes, or a great deal if a new angle emerges from the locker-room chats. Of course, deadline determines how much you can revise.

- Describe drives. What was the average length and number of plays for a team's drives through the game? Did a team move the ball more effectively in certain quarters? On what yard line did most drives begin? How many plays did each drive average? Which drives were not average, resulting in more yardage and time off the clock? Dissect these drives to explain the reasons for a team's successes and failures on the field.

- The game may appear to have been won on a play during the final minutes, but many other plays during the game put this team in position to win. Try to find these other plays – the block by a fullback that allowed a tailback to score, the poor snap saved by the holder on a field goal in the third quarter, the pass deflection made by a cornerback against a much taller receiver in the end zone in the first half. Dig below the surface for these key plays.

- Obviously, focus on great individual performances – a running back who rushes for 200-plus yards, the defensive lineman with three sacks and countless tackles, the quarterback who tosses four touchdowns, the receiver with 100-plus yards and the kicker who hits five lengthy field goals. But don't forget to mention the linebacker with 15 tackles or the defensive back who limited the opposing team's top receiver to a few catches and yards.

ASK

- Ask players and coaches for roster changes. For example, you could ask why Ravens quarterback Steve McNair was removed from a game in the fourth quarter. "I could tell he was favoring [his groin] a little bit," Baltimore coach Brian Billick said.[1]

- Ask offensive linemen about the opposing defense, seeing the game through their perspective.

- Ask defensive linemen about the opposing team's offensive line or running backs. As a result, you may get a response like the following that ran in the *St. Louis Post-Dispatch:*

> But the Buccaneers were surprised not to see the Rams stretch the field.
> "I really thought they would try to go down the field more with their talented receivers," said Bucs defensive end Kevin Carter.
> "The one thing I was surprised about is they didn't go downfield more," Bucs linebacker Barrett Ruud said. "Because that's kind of what their passing game is known for – the real deep digs, the deep comebacks."[2]

- Ask players how they were able to come from behind to win. Here's a comment, published by the Associated Press, from Houston cornerback Dunta Robinson after a Texan rally fell short: "It's a new team. There's no quit in us. In the past, the game might have got out of hand. But now we expect to win football games, no matter who we are playing, no matter who is injured."

- Talk to coordinators and assistant coaches as well. Did the defense have to make adjustments at any point? Did the offensive line drive the defense off the ball on running plays? How was the other team able to run so well on kickoffs and punts? These are questions better posed to coaches who specialize in these aspects of the game.

- Ask players to walk you through key drives. What did players notice as they moved down the field? Did defensive backs play much farther off receivers, giving them a five to 10-yard cushion? Did a team rush fewer players through the tackles? Did the opposing team blitz more?

- You can also ask players to describe disappointing starts to seasons. Yes, it is difficult to ask people why they have failed, but that is part of the job. Here's what LaDainian Tomlinson said after the Chargers lost to go 1 – 2. "It's still a long season. But I mean, right now we just – I don't know. I'm lost." This tells readers much about the mind-set of the team.

- Essentially, you want to offer fans a perspective they cannot get by watching a game in the stands or on television. That means asking players and coaches how they felt, what they saw and why did they acted as they did. Speak with as many people as possible – and make sure you speak with players and coaches from both teams to get a well-rounded perspective. Otherwise, readers will be stuck with a single perspective, typically the home team's perspective. That won't impress fans or potential employers.

- Interviews in high school football go much differently than in college and the NFL, where players are brought out for press conferences. At the high school level, you'll have to scramble to speak with players and coaches before they hit the locker rooms. "The entire atmosphere of a high school game is less structured than the pro/college setting," Ruppert says. "On the high school level, you're on your own to get interviews with players and coaches. You have to remember you are interviewing 16 – 17-year-old kids who might not realize how their words will look in the paper the next day."

- On tight deadlines, grab the most important player and compile your game stats. Then interview a coach, asking what did and didn't work before you race off to file the game story. These are not times for a rambling conversation.

▶ Ask quarterbacks about their reads. Did the safeties stay back, trying to prevent the deep pass? Did linebackers get forced to cover receivers on shorter patterns? Did the defensive line try putting extra pressure up the middle? Let the quarterback show you how and why he made his decisions.

WRITE

▶ Cite key plays. There were several key plays in the Giants' victory over the Redskins. This AP writer also included a trend:

> The Giants converted seven straight third downs to put together three touchdown drives in the second half, the last a 33-yard pass from Eli Manning to Plaxico Burress with 5:32 to go. Washington responded by driving to the Giants' 1-yard line in the final minute, but running back Ladell Betts was stopped on third and fourth down runs.

▶ Focus on key drives. Include number of plays, yards and time expired, especially if the latter two elements are significant. Drives that last more than 10 plays, that cover more than 75 yards and that run off more than eight minutes are particularly interesting. That's what the AP writer focused on in a key drive during the Jaguars' victory over the Broncos:

> Jacksonville started with a methodical 80-yard, 18-play drive that lasted 11 minutes, 44 seconds, which was capped by a three-yard touchdown pass from David Garrard to Reggie Williams.

▶ Cite turnovers. See how many times a team, or player, fumbled the ball, particularly if these turnovers led to opposing scores or if they halted a drive inside the 20-yard line. Check past games to see whether this is unusual or is a trend.

▶ Cite trends. Perhaps a quarterback threw several interceptions during the game, which allowed the opposing team to score or halted scoring drives. Maybe a defensive lineman made several key plays, tackling running backs before they could get first downs and sacking the quarterback. Or maybe, as in the following report by the AP, a player lost his composure:

> The Panthers came up with the victory largely because DeAngelo Hall lost his cool. Atlanta's Pro Bowl cornerback picked up three penalties for 67 yards on Carolina's tying drive.

Isolate a moment. Consider this play, reported by the AP, in a game between the Browns and Raiders.

> As Phil Dawson lined up for the potential winning field goal, Oakland coach Lane Kiffin told the line judge he wanted to call a timeout before the kick. He had watched Denver coach Mike Shanahan use the same strategy to beat his Raiders in OT the week before. So Kiffin decided he'd try it himself. The move paid off when Tommy Kelly blocked Dawson's last second attempt, allowing the Raiders to snap an 11-game losing streak.

What's the big picture? What does this game mean to the teams involved? How does it affect them? Why is the game important?

Avoid holiday leads. Football games covered on Halloween should not be filled with players galloping or flying like ghosts or about a monstrous defense or a ghoulish finish to a game. Please, avoid these. Readers will get bored with so many references in so many games, and copy editors will tear out tufts of hair with each succession of trite, clichéd references. Find a more creative way to approach the game.

Sometimes, the best lead is the straightforward approach that focuses on a key play or key stat, along with the game's result. The AP follows this formula when filing its initial game story for NFL and college games, knowing that many newspapers rely on these tight stories for roundups, where only the first 1 – 2 paragraphs are used. Only later does AP file the more featurized game lead. So feel free to write a straightforward lead like the AP lead that follows, especially if you are filing your story for the next day's editions or for your online editions.

> Tony Romo threw touchdown passes to Jason Witten and Marion Barber as the Dallas Cowboys defeated the Chicago Bears 34 – 10 on Sunday night.

If you are writing a story that will be published a few days after the game, find an angle that focuses on why or how your local team fared. If you are writing for online editions, you can still use most of the original story; you can just revise the lead elements and keep the remaining analysis and play-by-play.

A few other straight leads from NFL games filed by AP:

> Randy Moss had touchdown catches of 45 and three yards as New England posted its third straight rout, a 38 – 7 win over Buffalo.

> Joseph Addai ran for two scores and Adam Vinatieri kicked three field goals to lead Indianapolis past Houston, 34 – 20,

(continued on page 142)

Use different color ink when recording notes for each team, which allows for easier, quicker reference on deadline. For example, you could use black or blue ink for New York's drives and red or green for Indianapolis. Bring at least 12 play-by-play sheets to each game, stapling the to use on the same clipboard as the stats sheet. As you record each play here, add the results to the stats page as well. That means after No. 32 runs for 4 yards, you'll also add "4" to this running back's total on the teams state page. Practice on several TV games before heading out to a live game.

1. Player (32) who advanced the ball. Add brief descriptions of plays as reminders.

2. Total yards gained on the play.

3. Field position. Where the ball is set before the play begins.

4. Down in the series and yards needed for a first down.

5. Record scoring plays such as this 47-yard field goal.

6. Write the score after each scoring play, circling it so it stands out for review on deadline.

7. Time remaining in the quarter when the team scored. Add time at the start of drives as well, which can reveal time elapsed (another nice detail for game stories).

8. Change of possession. Now the stats are reversed with the down on the left side. Don't forget to use a different color ink as well.

9. Record incomplete passes like this. Keep updating totals on the team stats page as well.

10. Record reasons for change of possessions, such as a punt here. Other reasons – interception, fumble, missed field goal, and failure to gain 10 yards on four downs.

New York ①	1st Qtr	Indianapolis	
32 (up middle) ②	4	NY20	1-10
44	② 2	NY24 ③	④ 2-6
12-84	11	26	3-4
32	3	37	1-10
12-88	21	40	2-7
32	4	IN39	1-10
44	3	35	2-6
32	2	32	3-3
Times 47 FG ⑤	⑥ 3	30 0	8.04 ⑦ 4-1
1-10 ⑧	IN28	3 (left side)	34
2-7	IN31	4	34
3-3	IN35	0	⑨ 12 inc
4-3	IN35	⑩ PUNT 31 yds	
32 (sweep left side) 9		NY38	1-10
44	2	NY47	2-1
		NY49	1-10

1. *Each time a player carries the ball, add it to the previous total, crossing out the previous yardage. Johnson had 3 yards on his first carry and 1 yard on his second carry, meaning he had 4 yards on two carries.*

2. *Put a square box around halftime totals to better evaluate performance by half. Johnson had 31 yards on nine carries in first half, a 3.44-yard average per carry.*

3. *You can determine total number of carries by counting numbers in the row. Johnson ran for 119 total yards on 20 carries, revealing a much better second half of 88 yards on 11 carries, an 8.0 average per carry.*

4. *Record carries even when a runner does not gain any yards. Montes gained no yards on his fifth carry, so 19 is crossed out and rewritten.*

5. *Deduct from totals when runners lose yardage on a carry. Here, Palmer lost two yards for minus-1 yard total on three carries.*

6. *Use tally marks to record passing attempts.*

7. *Put total completions or attempts at halftime in a box for easier reference.*

8. *Use tallies to denote first downs. Teams can record only one first down at a time, meaning a 40-yard run is not worth four first downs.*

9. *Determine how a team best advanced the ball. This team relied more on the running game. But, sometimes, a team may have far more first downs from passing.*

10. *Total yardage for punts as you would carries for a running back. At the end, divide the total punts into total yards for the average per attempt – in this case 33.6 yards per punt.*

11. *Penalties are also tallied like rushing attempts. In this case, the team was called for seven penalties for 60 total yards.*

KEEPING SCORE FOOTBALL stats

Individual Statistics ①

RUSHING ② ③

Johnson (32)	5	4	7	4	18	25	26	26	31	21	44	44	48										
Franklin (34)	1	3	2	5	8	10	15	18	21	29	34	39	52	56	46	70	89	107	105	106	119		
Montes (44)	8	10	15	14	14	25	28																
Rodriguez (45) ④	4	5	4	8	7	11																	
Palmer (12) ⑤	12	14	15	16	2																		

PASSING

	Attempts	Completions	Yards
Palmer (12)	HH HH HH ⑥	HH 11 3 ⑦	8 12 33 40 45 84

RECEIVING

Brown	8	24	41	46
Martin	4	9		
Camarillo	7			

FIRST DOWNS

by RUSH	HH HH 1 ⑧
by PASS	IIII ⑨
by PENALTY	II

PUNTS	20	28	96	130	168 ⑩	
PENALTIES	5	10	25	40	56	60 ⑪

FIRST HALF STATS

Total yards
Rush Yards/Att
Pass yards
Att/Comp
First Downs
Penalties
Punts/avg.

TOTAL STATS

Total yards
Rush Yards/Att
Pass yards
Att/Comp
First Downs
Penalties
Punts/avg.

FIELD GUIDE TO COVERING SPORTS Copyright © 2010 by CQ Press.

Donovan McNabb threw for 381 yards and four touchdowns, Kevin Curtis had 221 yards receiving and three scores as the Eagles earned their first win.

▶ Some final advice: "With covering major or pro sports, it often gets to be about the writer/reporter's ego," says Bryan Black, the high school sports editor for *The Virginian-Pilot* in Norfolk, Va. "With high school sports, you need to stay in closer touch with your audience. It's not about you, and it's never going to be about you. It's about the kids you cover and their schools. And for high school reporters who think it is about them, they're on the wrong beat."

▶ Show, don't tell. Show how a freshman was the player of the game by describing how he played in key moments. Don't just write that the freshman was "the player of the game." Show how this player performed better than everyone else.

▶ Focus on defensive stats. Did a team record a number of sacks, interceptions or limit the opposing team to few yards? Determine the reasons for this, and cite a key play or two to illustrate.

▶ Focus on punts, especially when one team (or both teams) boots it frequently during the game, something that usually signifies tough defenses or inept offenses.

▶ Focus on special teams.

▶ Focus on the key stats, whether that's the average yards per pass play, the total yardage in penalties, or the number of 20-plus-yard running plays. Determine the most significant stats for this game.

▶ Spell out RB (running back), WR (wide receiver) and QB (quarterback) in first reference. Here is the correct spelling for other commonly used football terms: ball carrier, end line, end zone, field-goal attempt, fair catch, fullback, goal line, goal-line stand, handoff, kick off (as verb), linebacker, pitchout (noun), place kick, place-kicker, tailback, tight end and touchdown.

▶ Use numerals for yardage. Write 9-yard line, 8-yard pass, and he ran in from 4 yards. But use words for downs, such as fourth-and-2 and second-and-8. But check with your local sports editors to make sure local style does not usurp AP Style.

▶ As always, avoid clichés, such as "coughing up the ball" instead of fumble, and "airing it out" for passing the ball.

GOLF

G olf's rules can be bizarre.

A breeze rocks a ball as a golfer hits it? That's a one-stroke penalty.

A caterpillar crawls onto a ball? Better whack it aboard, or hope it gets off quickly. Brushing the bug off the ball costs two strokes.

A hawk picks up a moving ball and carries it off into the woods or drops it in a creek? The ball must be hit where it falls.

And don't even think about tearing off the cap of a mushroom when a ball lies against the toadstool's stem. That would be a stroke penalty because the morel is a fixed impediment, not loose like a twig, leaf or candy wrapper.

Golfers have been disqualified for putting a towel down while hitting a shot from the knees, for having a toy putter at the bottom of a bag inadvertently dropped in by a child. (Golfers are limited to 14 clubs on tour, so clearly this was an advantage.)

Golfers also get disqualified for failing to sign their scorecards. Padraig Harrington forgot to sign a card in which he shot the lowest score, giving him a five-shot lead entering the final round. Gone. Robert de Vicenzo was not allowed to compete in a playoff for the 1968 Masters when he signed a card that inadvertently added an extra stroke to his score.

Lee Janzen failed to add a stroke when a ball fell into the cup a few seconds past the 10-second rule at the World Series of Golf, although he and partner Vijay Singh believed they had abided by the rule. A TV viewer later phoned the Professional Golfers' Association of America, prompting a disqualification for signing a card with the wrong score.

"Golf's a game where people call penalties on themselves," said Mark Russell, a PGA Tour official at the event. "Offensive lineman don't say to a referee, 'I was holding, you should throw a flag.'"

Players can also be penalized for actions taken by others. A player on the Canadian PGA Tour was penalized because his caddie stood behind him while he putted, which is a two-stroke penalty. The player, who shot 8-under-par 63, never noticed the caddie. His opponent did, waiting until the card was signed to lodge a complaint. This player then won the tournament.

Bart Bryant was penalized two strokes because another player fixed a divot, or pitch mark, on the fringe of the green that would not have really been in his shooting line. Bryant, in the rough, needed to chip the ball well over this mark to reach the green. But that did not matter to tournament officials who assessed him a two-stroke penalty. Sometimes, though, karma kicks in. During the next round, Bryant aced a par-3 hole, essentially getting both strokes back.

Golf has many draconian rules, so carry an official United States Golf Association book to all golf events. You never know when a bug will hop on someone's ball.

PREPARE

Know the Basics

▶ Most golfers carry eight to 10 irons in their bag, numbered from 1 to 9. Golfers also carry wedges that are unnumbered. Overall, PGA golfers are allowed a total of 14 clubs. The higher numbers indicate a higher-angled head face, meaning the ball is more likely to loft high as opposed to clubs with lower numbers, whose lower loft angles help golfers drive the ball farther.

▶ Golfers must stay within the set boundaries of a course, usually marked by white stakes. Balls landing outside this area, or out of bounds (O.B.), are penalized one stroke, and the ball is returned to the original location. The shot also counts as a stroke, so a golfer has really lost two strokes before taking the shot over again.

▶ Courses vary widely for length, layout and landscape. Some are straighter and longer, while others have tighter fairways and sharper turns. Courses sometimes have unique features as well, such as No. 18 green at the TPC Sawgrass course that is set on a tiny island. The average distance for PGA courses is just over 7,000 yards for 18 holes, while Ladies Professional Golf Association courses are typically in the mid-6,000s. Many high school, college and LPGA events are more likely to be somewhere between 5,500 and 6,500 yards.

▶ Several statistics offer an overview of each player's strengths and weaknesses. The primary stats include scoring average (average strokes per round), driving accuracy (percentage of times a tee shot rests on the fairway), driving distance, greens in

sports insider

Because the best scores are the last to tee off, the players most likely to lead or win are going to be in the final few groups. If you have a serious deadline, as I always do, I can't afford to walk the back nine on Sunday because someone could do something heroic that I miss. If you have more time, it's easier to do and recommended. So you miss the great eagle putt. You'll be able to hear the cheer from 1,000 yards away, sense how it affects the tournament and have better detail. Plus, you'll see highlights later. Years ago, I was with Larry Dorman of *The New York Times* as we watched the final group at The Players Championship. We were on the 15th hole when an enormous cheer rung out – Fred Couples had just made eagle on the 16th hole. The look on the leaders' faces on the 15th hole as they stepped away from their shots was priceless, and it became a big part of the story.

Doug Ferguson,
golf writer, Associated Press

regulation, putts per round, and scrambling (percentage of time a player misses the green in regulation but still makes par or better). Greens in regulation is a little more complex. A green is considered hit in regulation, according to the PGA, if any part of the ball touches the putting surface and when the number of strikes taken is two fewer than par for the hole. That means a golfer would need to drive on the green of a par-3 hole $(3 - 1 = 2)$ or hit the green on the third shot of a par 5 $(5 - 2 = 3)$. Each stat reveals different strengths. Before a tournament, review the leaders for each stat. Then see whether the course plays to a golfer's strengths or weaknesses. For example, a longer course would help a player ranked high in driving distance rankings.

▶ In professional tournaments, players compete against the field, trying to shoot the lowest possible score during the prescribed rounds where each stroke is counted. Rounds consist of 18 holes. Most PGA events are scheduled for four rounds, or 72 holes. The player who takes the fewest stokes wins. In college tournaments, the team with the lowest combined score for its top four golfers wins. College events usually go three rounds, or 54 holes.

▶ Fields for PGA Tour events are set for either 132, 144 or 156 players. After the first two rounds (36 holes), the field is reduced to 70. Ties may increase this number by a few golfers who qualify to play the final two rounds.

▶ In match-play events, golfers compete against one another to earn points (or holes) across the prescribed length, usually 18 holes. Golfers earn one point for shooting the lowest score on a hole, but players each earn one-half point if they tie, shooting

digital assist

That's what the *Arizona Daily Star* did for the World Golf Championships – Accenture Match Play Championships. Readers could click on any of the 18 holes to learn more about it (distance, par) or readers could click on the flags to view a panorama of each hole. The site includes tips from pros for playing the hole and suggestions for the best place to watch. Check it out at azstarnet.com.

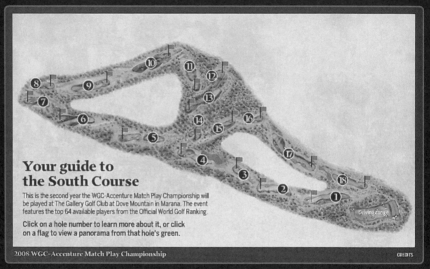

Your guide to the South Course

This is the second year the WGC-Accenture Match Play Championship will be played at The Gallery Golf Club at Dove Mountain in Marana. The event features the top 64 available players from the Official World Golf Ranking.

Click on a hole number to learn more about it, or click on a flag to view a panorama from that hole's green.

2008 WGC-Accenture Match Play Championship

CREDITS

identical scores on the hole. The player who earns the most points wins. Players frequently clinch a match-play victory before 18 holes are completed. Scores are recorded by citing the number of holes the player is ahead, followed by the number of holes remaining – meaning a player who has won 4 and 3 is four points ahead with three holes remaining, making it impossible for the other golfer to tie or win the match. This format, played in very few tournaments, is used in the main team competitions – Ryder Cup and Presidents Cup – where a team can pair up in team competition, using a best ball format.

▶ Best ball format means a team of two to four players uses the lowest score recorded by any member, measured against the lowest score posted by the opposing team.

▶ A skins game is a sort of match play where players compete for prize money on each hole. The player with the lowest score wins the hole, or the skin, meaning the player wins the money set aside for that hole. If all players are tied, the prize money is awarded to whoever wins the next hole.

You're more likely to come across the Stableford scoring format in a club championship than a professional event. The PGA no longer uses it, neither do the LPGA or Senior tours. This system, which has several variations, rewards risk taking, usually yielding two points for birdies, five for eagles and eight for double eagles, but no points for pars. Players lose a point for bogey and three for double bogeys or worse. The highest score wins.

Familiarize yourself with the following terms:

▶▶ **ace:** term for a hole-in-one, where a shot goes into the hole off the tee.

▶▶ **address:** how players position themselves before shooting, taking a stance and putting the clubhead behind the ball. Players are assessed a one-stroke penalty if the ball moves before they hit it.

▶▶ **approach shot:** shot intended to land the ball on the green, usually from the fairway.

▶▶ **apron:** grass surface on the perimeter of the green, separating it from the fairway.

▶▶ **birdie:** a hole played in one stroke less than par.

▶▶ **bogey:** a hole played in one stroke more than par. Players who require additional strokes double-bogey, triple bogey and so forth.

▶▶ **bunker:** a hazard where sand fills a depression that's also called a sand trap.

▶▶ **caddie:** person who carries clubs, offers advice and helps with strategy. Professional players usually retain their own paid caddies.

▶▶ **chip:** shot usually shorter than 20 yards played close to the green and intended to fly and roll close to the hole.

▶▶ **club face:** surface of the club's head, at the bottom, that makes contact with the ball.

▶▶ **dogleg:** a right or left bend in a fairway.

▶▶ **double eagle:** a rare feat where a hole is played in three strokes less than par, meaning a player has either aced a par-4 hole or completed a par-5 hole in two strokes.

▶▶ **eagle:** a hole played in two strokes less than par.

▶▶ **fairway:** area between the tee and green that has short grass, which typically offers the best lies.

- ▶ ▶ **gallery:** name for the fans watching a tournament.

- ▶ ▶ **grand slam:** A tour's major events. The PGA's version consists of the Masters, U.S. Open, British Open and PGA Championship, played in that order. The LPGA's majors are the Kraft Nabisco Championship, LPGA Championship, Women's British Open and U.S. Women's Open.

- ▶ ▶ **green:** closely mowed area where the hole is situated.

- ▶ ▶ **handicap:** calculates the number of strokes a player averages above par, meaning a player whose average score is 90 would have a handicap of 18 because par is considered 72 strokes per 18 holes.

- ▶ ▶ **hazard:** areas designed to make play difficult; they include sand traps and water (ponds and creeks, for example).

- ▶ ▶ **hook:** a shot other than a putt that unintentionally bends, or curves, left for right-handed golfers. Golfers may intentionally try to hit a slight curve, a shot called a fade.

- ▶ ▶ **lie:** location where the ball rests after a shot. A bad lie would be a location where trees block a direct shot to the green or where the ball rests in bunkers, high grass or between rocks.

- ▶ ▶ **LPGA:** Ladies Professional Golf Association, which runs both the teaching and tour aspects for women golfers.

- ▶ ▶ **medalist:** player with lowest score in a tournament. When two or more players are tied in championship events, a playoff is held.

- ▶ ▶ **par:** number of strokes most golfers would need to complete a hole based upon its total length. The standard score for holes shorter than 300 yards is 3, meaning a 220-yard hole would be a par 3 while a 540-yard hole would be a par 5.

- ▶ ▶ **PGA Tour:** organization comprising professional golfers that runs most U.S. men's professional golf events.

- ▶ ▶ **PGA:** Professional Golfers' Association of America, which is a teaching organization and should not be confused with the PGA Tour.

- ▶ ▶ **pin high:** fairways can drop below greens, and tee boxes can be set much higher than the fairway or green. When a golfer strikes a shot at the same level as the green, the hole is considered pin high.

- ▶ ▶ **scramble:** a format used primarily for club and amateur events involving teams where players each take a shot based on the best lie of members' previous shots.

> ▶ ▶ **shank:** a severely mis-hit shot that usually goes directly right after the ball hits an area other than the club face.

> ▶ ▶ **slice:** a shot that unintentionally bends, or curves, right for right-handed golfers. A pulled shot cuts even more severely left, without a curve.

> ▶ ▶ **USGA:** United States Golf Association, which hosts the U.S. Open and whose rules are used on most golf courses.

Get Ready

▶ You can't be everywhere at once at a golf tournament, so do your homework. Pick your spots to watch the opening rounds. Read player profiles and recently published stories. Find out who's been playing very poorly, who has faced some difficulties, and who might have a great story. For example, someone may be playing for the first time in five months because of knee surgery. A veteran may be playing a certain golf course for the first time in years. Or this could be the first tournament for a player who blew a six-shot lead in the final round of a previous tournament.

▶ Pick a group that is likely to yield a good story, and walk at least nine holes with them. If these players are not doing well, check the leaderboards throughout the course to find another person to follow for the next nine holes. Be flexible, though, because not everything will go as planned. Come to a tournament with several possible story angles.

▶ Walk the golf course to determine significant hazards, challenges and pin placements.

▶ Create a system for taking notes as you describe players' performances. Here's how Associated Press golf writer Doug Ferguson recorded a hole played by Vijay Singh, Camilo Villegas and Mike Weir:

> VJ – Fwy, rt. bunker, 12 ft, 2-putt (then his score in relation to par)
>
> CV – RR, short, chip to 3 ft, save
>
> MW – Fwy, 18 feet, birdie.

On this hole, Singh hit into the fairway, then the bunker on the right, blasted out to 12 feet and took two putts for a bogey. Villegas hit into the right rough, came out short, chipped to 3 feet and saved his par. Weir hit to the fairway, then 18 feet and made the putt.

▶ Check stats leading into tournaments, something professional tours and colleges provide. For high school tournaments, contact the coaches to request scoring averages.

▶ Bring a USGA golf rules book, something that can easily fit in a satchel or backpack.

▶ Golf has more course etiquette than other sports. For instance, fans (and sports writers) should remain silent and still when a golfer stands over the ball preparing to hit. Noises and movements can distract the golfer. Find a spot to watch the shot well before the player prepares to hit. In addition, always allow players to leave the green first toward the next green unless you are way ahead of them. And never stand in the player's line of sight during putts. Move a little to the left or right.

▶ Kneel as you watch. Don't block the view of fans who paid to watch this event. Do not engage fans in conversations, especially those holding beers or who make snide remarks. If someone asks how a player is doing, feel free to inform the person and continue on.

▶ Don't panic – or overreact. You can't possibly catch everything. Follow what you can, and then get the details about other players in the press tent or by speaking to players afterward. "We were in Dallas one year, a tournament that uses two golf courses, and a buddy of mine saw Mark Calcavecchia birdie two straight holes to grab the early lead," Ferguson says. "He went out to watch. By the time he crossed the street and walked nearly two miles to reach the fifth hole, Calcavecchia had made two bogeys and the guy leading the tournament was on the other course, a 20-minute walk away."

▶ For the final two rounds, follow the leaders. The players with the best scores are the last to tee off during these latter rounds.

▶ Note players' reactions during key moments. How did Ernie Els react just off the fairway when Tiger Woods sank that 20-footer to win? How did Annika Sorenstam react after she missed a four-foot putt to force a playoff? How did a player react after recording a third bogey in a row? How do players react when loud cheers ring out a hole or two ahead during the final round? Do they look beaten? Worried?

▶ Note players' body language. Some players slam their clubs on the ground, others curse after bad putts and others may high-five their caddies. See whether body language changes. Does it reflect a player's performance? Does it reveal how a player scores on the next few holes? Is the gesture a surprise for this usually low-key player?

▶ Focus on putting. Did a player make a great number of long putts, from about 15-plus feet away? Or perhaps a player missed several putts within six feet. Did someone miss a very short putt, or make a very long one, to win or lose an event? Putting is emphasized a great deal in a sport where the saying is, "Drive for show, but putt for dough."

▶ Focus on driving. Did a player gain a great deal by continuously hitting the ball farther than others? Did this set up some easier approach shots? Driving itself won't enable a player to win, but it doesn't hurt a player's chances either.

▶ Focus on the short game – particularly shots around the green, where masterful players like Phil Mickelson can salvage great shots out of bunkers or can consistently land the ball close to the hole for short putts. This part of the game can have a dramatic impact on one's overall play, just as accurate approach shots can.

ASK

▶ Don't request an interview until a player finishes the round, which means signing the scorecard. Afterward, players may need to decompress, putting away tees, yardage books and other stuff from their bags. Or they may need to chat with their caddies to set up the next day's schedule. Either way, give them space.

▶ Players who fail to sign a scorecard or who sign a scorecard that includes any mistakes are immediately disqualified, so golfers usually spend several minutes after a round verifying the scores for each hole.

▶ Tour officials in professional tournaments bring the top players to the press center at the end of their rounds. This is also usually the case for National Collegiate Athletic Association championships. These players will walk you through their rounds. You can ask questions to get additional details as well. Which club did you use for your approach shot? How did the putt break on No. 17? How far did you hit the driver on No. 8?

▶ Ask golfers to summarize their rounds. How did the course play (wet, windy, dry, hard)? Did this play to your strengths? Talk about the birdie on the fourth hole. When did you realize you were leading? What part of your game worked best today? Can you recall the club you used to hit the approach shot on No. 16?

▶ Show a little empathy for players who had a difficult time. Avoid blunt statements such as: How did you blow that putt? Or what happened on that double-bogey at No. 8? Use a little decorum, show a little empathy and phrase questions with that in mind, perhaps posing the following: Can you describe some of the challenges on the eighth hole?

▶ But don't console or pamper players, something the real professionals usually hate. If you have a question, ask it. "Instead of something like, 'Jack, we know you're the greatest major champion of all time, and nothing you do at the Masters will ever change that, but do you wonder if you can still compete at your age?'" says Ferguson, "I went with this one, 'Is part of you worried you won't break 80?' Jack knew what we and everyone else was thinking, and he appreciated the honesty of the question."

▶ Every question should have a purpose. Ask questions because you really need answers, not just to solicit quotes or to hear yourself speak.

▶ Listen to a golfer's opening statement, which can frequently be the most quotable part of the interview.

▶ Learn to read a player's mood, something easier said than done. Knowing how a golfer played the final hole of the day can help inform this assessment. The general rule: if you want to speak with someone, pray for a birdie. If someone wants to leave, ask, "Do you mind if I walk with you?" If players storm off, don't take this personally. We all need to blow off some steam. Let players hit some balls at the driving range or eat for about 30 minutes. Then respectfully request to speak with them again.

▶ Humor can sometimes break the ice with players – but be very careful if you try this. "A friend from Australia assigned to write about his Aussie mates was waiting on Steve Elkington, who finished with a double bogey and was furious," says Ferguson. "He bolted out of the trailer after signing his card, blew off everybody and walked toward the parking lot. My man chased him down and said, 'Steve? Steve? Do you have time for a quick word, or should I just go (expletive) myself?' Elkington laughed so hard he gave him 10 minutes."

▶ Ask how the course plays to someone's strengths and weaknesses, especially when writing preview stories. Check how players and teams have fared on courses during previous events.

WRITE

▶ Don't bury the lead. If a top golfer in a slump plays surprisingly well, focus on that instead of on the score for the leader. Start with the most interesting story.

▶ Focus on the news, which may not always be who's leading – especially during the first three rounds. A 69 by John Daly usually trumps a leading 67 by most players. Tiger shoots 77? That's bigger news than Mike Weir leading by two strokes. A player returning from appendicitis or a heart transplant? These are much better stories than who leads in the opening rounds. "Here's a good rule of thumb," says Ferguson. "If you were to call a friend who asked you, 'What happened at the golf tournament today?' then your answer is probably the story." Here are Ferguson's first two leads from the event:

> The most stunning collapse in golf gave way to the greatest comeback in the history of major championships.
>
> Paul Lawrie, 10 strokes behind when the final round began Sunday, became the first Scotsman to win the British Open in his native land in 68 years, but only after a three-way playoff caused by Jean Van de Velde's triple bogey on the 72nd hole.

> The cruelty of Carnoustie yielded to craziness at the end.
>
> The Scottish gallery sat in stunned silence as the greatest collapse in golf unfolded before their eyes. An hour later, they sang and swayed, celebrating the greatest comeback in a major by one of their own.
>
> Paul Lawrie became the first Scotsman in 68 years to win the claret jug on his native soil, an unremarkable champion in an unforgettable British Open.
>
> "A fairy story," he called it. But it was a horror story for Jean Van de Velde, the Frenchman who wanted to win in style and wound up losing in a shocking display of self-destruction.

▶ Describe spectacular shots by noting details about the landscape, people's expressions, weather conditions and the manner in which a golfer made the shot. You can also draw arrows to denote the direction of a blustery wind. Tiger Woods made an exceptionally tough shot like this during the 2002 PGA Championship at Hazeltine National Golf Club, hitting a 3-iron from a bunker over a tree to 12 feet of the hole before making the putt. Ferguson noted that Tiger's knees touched the edge of the bunker, that a 60-foot tree was 100 yards ahead of him, and the look on the caddies' faces when he made the birdie putt.

▶ Find a shot that defines someone's round. Chuck Culpepper started his story on Woods' return from an injury with this vivid description:

> It looked nauseating from contact. It screamed wildly right and ricocheted through a brutish array of cactuses and barged to the other side of a barbed-wire fence. Had the rattlesnakes in the hills not slept through February, one might've mistaken it for an egg and eaten it.

This zany tee shot on No. 15 Thursday epitomized Tiger Woods' back-nine inconveniences, quashed the momentum he'd gathered by holing from a greenside bunker on No. 14 and deflated the din he'd created around the Accenture Match Play Championship.

It also gave the loudest hint he would lose to the ruthlessly steady Tim Clark and exit in the second round, and that his noisy return to the PGA Tour after his eight-month absence would stall at two days and 32 holes.[1]

▶ Cite trends during a round, such as the fact a player birdied four straight holes or bogeyed four of six holes down the stretch. Perhaps a player started poorly, shooting 3-over for the first five holes, before shooting 7-under for the remaining 13 holes. If this golfer is a contender, ask the player the reasons for this sudden shift. You may also want to cite trends as they pertain to certain holes or times of the day. Did a par-4 hole play much easier for the round? Did few people score well on a par-3? Did players in the afternoon shoot better scores that those in the morning? Determine the reasons so you can include that information as well.

▶ In college tournaments, team results usually trump local individual scores. But that does not mean you can't focus on individual results as well. If a local player does exceptionally well, you can lead with that instead, but add the team scores soon thereafter. You can also break down the scores for individual golfers on the team to see who fares well to explain how a team rallied to win in the final round. Make sure you also speak with these golfers to gain further insights into their rounds. Otherwise, write mostly about the teams:

> Florida Southern rallied to shoot a 14-under 268 during the final round to vault past Tampa and Rollins and win the Sunshine State Conference women's title at Howey-in-the-Hills.

▶ Here are the main ways numbers are used in golf stories:

▶▶ **Use numerals for club sizes:** 9-iron, 3-wood. Clubs are divided into irons, drivers (woods) and putters.

▶▶ **Use numerals for par listings:** Hyphens should be used only as compound modifiers (par-5 hole, 4-under-par 68); otherwise a player had a par 5 or shot 4 under par.)

▶▶ **Use numerals for handicaps:** a 2-handicap golfer or he had handicap of 2 strokes.

▶▶ **Use numerals for match-play scoring:** Woods defeated Els 3 and 2.

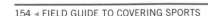

▶ ▶ Use regular AP style for most other golf references, which means spelling out numbers smaller than 10 – nine-hole course, fourth hole, second round, 12th hole. Exception: Use numerals if you write 'No.' before a hole, as in he bogeyed Nos. 2, 3 and 5.

▶ ▶ Some news organizations use numerals for distance even if they are fewer than 10, as the AP Stylebook requires. So check with your editors to see whether you'll need to write that putt was made from six (or 6) feet.

▶ Cite the leaders as early as possible in stories, along with the round just completed, name of event, and length of the course. But this does not have to be in the lead paragraphs, where you may want to focus on a more newsworthy or compelling story.

▶ Include total yardage and par somewhere in the story: Wie shot 2-over 74 on the 6,476-yard Turtle Bay course.

▶ Avoid clichés in all writing. Putts are not nasty and they are not drained. And the apron is not frog hair. Avoid using any term that is not precise enough for most people to understand.

ICE HOCKEY

Ice hockey is the only team sport that allows fighting during games.

In fact, fighting is so ingrained into the sport that teams have "enforcers," whose role is to defend their squad's top scorers against "goons" or "meat wagons" on the other team, players whose primary skill is scrapping.

"Grinders" are players whose mission is to wear down an opposing team's top players by playing physically and engaging in fights.

Goons and grinders body-check opponents, slam them into walls, and may even offer a "facewash" – rubbing a hockey glove over the face of an opponent. Ultimately, this may lead to players dropping mitts or fighting. These fights sometimes expand into a series of bouts where most everybody is battling in a "line brawl."

"There is a culture in hockey that still exists in which players are held accountable for their actions on the ice," says Chuck Gormley, hockey beat writer for the *Courier-Post* published in Cherry Hill, N.J. "If a cheap shot artist slashes a star player, either he will pay with someone going after him, or his star teammate will pay with a cheap shot from his opponent. Hockey players are very protective of their teammates and will do almost anything to right a wrong."

But hockey also has a poetic-artistic side: Players glide across the ice, make acrobatic moves and fire shots through narrow holes to score. And hockey beat writers regularly say hockey players are among the most polite and accessible of any sport.

"Hockey players are by far the easiest interviews I've had," says Cameron Eickmeyer, managing editor for USAHockey.com. "They are usually very honest and open and almost never a canned-quote machine. If you show them respect and listen, hockey players will really open up."

Learn the Basics

▶ Hockey's rules are not as widely known as those for baseball, basketball, football and tennis. Hockey writers need to immerse themselves in the basic rules and terms before covering a game. Hockey is a much more specialized beat than these other sports. "Hockey is still a niche sport," says Michael Russo, hockey writer for the *Star Tribune* in Minneapolis. "You can't take just anybody and have them cover hockey. This is one sport where you'd better know the rules."

▶ Games are divided into three 20-minute periods. Teams play a sudden-death overtime when games are tied at the end of regulation, meaning the first team that scores wins. The game goes to a shootout if nobody scores during a five-minute OT period. In the postseason, games are extended to 20-minute sudden-death periods that never go to a shootout.

▶ Three players compete for each team in NHL shootouts. If both teams score the same number of times, an additional player shoots for each team until one team gains the scoring advantage. Both teams get the same number of shots. Shootouts don't count toward any individual statistics.

▶ For standings, teams earn two points for a win, one point for a tie and no points for a loss. A team earns a point despite losing a shootout.

▶ Both goalies earn a shutout when games end 0 – 0 before shootouts.

▶ Goalies may be the most important players on the ice. A hot-handed goalie can seemingly lead a team into the postseason, and through the playoffs, by himself. Goalies are evaluated primarily by two key stats – wins and goals against average. In some ways, they are like pitchers. Goalies who find a way to win, despite the score, are highly respected, as are goalies who regularly allow few goals – an average below 3.00 goals per game is considered excellent, much like a pitcher's earned-run average.

▶ Familiarize yourself with the following terms and stats.

▶▶ **backhander:** shot taken by using the back of a stick's blade.

▶▶ **blue line:** lines separate the rink into three zones – attacking, neutral and defending. The area in the center between the two blue lines is the neutral area.

▶▶ **breakaway:** describes a player driving toward the opposing goal with no defender between himself and the goalie.

▶▶ **crease:** the blue ice in front of each goal, an area designed for goalies to work unimpeded. If a player enters the crease before scoring, the goal is disallowed in most leagues.

▶▶ **deflections:** a redirected shot into the goal, something teams usually practice.

▶▶ **empty-net goal:** a score when the opposing goalie is no longer in the net, usually replaced by a forward during the final minutes of a game when a team needs a goal to tie the game.

▶▶ **faceoff:** restarts action after goals and penalties when both teams' centers fight for possession of a puck dropped between their sticks by an official. Faceoffs are also used after ice infractions such as offside and icing.

▶▶ **forfeits:** recorded as 1 – 0 victories.

▶▶ **goal line:** the puck must completely cross this line as it goes into the net to count as a goal.

▶▶ **hat trick:** term for a player who scores three goals in a game. A natural hat trick means the player scored three goals in a row without anyone else scoring during this time period.

▶▶ **icing:** when a player shoots the puck across the red line and the opposing team's goal line that isn't touched by a player and that doesn't go into the net. A linesman stops play, restarting it with a face-off in the zone of the team called for the penalty.

▶▶ **player advantage:** when a team has one more player on the ice than its opponent because of a penalty.

▶▶ **penalty box:** where players sit to serve time for penalties.

▶▶ **plus/minus:** used to measure how players contribute to the team's success. Players get one point, or (+1), for each goal the team scores when on the ice, and lose one point (−1) each time the opponent scores. Power-play goals are not calculated.

▶▶ **power play:** name for moments when a team has a player advantage.

▶▶ **screened shot:** shots where the goalie's view is obscured by opposing players, a strategy used during scoring opportunities.

▶ ▶ **shifts:** Players play for about a minute at a time, racing and sprinting to the point of exhaustion before jumping over the wall to the bench as the next line of players jumps out to play. The top players may be on the ice for about 20 minutes per game, one-third of the total length of play.

▶ ▶ **slapshot:** a hard shot fired toward the goal, usually preceded by a big windup.

▶ ▶ **snap shot:** a hard shot where players do not wind up, instead they take the shot while the stick is at hip level.

▶ ▶ **wrist shot:** as the name implies, players fire shots mostly with their wrists and forearms.

▶ ▶ **zamboni:** ice-resurfacing machine that cleans the rink before each period begins.

▶ Penalties are divided into several categories. Minor penalties are those where a player must leave the ice for two minutes, giving the opponent a power-play opportunity. For major penalties, players must serve four or five minute in the penalty box. For misconduct, players are forced to leave the ice for 10 minutes, but the team may replace the player on the ice. For severe penalties, players may be disqualified, meaning they must leave the bench and locker room area. Goalies never have to serve penalties; instead, a teammate must serve time for any infraction called on the goalkeeper. Here are some of the most commonly called penalties:

▶ ▶ **checking from behind:** hitting an opponent whose back is turned.

▶ ▶ **cross checking:** a player hits an opponent while holding the stick with both hands.

▶ ▶ **high sticking:** a player strikes an opponent while holding the stick above shoulder level.

▶ ▶ **holding:** a player holds an opponent.

▶ ▶ **hooking:** a player uses a stick to slow down, or hold, a player.

▶ ▶ **interference:** illegal body contact with a player who does not have the puck; called when a player knocks an opponent's stick out of his hands.

▶ ▶ **offside:** players are not allowed to be ahead of the puck in the attacking zone. If players are already across the blue line before a teammate who is carrying the puck, offside is called. This is enforced to prevent players from remaining near the opposing goal, which is sometimes called cherry-picking in basketball.

▶ ▶ **slashing:** hitting, or swinging, a stick at an opponent.

▶ ▶ **spearing:** stabbing an opponent with a stick's blade.

▶ ▶ **tripping:** causing an opponent to fall by using a stick or body part.

Get Ready

▶ Arrive early so you can review game notes that may include player profiles and game-by-game results to note a few trends and potential storylines for this game. Richard Chere, who covers the New Jersey Devils for *The Star-Ledger* in Newark, N.J., arrives three hours early so he can speak with players for an early story and to post information on the newspaper's National Hockey League weblog before the game starts. He also speaks with players during the 30-minute early skate, while players practice and warm up. In the game notes, check recent results to see whether a team has won or lost a string of games in a row. What were the scores? Did a team rally to win several games in the third period – or, conversely, lose several despite two- or three-goal leads entering the final period? You can address these angles if something similar happens during this game, or if a team halts a winning or a losing streak. If possible, read press guides and notes posted on team Web sites for college and NHL teams before arriving at the game.

▶ Determine whether the teams have any rivalries. Did someone get slashed the game before? Did two players fight in a previous game? Maybe someone delivered a hard hit that caused an injury.

▶ Look through stats and news to see whether a player is about to reach a milestone for a season or career.

- Determine if any key players are missing because of injury, discipline, trade or graduation. If so, whose playing time will be affected?

- Right before the opening faceoff, record the forward lines and defensive pairings for each team so you can see the offensive and defensive matchups preferred by the two coaches. It's easy to overlook who's on the ice with five playing for each team, along with about 18 players on the bench.

WATCH

- Review stats sheets distributed between periods to verify your notes to see if the stats reveal any trends missed while keeping score.

- Describe big goals for reference when writing the game story. For each, include time scored, scorer, who assisted and a brief description of the goal. In addition, describe defensive mistakes made by the opposition, which can lead to further analysis or to questions to ask after the game. Some hockey writers also note big hits.

- Determine how a goal happens. Sometimes, a goal is created from a play that few saw and that does not appear in a box score. Who made the big hit to start the play? Who stole the puck? Did the defense allow an open crease? Evaluate the assist that set up the goal. Maybe a second pass was needed as well. These are details you can't get from the box score.

- Record times between shots. This information can reveal a trend and can lead to post-game questions. What happened during that six-minute interval in the third period where you could not get off a shot? Did they play you any differently? Were you trying anything new?

- Observe which players go out on each line shift. Did a coach pull someone from the first or second lines? Was a player moved down to a third or fourth line? Did a player miss a shift or an entire period? Ask coaches afterward about the reasons for any line shifts.

- Watch for a general perspective as well, to get a feel for the game's flow. Is one team dominating? Is it a skating or a hitting game? Are referees blowing whistles? Are there lots of stoppages? Or is the game flowing unimpeded? These general impressions can lead to more specific analyses and post-game questions. "In time, you get to know which game suits the team you are covering," says Gormley.

- Injuries can be a big part of hockey. So keep an eye on the trainer and the tunnel that leads to the locker room. Players who get hurt frequently confer with the trainer on the bench, or they may just depart for the dressing room, depending on the severity of the injury.

- Record every scoring opportunity, even those that fail. Record shots that hit the post, a fact that's worth noting during a close game. Check the number of shots each line takes during the game, including those that go for scores. See which line is most effective.

- Record details about every penalty called – which player drew the penalty, which player caused the penalty to be called, the time the penalty was called. As the game progresses, determine whether certain players are called for penalties, or draw others into penalties, something that is significant in hockey because penalties give a team a player advantage.

- On power plays, record the number of shots taken for each opportunity. Games are frequently determined by a team's success on power plays. Did one team fire off numerous shots during each advantage? Did a team play well defensively, preventing many scoring opportunities? Killing power plays is as significant as converting them. Check each team's success rates on power plays. Did they play better or worse than their averages during this game? Get more details in the locker rooms after the game.

- Look for what Russo calls clutch goals, scores that put a team ahead by one or two goals. He keeps his own Excel spreadsheet on stats like clutch goals, which are not recorded by the league. "That way, if a clutch goal is scored, I can just flip to a page to see how many he has," he says. "Then, I can put it in the story."

- Record key plays, such as saves on breakaways, that may not always show up in stats sheets. Describe plays where a defense thwarts a scoring opportunity, especially if the defense then takes the puck the other way to score – something that is essentially a two-goal swing on one play. You should also describe key saves by goalies and last-minute shots. These plays may seem obvious when they happen, but they can be forgotten in deadline if you don't write them down.

- Determine the locations and types of shots. Those that are low and to the stick side can be more problematic for goalies. Wrist shots, while slower than slap shots, are usually taken more quickly and without a windup, meaning goalies have less time to react.

▶ Hockey writers brag how hockey players are down-to-earth, accessible and candid. Players may even invite you to their homes or the coffee shop, says Russo. After games, they usually don't hold back.

▶ For NHL games, head to the morning skate that lasts 30 minutes, a time when players are warming up and working on skills and are much more relaxed. This is a good time to shoot the breeze with players, asking them questions for features, notes packages and for that evening's game.

▶ Ask players to describe the opposing goalie's performance. Did he ever leave the net exposed by veering too far from the goal? How did he move in the crease? Why couldn't anybody score on him today?

▶ Ask questions, no matter how delicate. A goalie won't be happy after allowing the winning goal, especially one scored in the final minutes. But find a way to ask questions that help illuminate this key play and get his unique perspective. What were you focusing on when Tomas came flying down the right side? Where did it appear he was going to shoot? Do not ask, "How did you feel about that final goal?" The goalie's probably feeling angry, sad and frustrated – for having to field the question as much as having allowed the decisive goal. You may also want players to explain how opponents slipped away for breakaway goals or to describe a final shot that did not go into the goal.

WRITE

▶ Write a running narrative after each period, a mini game story that focuses on key plays and trends. After each period, write another narrative that should be placed above the previous one, meaning the running for the third period would be inserted first, followed by summaries for the second and first periods, respectively. At the conclusion of the game, write three to five paragraphs that include a general overview and can be used as the lead grafs for a story that can be quickly filed for early print editions and for the Web site. After interviewing players and coaches, work on a version that may be revised a little, with a few updates and quotes, or a great deal if a new angle emerges from the locker-room chats. Of course, deadline determines how much you can revise.

▶ Note winning and losing streaks in stories, particularly if a streak has been halted or has been extended for a long time. Three-game streaks are minor notes, but seven or more is much more newsworthy.

▶ Teams can also have winless streaks if they have both tied and lost games during a stretch. For example, a team that has gone 0 – 4 – 2 is on a six-game winless streak (not losing streak) since the team has tied two games along with the four losses. Same goes for a team that has gone 4 – 0 – 1. The team is not on a winning streak but on a non-losing streak. You can write around this: The Red Wings have not lost in five straight games, going 4 – 0 – 1.

▶ Third-period rallies are always worth noting.

▶ Record career stats plateaus, usually in increments of 50 – for example, a player's 150th career goal, a 300th career assist, or a 200th career victory for a goalie.

▶ Note season highs for any team or individual statistic – team goals, individual assists, accumulated penalty minutes, shots on goal. Avoid writing season-high until about a month into a season. It's silly to write "season high" five games into a season.

▶ Mention saves for goalies who have disallowed many goals during a close game, particularly after a goalie stops 25 or more shots in a game that ends either 1 – 0 or 2 – 1. That a goalie made 26 saves in a 7 – 4 victory is not as compelling. In addition, note when a goalie rebounds from a poor performance to a victory. An Associated Press writer described one goalie's turnaround this way:

> Osgood recorded his 31st career save four days after allowing five goals in a 6 – 3 loss to the Islanders.

▶ Mention a team's record against an opponent, particularly when it involves a string of wins or losses or when it precedes another showdown that could determine a post-season loss.

▶ Don't describe every goal in detail, only the ones that took amazing skill or that involved something unusual during the play. For most goals, you can just write that someone scored along with the time and the team score. "If it's a really sick goal, I'll describe it to a tee," says Russo. "In Atlanta, a player drilled a goal into the top corner post. That was the only opening, the only place he could have put it – and he did, right in the top shelf." Here's how the AP described one sensational goal: "Sidney Crosby shifted the puck from backhand to forehand before sliding it along the goal line and into the net behind goalie Martin Brodeur, who had deflected the previous 20 shots in the game." Here are some other descriptions from AP stories:

> Tampa Bay goalie Olaf Kolzig misplayed the puck behind the net, which allowed Frans Nielsen to gain control and feed Hunter, who was alone in front of the goal.

> Rolston scored a power-play goal late in the second period, knocking in his own rebound after Kari Lehtonen made the initial save.

> Stastny scored his first goal of the season 2:57 into the period to make it 3 – 1, banking a shot off a surprised Turco, who lost sight of the puck.

▶ Cite a team's record in overtime games, when the extra period is required: "Alex Ovechkin's goal tied the game, sending the Capitals into their eighth overtime in 14 games. They are 5 – 3 in OT." (Associated Press)

▶ You can describe rallies briefly, showing the progression of goals in a single sentence or two, as Gormley does here: "Carter started the comeback at 7 minutes, 46 seconds into the second period. A minute later, Gagne cut through Goligoski and Malkin on a short-handed breakaway and, with Malkin draped on his shoulder, put a backhander past Fleury." (Associated Press)

▶ Note when a player or line shoots infrequently: "Petr Sykora took only one shot in 14 shifts during the first two periods." (Associated Press)

▶ Note scoring trends. Has a team had trouble scoring recently, averaging fewer than two goals over an extended period? If so, ask coaches and players for the reasons. Are defenses setting up differently? Has the team shot poorly? Are players hustling for loose pucks?

▶ Avoid using clichés like "light the lamp" or "ripple the twine" for goals.

▶ Address a team's power-play performance, especially if the team does far better or worse than its average with a one-player advantage.

> The Lightning, who entered the game third in the NHL in power-play efficiency at 43.2 percent, failed to convert on six attempts. (Associated Press)

► Focus on the play of goalies, who, like quarterbacks and pitchers, can carry a team through a season or the playoffs. Coaches usually pick a single goalie to carry them through the final weeks of a season and on through the postseason:

> Heading into the game against Colorado, Turco was 6 – 1 – 0 in his last seven games, with a 1.70 goals against average and .934 save percentage. Those are the kind of numbers that can carry a team a long way.
>
> "I feel good right now, that I've come a long way," Turco told Heika. "My ability to stay on my feet longer to react to second plays or even third plays from a balanced position has been a great feeling for me lately."[1]

LACROSSE

I f you're familiar with men's lacrosse, your first glimpse of a women's game may confuse you. Where are the helmets and shoulder pads? Where's the slamming and rattling of sticks? In covering lacrosse, it's crucial to remember that rules for women and men differ greatly – more than in any other sport.

While men regularly body check, push and shove, women are not allowed contact. So women wear only mouthpieces and goggles, not the helmets, shoulder pads and leg pads the men wear. Men wear helmets, shoulder pads and leg pads to protect their bodies from regular contact with sticks, players and balls shot toward the goal. Women, meanwhile, wear only mouthpieces and goggles since they are not allowed contact.

"It's not like covering men's and women's soccer," says Brian Logue, director of communications for U.S. Lacrosse and editor of *Lacrosse Magazine*.

In addition, because they are heavily padded, men can leap in front of the net to block shots on goal with their bodies, a tactic denied women.

Face-offs, which can be decisive in games, are played much differently by men and by women. Men battle each other, keeping their sticks on the ground to anticipate the referee's motion to drop the ball between them. Players smack sticks and slam bodies in an attempt to gain possession. Referees, meanwhile, hold women's sticks together in the air until the whistle blows.

Women also field 12 players, two more than in men's games.

Men use both long and short poles that can range from 40 to 72 inches, while women's lacrosse poles are all about the same size, from 35 to 43 inches.

There are several other differences between men's and women's lacrosse, but they are too numerous to note here.

Learn the Basics

▶ There are two main versions of lacrosse played in the United States – box and field lacrosse. Box lacrosse is played indoors, usually on a covered ice hockey rink using six players. Field lacrosse is played in a larger field outdoors using 11 players in a more wide-open game.

▶ A lacrosse ball, made of solid rubber, can be white, yellow or orange. The ball weighs 5 to 5¼ ounces and is 7¾ to 8 inches in circumference.

▶ In field lacrosse, a field is 110 yards long by 60 yards wide, roughly 10 yards longer and wider than a football field. Women's fields are 10 yards longer and five yards wider, an attempt to create more room to avoid contact. Both fields include 10 yards of space behind each goal.

▶ Men's teams field 10 players, but they really play six-on-six offense because the three defensemen are not allowed to cross midfield. The three attackmen can't go past this midfield line to play defense either. Only the three midfielders are allowed to move freely across the field. Women officially use attackers, midfielders and defenders, but they can all move freely.

▶ Defenders and attackers use sticks of different sizes. Four players on the field use the longer sticks, measuring 52 to 72 inches. Only four players can use the longest sticks, which, at 6 feet, may be taller than some defenders who can better reach in and knock away balls and shots with them, But they are rather clunky, making it difficult to pass or shoot with them. Usually one midfielder will also have this longer stick. Attackers use shorter sticks, measuring 40 to 42 inches.

▶ Collegiate and professional games last 60 minutes, divided into four 15-minute quarters. High school games usually last 48 minutes. Halftimes run anywhere from 10 to 15 minutes, while breaks between quarters are set for about two minutes. Teams are awarded two timeouts per half.

▶ Teams must cross the midfield line in 10 seconds after they gain possession, just as in basketball, or they lose possession of the ball. Teams can't go back over that line afterward, an infraction that forfeits possession of the ball. These rules are used to keep the game flowing, to avoid a keep-away approach to the game.

During the final two minutes, teams are required to keep the ball in the attack zone or relinquish possession.

Overtime periods are played in sudden-death format, where the first team to score during the four-minute extra session wins.

Players can move behind the nets as in hockey, although the space is much wider and deeper on the lacrosse field. Goal nets for field lacrosse are 6 feet by 6 feet, while box lacrosse nets are 4 feet by 4 feet.

Balls that drop out of a stick, called ground balls, remain in play.

Players may bounce shots into the goal, often doing so off the trampled dirt area about 15 feet in front of the goal.

On shots that go out of bounds, the player nearest the sideline where the ball went out gains possession of the ball.

Passing is an integral aspect of the game, allowing teams to more quickly move the ball to set up shots. Players can throw either overhand or underhand, but passes thrown higher are better than those tossed low or those that slowly roll on the ground, making them easier to intercept.

Face-offs are significant in lacrosse because the team with the ball can score frequently. The sport is not like basketball or soccer, where the other team automatically takes position after each goal. Face-offs are used to restart the game at the start of each quarter and after each goal. In some ways, lacrosse can turn into a make it – take it scenario if the scoring team continues to win face-offs. As a result, teams often go on scoring runs of three, four, even eight goals in a row – and sometimes before the other team can even gain possession of the ball. So, clearly, players fight hard for the ball. "Once the ball is in the air," says Logue, "all the players are really going for it." Face-offs take place after goals, at the start of each quarter, and after certain dead balls when two opposing players crouch down at midfield, hold their sticks flat on the ground and press the backs of their stick pockets together. Players rake or claw at the ball to gain possession or may flick the ball to a teammate.

- Game flow is similar to a mix of basketball, hockey and soccer. As in basketball, teams try to execute drawn-up plays. Lacrosse's offensive schemes are also like hockey, but lacrosse teams go on runs more like a basketball team. Look for a few other similarities to basketball. First, players shoot, pass or attempt to fake out defenders. Second, teams can either race downcourt on fast breaks or they can more slowly set up shots in a half-court offense.

- Lacrosse is a physical game, much like hockey, where players may bodycheck one another or smack another's stick to steal the ball. Unlike in hockey, fighting is not tolerated. Players are assessed a five-minute penalty the first time they engage in brawls. After this, players could be suspended for several games.

- In box lacrosse, teams use five players plus a goalie. The left and right creasemen are the team's top scorers who stay more on the offensive side, leading fast breaks. Left and right cornermen spend more time at midfield, while the pointman moves up and down the middle lanes of the field.

- Defenders try to dislodge the ball from the ball carriers' net by jabbing a stick into the net, something called a poke check.

- Defenders may also slap their sticks against the ones held by ball carrier; this is called stick checking.

- Teams run picks and switches in order to create matchups against a defender with a shorter stick. An attackman can shoot more easily against a defenseman who doesn't have an extra two feet of stick.

- Mismatches are created when teams use picks to block, or impede, a defenseman from following the person the player is assigned to cover. This can be particularly frustrating to teams playing man-to-man defense. But creating picks can also work well against teams employing zone defenses, where players are assigned to cover an area, or zone. A pick, though, creates an even larger gap between defenders. But teams are counting on a defenseman with a smaller stick to slide over, creating a two-foot mismatch and, therefore, a better scoring opportunity.

- Teams also rely on screens to create scoring opportunities, where an attacking player will move in front of the goal crease and obscure the goalie's view.

- Balls are knocked loose by defenders, are dropped by attackers and roll around after errant shots. Whichever team grabs, or controls, these loose balls the most usually wins.

Penalties can be difficult for novices to discern. Rules allow players to smack, or slash, an opponent's stick. But players are sometimes called for slashing. Officials try to assess whether players are seeking to steal the ball or to inflict injury. Like most calls, penalties are judgment calls. (In all sports, don't unfairly judge officials in your stories. Try to understand the game and speak with referees, even off the record, to better understand the games first.) You may want to track total penalties and note when they prove decisive in a game, though. That's worth writing about.

Players may not enter the semicircle around the goal. Goals are dismissed if a player even steps on this line during a successful attack.

In box lacrosse, teams must shoot every 30 seconds or face losing possession, the same way the NBA enforces the 24-second shot clock.

As in hockey, lacrosse players can substitute freely, running on and off the field at designated areas.

In box lacrosse, most penalties are two minutes long. More serious penalties, such as fighting, are assessed five minutes in most leagues and games. Players can foul out in some professional leagues after five fouls, as in basketball. At the high school and college levels, yellow and red cards may be issued for major infractions, prompting expulsions and suspensions.

Review stats before each game to find trends and to identify the top players. The key stats in lacrosse include assists (A), goals (G), loose balls grabbed (LB), power-play goals (PPG), power-play assists (PPA), shots (S), shooting percentage (SPCT), shots on goals (SOG), short-handed goals (SHG) and short-handed assists (SGA). Shooting percentages over .200 are considered excellent. This is calculated by dividing total goals by shots on goal.

Familiarize yourself with the following terms:

> > **attackmen:** primary offensive players in field lacrosse.

> > **ball carrier:** term used for player carrying the ball on the stick.

> > **body check:** players may hit a ball carrier or while contesting a loose ball but only above the waist and never from behind.

> > **box:** rectangular-shaped area around the goal. Shots are seldom made outside of this area, so defenders don't press attackers until they enter this area. Teams that are ahead are required to keep the ball, preventing what could turn into a game of keep-away during the final minutes.

► ► **clearing:** when defensive players run or pass the ball away from their goal areas, usually by traveling down a sideline.

► ► **cradling:** players can turn their wrists and arms to hold the ball in the stick's pocket to maintain control while running on the field.

► ► **crease:** nine-foot semicircle surrounding each team's goal where offensive players are disallowed except to reach in and scoop loose balls.

► ► **creasemen:** take face-offs; primary scorers in box lacrosse.

► ► **cross-checking:** using the handle of the stick to hit an opponent.

► ► **cutting:** a tactical move where players dart, or cut, toward the goal in order to receive a pass and shoot.

► ► **man down:** teams that have lost a player to the penalty box and must play with one fewer person on the field.

► ► **offside:** an infraction called when one team does not have at least four players on its defensive side or at least three players on its offensive side.

► ► **slashing:** hitting another player with a stick.

► ► **tripping:** obstructing, tripping or hitting an opponent below the waist.

Get Ready

► Read about the players and teams involved to find storylines and to better analyze the game. What happened the last time these teams played each other? How well do these teams convert their shots? Has one team won or lost several games in a row? Try to discern the reasons for either streak.

► Teams usually rely on one to two main scorers, so look through each team's stats to see who's scored the most – or taken many shots. Odds are this person will continue to take most of the shots – and that the opposing team's top defenders will cover this person. During the game, focus on matchups like this. Who won the battle? Did teams play man-to-man or zone defense to stop this player? Did this matchup yield any key plays? Be careful. Just because someone scores several goals doesn't mean the defender failed. If a player who averages five goals a game scores three – is that a victory for the defense? Did the defense force this player to take awkward shots? Did they limit scoring opportunities? In most instances, you may have to ask the defenders and the coaches, who can offer examples from the game and insights on the coverage.

► Prepare yourself to follow the ball as much as possible. In lacrosse, the main action centers on the shots on goal, passes, face-offs and loose balls.

▶ Odds are, you won't know enough to break down offenses or analyze defensive alignments until you've covered lacrosse for a while. Instead, take notes on the key events, which, in lacrosse, means scoring. As you take notes, keep a running summary that includes references to goals scored, fine defensive plays, saves by the goalie. In addition, offer a brief description of each whenever possible (No. 12 cut right for a few steps, then cut left, shot ball into lower left side of net for score.).

▶ After each period, look for trends in scoring. Did one team, or player, score several goals in a row? Did a goalie make a series of saves? Note these for the game story.

▶ Beat writers like Budd Bailey, who covered the National Lacrosse League for *The Buffalo News,* go to morning practices to gather information for a notes package and to find key angles for that night's story and live-game blog. He'll also check the league Web site, read releases and evaluate team stats.

▶ Also, keep track of all shots on goal. Record where on the field they were taken and the reason they did not go into the net. Did a team take far more shots from the right side? Did a diving defender deflect the shot? Did the goalie use her stick to deflect a low, hard shot?

▶ Record physical plays to illustrate the tone of the game. If you see few aggressive or physical displays, that can also be an angle for the story, something that can lead to questions after the game.

▶ Keep track of shot selection. Were a majority of the shots taken from longer distances or from the same part of the field? Did one team take mostly off-balance or awkward shots? Did players force shots? These are probably caused by a solid defensive effort. Address than in post-game interviews.

▶ Keep track of decisive goals to reference when writing the game story. For each, include time scored, scorer, who assisted and a brief description of the goal. In addition, note defensive mistakes made by the opposition, which can lead to further analysis or to questions to ask after the game.

▶ Take note of penalties. Did one team get called for far more infractions? Did any penalty prove decisive in the game? If so, explore the reason for the penalty call. Describe the play that prompted the penalty as well as the one that led to the decisive goal.

ASK

▶ Ask coaches and players how they spread the ball around on offense. Lacrosse teams usually have a go-to scorer, someone who can be relied on when a goal is needed. Observe who gets the ball during the final minutes of each period.

▶ Ask goalies about the opposing team's shooting proficiency. How accurate were their shots? What sorts of things did they try in order to set up shots?

▶ Ask coaches about strategy, such as adjustments made to counter the opposing team's tactics. What was the team's game plan? What did you do to adjust as the game wore on?

▶ Look for a mismatch in personnel, defenders who cannot keep up with attackers or midfield players who cannot keep up.

▶ Take note of whistles. Did it appear many were blown during the game? Ask both coaches.

▶ Ask about the tempo of the game. Did a team take a big lead in the first period before slowing the game in the second half? Did a team start slowly before being forced to play more aggressively (and perhaps more sloppily) in the later periods? Ask coaches and players about the pace of the game.

▶ Lacrosse players are not always comfortable speaking about themselves, perhaps because the sport is not in the limelight like football or basketball. So you may want to ask questions about teammates or the team's overall performance. Ask them to describe how their teammates were able to set up so many scores. What went right in today's game?

▶ Focus on face-offs. What did you do differently today to win more of the face-offs? Ask an opposing player: What did she do differently to win so many face-offs today?

WRITE

▶ Start with the bigger picture: who won and why. "Usually with so many goals scored, the scoring or goaltending writes a lot of the story," says Budd Bailey, who covers lacrosse for *The Buffalo News*. "In a 17 – 16 game, one play usually doesn't dictate much. However, last week Buffalo erased a six-goal lead to tie it in the last minute and then won in overtime. After starting my story with the comeback, I quickly got into a description of the game-winning goal. I've written more stories about hockey than anything else, and you can't quite approach it the same way because there is so much more scoring in lacrosse. The basketball analogy works better, because teams can go on 'runs' that help determine the final outcome."

▶ Focus on game-winning goals and on players who've scored several goals or recorded several assists. You can also describe goals that just missed during close games, citing how the ball bounced off a crossbar, deflected off the goalie's shoulder or went so high that it landed in the stands.

▶ Focus on a key defensive play, describing it and explaining its impact on the game's final outcome.

▶ Cite runs of unanswered goals, offering the score either before or after the run as well: "Johns Hopkins scored six straight goals to take a 12 – 9 lead midway through the third quarter."

▶ Describe a great performance by either goalie, citing a few plays to show this.

▶ Describe key plays anywhere on the field.

> But Greer made sure that his Duke team did not have similar heartbreak.
> After the Duke freshman Terrence Molinari won the game's final face-off, he passed the ball to midfielder Peter Lamade.
> Lamade tossed the ball to Greer, who was about 8 yards in front of the net and guarded by short-stick midfielder Danny Nathan.
> Greer snatched the ball from the air, spun to his left and beat Cornell goalkeeper Matt McMonagle to the near side of the cage.[1]

▶ Describe unusual plays.

> Nathan Kenney cut the lead to 12 – 8 on a strange goal with 4:21 left in the quarter. Kenney ran down the left wing and raised his arm as if he had scored, but the ball went sailing into the corner of the stadium. The officials correctly saw, however, that the ball had gone through the net and signaled the goal.[2]

ROWING

The key to rowing is the coxswain, a word that most people outside the sport can't even pronounce, never mind define. The coxswain functions like a race-car driver, steering the boat through the fastest path, using crew members as accelerators. Though by far the smallest person on the boat, the coxswain has the biggest role – part coach, part teammate.

Coxswains are charged with steering lengthy, awkward boats down a straight course while directing crews of two, four or eight to follow any order. They sit facing their rowers, surveying the water to see what to do next, whether the boat is on line and what is needed to pass boats in other lanes.

Plus, they need to be able to execute the race plan, be aware what's going on around them and confidently make changes to positively affect the crew.

Coxswains always straddle this line between their disparate roles in a sport that requires sheer strength, endurance and mental toughness. They need to be leaders yet fit in with the crew. They're cocky and aggressive – yet calm, depending on the situation.

Coxswains also protect their crew's interests but also correct their faults during tense competitions. They must be skilled technicians who respond to unfamiliar situations such as an oar getting stuck or a headwind causing problems.

Coaches say they must be psychologists, knowing when to motivate and when to relax, determining who on board can be trusted to come through when asked, and learning what makes a crew member tick. The cox needs to possess an innate feel for what the boat needs.

"A good cox is observant – and knows when to crack the whip and when to be quiet," says John Fuchs, whose women's teams at Western Washington University have won four consecutive National Collegiate Athletic Association Division II national titles.

Coxswains are like quarterbacks in some ways, frequently calling the shots out on the water. "A lot depends on how much confidence I have in the coxswain's ability to know what I would want at the moment," says Bebe Bryans, a former national coach now running the women's program at the University of Wisconsin. "If that confidence is high, I give them quite a bit of latitude to respond to what's going on moment to moment."

Coxswains need to sense the crew's emotions. Shorter breaths usually mean panic has set in, that members are struggling to keep up. At this point, an experienced coxswain may call for a slower and harder stroke to force the crew to settle down.

"One year our plan was to take a power move 10 strokes or so before the half way mark," says Bryans. "The coxswain could feel that the boat was going really well and actually getting faster without the call – so she decided to put it off as long as possible until the other boats around her had finished theirs, and then we took ours. She told the rowers exactly what was happening and why, and encouraged them to hold the other boats off during their moves and fly away on ours. It worked really well in that particular situation. If she senses breathing becoming short, that usually says that panic might not be too far behind, so calling something to breathe and lengthen would be appropriate at that moment."

In most competitions, coxswains need to meet both a minimum and maximum weight, meaning sometimes they'll need to sweat off weight. At other times, they'll need to pack on some pounds – yet another seemingly incongruous challenge.

One thing is not difficult to reconcile: the essential role coxswains play in any crew's success.

PREPARE

Learn the Basics

▶ The standard length for races is 2,000 meters, about 1¼ miles. Many high school associations race 1,500 meters. Other distances may be used in regattas and other races. A few older races are much longer.

▶ Races are really divided into three main parts – start, body and sprint. In a 2,000-meter race, the start lasts for about 500 yards, where crews try to stroke hard and fast to get out front and to establish a good rhythm. In the body, or middle 1,000-meter portion of the race, the focus is on power and boat speed. Boats try to establish their position on the second 500-meter section. By midway, the rowers may be distressed.

"The third 500 is mentally the most difficult," says Ithaca College coach Becky Robinson. "It tends to hurt the most and requires good focus and confidence to row through strongly." On the final 500-meter sprint, boats increase their stroke rate and their speed for a final, furious push to the finish line. Boats then start their sprint somewhere close to 500 yards from the finish line. Crew teams must exhibit power, efficiency and mental toughness during a race. "Everyone feels really good in the first 500 or so – so teams need to pace well," Bryans says. "There are also different strategies that may involve the other boat. Just reacting to what other boats are doing can pull you away from what you should be doing. Just because the other boat is ahead at any given point doesn't mean they will stay there."

▶ A stroke can be broken down into two main parts – the drive and the recovery. The drive is when oars are in the water, giving the boat its acceleration. The recovery is equally important, allowing a boat to propel forward with no additional effort. Crews practice on their pace to determine effort needed to move at the highest speed and to figure out how long they can drive forward at top speed before requiring the next stroke.

▶ You'll hear coaches talk about patience during races. By that, they mean a crew should not get overly excited and try to paddle, or stroke, faster than its set pace. Boats glide down the course each time the oars leave the water, something coaches call passive speed. Rowing too quickly can disrupt the smooth flow down the course. Coaches want teams to stick to the pre-race strategy in regard to strokes per minute and not react to other boats. "Patience is sticking to your race plan no matter what," Fuchs says. "If another crew has taken a lead, the crew needs not to panic and have patience knowing that their race plan will pay off later in the event. The crew only needs to be ahead when crossing the finish line."

ON TALKING WITH COACHES

sports insider

"I always take for granted that the reporter knows nothing about rowing. I am usually pretty correct, and for the most part it isn't a big deal. It just seems to me that doing a little homework about the sport will help the writer make more sense of the information they get. The basic terminology is also, well, basic. Knowing that the reporter cares enough about the story to come in somewhat prepared encourages me to be more thoughtful about my responses."

Bebe Bryans,
women's rowing coach, University of Wisconsin

- In college, teams usually compete in 4s and 8s only. (These numbers refer to the number of rowers in the boat. The coxswain is not counted.) In the Olympics, rowers compete in the following categories:

  - ▶ ▶ **men:** quad scull, double scull, single scull, eight, coxless four, and coxless pair.

  - ▶ ▶ **lightweight men:** coxless four and double scull.

  - ▶ ▶ **women:** quad scull, double scull, single scull, eight, and coxless pair.

  - ▶ ▶ **lightweight women:** double scull.

- Rowers' positions are numbered, depending on where they sit in the boat, from bow (front) to stern (back). The rower nearest the bow is called No. 1, followed by No. 2 and so on. The rower closest to the stern in a four- or eight-person crew is called the stroke, a rower who must be especially strong and skilled in techniques – and someone who is capable of setting the rhythm for the boat.

- Unlike track, rowing does not always put its fastest qualifiers in the middle lanes, where crews can better see their main competitors. That's because each course is different. At some races, the fastest lanes are those nearest the shore, protected from the elements. At others, geography may protect outside or inner lanes from prevailing winds. Check the winds from a bridge, or walk to both sides of the river, to get a sense of which lanes work best. And ask crews and coaches about this afterward.

- Rowers compete internationally in many events – FISA events, world championships, world cup and the Olympics.

- Don't always compare race times held on different days or years on the same course because water and weather conditions rarely remain the same.

- Familiarize yourself with the following terms:

  - ▶ ▶ **bow:** forward end of the boat pointed toward the finish line.

  - ▶ ▶ **FISA:** Federation Internationale des Societes d'Aviron, the governing body for the sport of rowing in the world.

  - ▶ ▶ **heavyweight:** crews don't have any weight limits.

  - ▶ ▶ **hull:** exterior of the boat that sits in the water.

  - ▶ ▶ **lightweight:** for men, no rower can weight more than 160 pounds, and the crew cannot average more than 155 pounds; for women, rowers must weigh less than 130 and average less than 125 pounds.

▶ ▶ **port:** the left side of a boat from the coxswain's perspective. This is actually to the right of the crew, whose backs are to the finish line.

▶ ▶ **power 10:** a strategy used in races when a crew increases the power for 10 strokes in order to pull ahead or to hold off a competitor. The stroke rating doesn't necessarily change, only the force behind each stroke.

▶ ▶ **puddle:** swirl of water that follows each stroke.

▶ ▶ **repechage:** essentially a second-chance race for boats that failed to advance from the preliminaries to the semifinals and finals.

▶ ▶ **rudder:** the steering device at the stern.

▶ ▶ **run:** distance the boat moves, or glides, during one stroke.

▶ ▶ **scull:** rowers use two oars, one in each hand.

▶ ▶ **starboard:** the right side of a boat from the coxswain's perspective. This is actually to the left of the crew, whose backs are to the finish line.

▶ ▶ **stern:** trailing end of the boat, anchored by the coxswain.

▶ ▶ **stroke:** one cycle of the oars.

▶ ▶ **strokes per minute (SPM):** the number of strokes a boat completes in a minute, which varies through the three stages of a race. Typical crews have higher stroke averages at the start of a race, going about 38 to 45 SPM. Crews then usually settle into a cadence in the 30s through the middle part before picking up the pace for the final sprint. SPM is also referred to as stroke rating.

▶ ▶ **sweep:** when rowers line each side of a boat, using one oar apiece.

▶ Rowing uses several formats for competitions – match race, championship regatta, head races and Henley races.

▶ ▶ **match race:** two or three schools line up abreast for match races, starting from a standing stop before taking off down a straight course.

▶ ▶ **championship regatta:** up to six boats race at a time in championship regattas that may also require qualifying heats to reach the finals. The top six boats qualify for the grand final, followed by the second six competing in the petite final. A repechage may enable nonqualifying crews a second chance to qualify for one of these heats.

▶ ▶ **head races:** boats line up single file to compete in the longer head races that usually cover distances of approximately three miles. Crews get timed individually as they negotiate sometimes narrow rivers and tight bends. The fastest time wins.

▶ ▶ **Henley races:** boats compete in head-to-head matchups for Henley races, named after the famous regatta in England. The winners advance to the next round and the losers are eliminated, similar to match-play golf.

Get Ready

▶ You can't write a very good story without description. Arrive early enough to walk the course. You'll need to survey the best location to see the race, a place that will enable you to see the finish as well because you probably won't be able to keep up with boats that travel around 12 to 14 mph – a running pace under five minutes per mile. Some larger races may offer a way to follow the action – flatbed trucks with bleachers, or bike baths and separate roadways where media and coaches are chauffeured along with the action. A century ago, trains used to carry fans along the course to follow races at Yale. You may also want to determine if a film boat will transmit live video to monitors at the finish line. For most races, though, you'll need to find a spot to watch the action come to you. That is probably around the 1,200-meter mark. "In many races, not much changes between the 1,200 mark and the finish," says Claus Wolter, a former Canadian Olympic coach now at Franklin & Marshall College.

WATCH

▶ Look to see which boat appears to flow the easiest across the river. That's probably the boat that will win.

▶ See whether a crew is sitting straight up or laying back more, techniques used to take advantage of wind conditions. Crews tend to lay back when battling head winds, sitting straight up for tailwinds. Generally, stronger crews perform better in headwinds while more technical crews battle flat or tailwind conditions better.

▶ See whether a boat gets a clean start, heading out strongly, or whether a team falls far behind at the beginning. Afterward, you can ask the crew about the beginning.

▶ Rowers are less focused on individual goals than almost any other athletes; their success relies entirely on the team's collective effort. There are no 50-point scorers, 200-yard runners or any three-homer performances. A team's finish is the only number that matters. As a result, rowers are not accustomed to speaking about themselves very often. You can start with some simple questions about the team's performance that coaches usually ask when they debrief their crews. What went well? What didn't go well? Did the team execute the race plan? Where could the team improve next time? Most rowers will be accustomed to answering these questions after every race.

▶ Coxswains have the best view of races, able to watch both their own crew and the progress of the boats around them – much better than the coaches. Ask them to walk you through the race. How did the team start? Did the team do any power 10s? At what point did they, or another team, challenge the leader? How did these boats respond during the sprint? Which boat was the smoothest during the middle, or body, of the race?

▶ Ask coaches for their strategies entering the race. Did the team follow this strategy? If not, how did the team alter it on the course?

▶ Ask about surprises during the race. Was the course windier than they had anticipated? Did another crew do much better than expected? Did other boats go out faster than anticipated?

▶ Ask the coxswain when the crew started each phase of the race.

▶ Coaches train their crews in hopes they can put together a "whole race," meaning the team planned and executed a solid race strategy. What was the race strategy? Did the team follow it? If not, how and why did the crew make adjustments? Physically, how did the team feel down the stretch?

▶ Ask coaches whether they felt prepared for this race. How did they physically prepare for this race? Did they feel the training carried them through? How did they mentally prepare?

▶ Focus on the sprint, describing how a crew moves ahead, holds off a challenge or falters during the final stretch. Use physical description to offer the margin of victory, stating that a team won by a half-boat length. Time margins mean little to casual fans. Writing that a crew won by five boat lengths is much easier to visualize, and understand, than saying a team won by 10 seconds.

▶ Focus on moments when crews challenge, or get challenged, for the lead. Describe how the boats responded. Did one team move from a full length back to within a few feet of the lead? Did the teams move back and forth, exchanging the leads with each stroke? Did one team slowly pull away, a few feet at a time, until it had nearly a half-boat-length lead? Describe this key moment.

▶ Too many rowing stories recite race results, sending readers racing to other stories. For racing, you need to find stories and then describe the key moments, or scenes, that help propel the tale.

▶ Describe weather conditions, which are especially important when they affect the race's outcome. Did gusts cause trees to sway or reeds along the river to bend over? Did the river have whitecaps? Did fog limit visibility? Coaches and crew prefer calm conditions and moderate temperatures (55 – 75 degrees Fahrenheit). That's when a team will usually perform at its best. Ideal conditions? Flat water, no winds and temperature at about 70.

▶ Describe head-to-head matchups.

> The Czech Republic's Mirka Knapkova set the pace for the first half of the race, with Neykova just behind. As Knapkova faltered, the Bulgarian took the lead in the third 500 meters, with two-time Olympics champion Ekaterina Karsten of Belarus stalking her. However, Guerette stayed right with Karsten and rowed through the three-time defending world champion during the final 500 meters. Guerette continued to close on Neykova but ran out of room, crossing the finish line in second. Neykova finished with a time of 7:22.34, with Guerette finishing in a 7:22.78. Karsten took the bronze medal in a 7:23.98.[1]

▶ Spell out times in first reference: "Wisconsin led the entire race, clocking in at 6 minutes, 8.41 seconds to defeat Indiana by 3.9 seconds. Michigan finished third in 6:15.9, followed by Minnesota (6:18.1) and Northwestern (6:19.9)."

▶ Focus on a crew's reaction right after it wins or loses – or even after members get to shore or receive awards. This can show what the victory or defeat meant to each team's rowers. Sean Ingle of *The Guardian* captured the spirit of both the champion doubles team and Britain's entire rowing entourage in the following lead:

> Zac Purchase smiled on the podium, smiled in his press conference, and smiled roughly every 30 seconds thereafter as a flash-mob of Chinese volunteers passed their cameras to his girlfriend Felicity and asked her to snap them with a British Olympic rowing champion.
>
> While they did so, Purchase's partner in the men's lightweight double sculls, Mark Hunter, articulated just what the gold medal meant to him. "I've been dying for this day since I started rowing," he said. "The national anthem, the flag, it's a dream come true."
>
> Before these Games, the British Olympic Association had set the rowers a target of four medals; they ended up winning six – two golds, two silvers and two bronzes – not just their finest result in an Olympic regatta for 100 years but good enough to top the medal table to boot. No wonder the team leader David Tanner sounded a proud man. "It has been fantastic," he said. "Only two nations won more than one gold medal and we were one of them. Twenty-three of our 43-strong squad have won a medal. It's fabulous."
>
> Purchase and Hunter were thumping favorites for the lightweight double sculls having set the fastest time in qualifying – and they soon showed why. After a steady first 500m they accelerated over the next 1,000m to move 1.77sec clear and a boat length up. And though the Greek and Danish teams closed in the last 500m, the British pair held on to win in 6min 10.99sec – an Olympic record. "I just kept pounding away," explained Hunter, who collapsed to his knees and threw up when he stepped back on terra firma. "I was in a dark place but there was just so much belief and that was what kept us going."[2]

RUGBY

Rugby is not a sanctioned varsity sport at any level anywhere in the United States. No state high school sports association hosts a high school rugby tournament. The National Collegiate Athletic Association does not host a national championship.

As a result, rugby remains a club sport, where students recruit, schedule games and direct the program. Sometimes, a volunteer coach assists.

But that may be changing.

Eastern Illinois University and West Chester University are among a handful of teams fielding varsity women's teams, part of the NCAA's emerging sports initiative that enables colleges to administer these newer programs.

Like the other emerging sports, rugby gets 10 years to attract 40 total teams and be adopted by the NCAA.

Rugby faces many challenges in its pursuit to earn full status, not the least of which is its image. The sport is unfairly portrayed as a reckless, violent sport, played by brutish women and men with few teeth and many broken bones. Nothing could be further from the truth. In reality, players do not suffer any more injuries than athletes who play football, soccer or basketball. And in rugby speed can play a far more important role than power, allowing wings to race past slower-footed forwards and allow fullbacks and centers to cut off angles for ball carriers. Some universities even sign on sprinters from the track team during the fall season.

"The team with the best, fastest, most powerful runners always has the advantages," says Frank Graziano, a former national coach who started the first women's varsity program at Eastern Illinois University. "There is no blocking in rugby, so running the ball is even more crucial than in football. Good blocking in football can make even an average running back do well. With no blocking, it's all about the running."

Rugby is an exciting sport that has the grace of soccer, the power of football and the speed of track.

So don't concentrate on the clichéd, stereotypical aspects of the game – the blood, violence, and the fact that women play this sport. Instead, focus on rugby games the same way you would any other beat, covering the big plays, featuring the unique players and addressing the scoring trends and rallies.

PREPARE

Learn the Basics

▶ The field is a little larger than a football field, roughly 20 yards wider and 10 yards longer. The field has a midfield line and two 22-meter lines, two 10-meter lines, and a goal line. A player must pass across this goal line as well as touch the ball down to record a five-point try. The spot where the two-point conversion, or extra point, is kicked is based on where the ball is touched down in the try (or goal) zone. Obviously, a spot right in front of the crossbars is the best choice, so ball carriers may keep eluding defenders and running around until they get to a prime location. Of course, players can be tackled and stripped off the ball before reaching this spot, which is one reason why some scores are registered in the far corners. These difficult conversion kicks are almost always off line.

▶ Scores, called trys, are worth five points. Conversion kicks, which are essentially like points after touchdowns in football, are worth two points. And field goals, or drop kicks, are worth three points.

▶ Teams may also kick field goals, three-pointers, from a spot on the field where a penalty has been assigned. Teams usually prefer to keep going for the five to seven points when this happens near the goal area. But, in tough games, some teams will go for the easier three-point kick instead.

▶ Here are the other main statistics used in rugby – assists, runs over 20 yards (ROTs), total points, tackles, assisted tackles and steals after tackles.

▶ Teams get the ball back after scoring – receiving another kickoff in a sort of "make it, take it" manner.

ON AUDIENCES

"Write a rugby story as if you have an educated audience. Rarely do I read an article about field hockey or lacrosse where the rules or terminology are explained. Rugby is an invasion sport like soccer, lacrosse, field hockey where possession changes at any moment, and field position and momentum change constantly."

Frank Graziano,
women's rugby coach, Eastern Illinois University

▶ A rugby ball is very similar in shape and size to a football, except it doesn't have laces for gripping and the nose is not as pointed.

▶ Teams consist of 15 players, whose roles are unique but also overlap. As in football, certain players push and create spaces for the runners. These players are the front-line players (props, hookers). Unlike in football, any rugby player can receive passes and run with the ball, although the flankers, scrum half, fly half and fullbacks are more likely to do so.

▶ Traditionally, players wear uniforms with numbers that correspond to their positions. No. 1, for example, is typically a loose-head prop, No. 9 is a scrum half and No. 15 is the fullback. The sport even has a position called the No. 8 whose main role is to direct and control rucks from the rear. If the sport is adopted by the NCAA, players won't be assigned jerseys that correspond to their positions. So a fly half might have to wear No. 23 and a prop No. 32, otherwise there could be much confusion as to who is actually on the field.

▶ College and international games run two 40-minute halves. Time is cited progressively, the same as in soccer, which means a try with five minutes left in the first half was officially scored in the 35th minute. For clarity's sake, though, you may want to cite the time left in a half or the game because readers are more familiar with those references.

▶ Scrums are frequently referenced but rarely understood. Here are some basics: Scrums are a way to restart play after minor infractions, sort of like when football centers hike the ball for a new play. But instead of hiking the ball to a quarterback, a player (scrum half) rolls the ball in the middle of two groups bound together by locking arms and facing one another. Teams line up eight players in three rows – three in the front, four in the second row, and one in the back, whose arms are locked around one another's shoulders or hips. Two people in the second row (loose head prop, tight head prop) position their heads on either side of the hooker, who is in the center. After the ball is rolled in by the scrum half, the two sides engage each other, driving forward to gain possession of the ball. Eventually, the players use their legs to kick the ball back to the scrum half, now repositioned behind the line – and the passing and running begins anew.

▶ Players must release the ball right after being tackled to the ground, leaving it there for whoever is closer – although players tend to place it near teammates. If players from both teams are over the ball, a ruck forms where players jump in to the help push forward and grab the ball from the ground. A ruck is another way to restart play without pausing. After a tackle in football, play stops. Rugby allows the ball to be quickly recycled back into play – and, unlike football, both teams can compete for the ball after a tackle.

▶ Rugby is an invasion sport like soccer, whose game flows freely up and down the field.

▶ The ball can't be passed forward, only backward and laterally – like early American football. Teams draw up pass plays to swing the ball from one side of the field to the other, trying to catch the defense off guard. Speed is essential in this passing and running game.

▶ Blocking is also disallowed in rugby. That means no screens or picks either.

▶ Kicking is another important part of rugby. "The two main set pieces – the scrum and lineout – can create a positive fall back at change of possession," Graziano says. "For instance, if I cannot run through the opposition's defense and choose to kick over the top to gain territory, this is a great strategy, especially if I am dominating the lineouts. (Even though the change of possession is at the lineout 40 yards down the field.) If I stand a better than even chance I can steal the lineout, then I put the opposition under pressure and remove one of their strengths, their midfield running defense."

▶ Stamina is also vital. Rugby is played on a field that is about 10 yards longer and more than 60 feet wider than a football field. It's the width of the field that creates more of the scoring opportunities and, as a result, causes the most fatigue. A football field is 160 feet wide, which creates just enough space for players to move and cut past 11 defenders who are attempting to tackle him to the ground. But the width is narrow enough to prevent fast runners from heading to a side and then simply out-running everybody to the end zone for an automatic touchdown. More often, football defenses can effectively contain players who possess even blistering speed. Eleven players are sufficient for plugging up the sidelines and then clogging many of the empty spaces on the field. That is not the case in rugby, where four extra players are expected to cover the 60-plus extra feet. A fast runner can make one little fake to the right and then head left down the sidelines. Once past this outside defender, a rugby player can more easily race untouched down the field to the try zone for an easy five points. The wider field makes it much more difficult for a defending player to reach a runner on the other side of the field. Even among the fastest female players, that extra 20 yards is going to take two to three seconds to cover. Elite collegiate football players (especially wide receivers and defensive backs) can run the 40-yard dash in 4.4 to 4.5 seconds, whereas typical club rugby players run the 40 in five-plus seconds. Some are significantly slower. So two seconds is a significant head start. Slower defenders rarely make it across the wider field.

▶ The fly half is a team's playmaker, directing the offense to run, pass or kick. Like a point guard or quarterback, the fly half barks out orders and creates scoring opportunities while leading the backs. This player must assess an opponent's defense quickly and efficiently, reacting to pursuit and anticipating running lanes. In addition, the fly half should be an exceptional kicker, able to send the ball far enough so that the defense has to scramble to try and recover. Ideally, the fly half also directs kicks where only quicker backs can recover them. Passing is also essential for a player who literally gets the ball rolling on running plays. "While the scrum half actually handles the ball more than the fly half, the fly half has better vision of the entire field," says Graziano. "It's this vision coupled with [the fact that] it's the first back position that puts the decision making in the hands of the fly half."

▶ The scrum half, usually positioned just ahead of the fly half, directs the forwards' movement during plays in and rucks and mauls. Usually the smallest player, the scrum half is wily, fast, fit and an exceptional passer – and frequently has to tackle bigger players. The scrum half communicates with the fly half, sometimes through hand signals, to call offensive plays. The scrum half also must be a superior kicker.

▶ Women's rugby is one of seven sports on the NCAA's list of emerging sports, a program created in the early 1990s to increase the number of athletic opportunities for young women. Since then, bowling, rowing, water polo and ice hockey have moved through the process to championship sports status. Like the other sports on the current list, rugby must attract 40 teams within 10 years to earn championship status or be dropped for consideration. Right now, with four years remaining, only four women's teams in the United States play varsity rugby. Bowdoin College in Maine and Southern Vermont College, both with Division III programs, are also considered varsity. Becky Carlson, the emerging sports program manager at USA Rugby, is working with coaches in the Big 12 Conference and across California, where state Sen. Dean Florez is pushing for increased gender equity compliance following sex bias suits that cost the state millions of dollars.

▶ Kicking, biting, gouging and raking one's cleats across someone's body are not allowed, although some try to do this in rucks and scrums. Players can be penalized or ejected for such actions, despite stereotypes to the contrary.

▶ Familiarize yourself with the following terms:

▶▶ **advantage:** when referees allow play to continue even though an infraction, or penalty, occurred, to give the nonoffending team the chance to do something positive – such as when football referees allow play to continue when the defense moves offside. If the team cannot advance the ball, the refs blow the whistle and restart the game from the location where the violation took place. In football, a team gets a do-over if a player makes a mistake on defensive offside, the same as in rugby.

▶▶ **backs:** three players on the back line who are usually the fastest. The two wings are often a team's best scorers, able to slide through defenses, make sharp cuts and race downfield. The fullback is usually more defense oriented, like a sweep in soccer.

▶▶ **center:** each team has two – inside center and outside center – who usually take on more ball carriers, meaning they should also record more tackles than other position players.

▶▶ **chip:** players trying to avoid getting tackled sometimes kick the ball a short distance ahead (or even over a defender's head) while running nearly full stride, believing they can beat everyone to the ball, pick it up and keep running downfield.

▶▶ **conversion kick:** worth two points. Unlike football, this kick is positioned on angle from where the ball is touched down in the try zone.

▶▶ **field goal:** occurs when a player drops the ball, usually in full stride, and kicks it through the goalposts after it bounces up to earn three points, the same as a dropkick in football.

▶▶ **goal line:** outlines the scoring area on each side of the field, much like a football end zone, where the ball is touched down for try. This is also called a try line.

▶ ▶ **hooker:** versatile front-row player who plays between two props in scrums, but whose most important duty is throwing the ball in during lineouts.

▶ ▶ **injury time:** time recorded by the referee after an injury that halts play. Referees, not the scoreboard, keep the official time in rugby and soccer, so don't be surprised when you see play continue for several minutes after the clock has wound down.

▶ ▶ **knock-on:** an infraction called when a player either fumbles the ball forward or hits it ahead in any way, giving a team an advantage. Play is restarted with a scrum.

▶ ▶ **lineout:** restarts play when the ball or ball carrier goes out of bounds, similar to a jump ball in basketball. A player throws the ball into teammates, as in soccer, except the receiving team usually picks a player up to catch the ball in the air. No contact is allowed during lineouts.

▶ ▶ **maul:** almost a reverse tug-of-war, when players on each side are trying to push a ball carrier who has been held up by the defense, usually in an attempt to steal the ball.

▶ ▶ **No. 8:** this player usually make a big impact in the game but rarely gets noticed. Sometimes this player might have the most tackles (if you track them), but, more often than not, this is a person who does all the little things well, especially those that go unnoticed – like a combination of offensive lineman and inside linebacker.

▶ ▶ **offside:** players cannot be ahead of the ball carrier for any reason, although this may not be called if a player is well away from the play, perhaps on the other side of the field.

▶ ▶ **penalty kick:** teams may attempt these kicks after gaining possession following a penalty near their opponent's goal. Like field goals, these are worth three points.

▶ ▶ **props:** large, strong forwards who support the hooker during scrums and who lift the jumpers during lineouts. Loose head props stand on the left side of the scrum half during scrums when their team puts the ball in play. The tight head props stand on the right side.

▶ ▶ **ruck:** when players circle a ball during a restart on the field (this is different from a lineout).

▶ ▶ **scrum half:** mix between an option quarterback and a defensive back, a player who needs great hands for passing and quickness for slipping through tight places like rucks, scrums or lines of defenders.

▶ ▶ **scrum:** a restart when teams fight for possession of the ball; involves eight players who lock arms and push against the other team's eight players. The ball is then rolled into the scrum. Each team pushes forward so the scrum half can get the ball and put an offensive play in motion. Scrums are a way to restart play after a minor infraction or penalty.

▶ ▶ **sevens:** a shorter game in which each team fields seven players for two seven-minute halves. This is much more of a speed game where teams essentially sprint across the field in an exhaustive, higher-scoring game.

▶ ▶ **tackles:** Players must immediately let go of the ball when they hit the ground so that play can continue. If they stay on top of the ball, a penalty is called. Players may not tackle below the waist.

▶ ▶ **throw-in:** lineouts start when the ball is thrown in from the touchline.

▶ ▶ **touchline:** lines down the sides of the field, outlining the field and denoting out of bounds.

▶ ▶ **try:** worth five points. Players literally have to touch the ball down in the goal area. Plural spelling is trys.

▶ ▶ **yellow card:** given to a player guilty of repeated infractions or dangerous, foul play. A yellow card results in a penalty of up to 10 minutes in most leagues.

Get Ready

▶ Verify rosters from both team along with correct spellings of names. Covering club games can be more than a little challenging because players share uniforms, depending on the positions they're playing. Anybody who plays scrum half wears No. 9 in these games, exchanging the shirt during substitutions. The same goes for every position, making it difficult to chart the game unless you're standing next to a coach or the bench and can see, or ask, who gets inserted in the game. Typical club games don't have proper rosters or any other programs, further hindering coverage. So make sure you remain on the sidelines, moving between team benches to get the right information. These club games usually don't have a scoreboard, so keeping score will also be a challenge. Bring a stopwatch and try to keep time as best you can. At NCAA-sanctioned games, this information is more readily available.

▶ Speak with coaches before you go to your first game to get additional information about the team, game strategy and the sport itself.

WATCH

▶ Rugby is simple, says Andy Wilson of *The Guardian* of London. Watch the ball and the player handling it. Obviously there is much more than this.

▶ Covering rugby is a lot like covering soccer, where play flows with few stops and restarts. That means you'll have little time to write lengthy notes or to keep many stats on your own.

▶ As with soccer, you will want to takes notes on key plays and scores. Usually there won't be an official scorer, so take detailed notes. Check uniform numbers and names before games start. If there is no official clock, bring a stopwatch to get a sense of time remaining in each 40-minute half.

▶ Reporters might want to stand next to a coach to listen to instructions. That way you can start viewing the game more like a veteran. You can also note key tackles, especially those near the end zone. Mark down the numbers for players so you can verify the names afterward (even if you have a roster).

▶ Keep watching the action after a player crosses the try line. Where the ball is touched down determines the angle for the conversion kick. Good players keep running toward the middle of the goal area to set up a relatively easy kick for the two extra points. Poor players allow the ball carrier to keep running in the goal area. In fact, defenders can still steal the ball or prevent a score until the ball is touched down.

▶ Frank Graziano, head coach of the only NCAA Division I women's rugby program, offers some advice on watching his sport; see the four paragraphs below. Graziano has served as assistant national team coach for the Women's National U-23 program and has been National Event Coordinator and Collegiate Director for USA Rugby. He played at Clemson, where he also created the women's rugby team in 1995.

To some extent, rugby is just like watching football. For all purposes, it's football with the free flow of "up and down" like soccer. First, the forward progress is key, just like in football. Going forward – or invading the opposition's territory – is crucial. And committing or creating turnovers while doing that shortens the field.

One team being able to break the defensive line is crucial, like in soccer and football. A soccer game stuck in the middle of the field is not so good, which forces soccer teams to go over the top. It's the same with rugby. If you cannot run through the opposition, then you have to kick down the field and try to gain field position, or maybe recover the ball or pin the opposition back. This is much like punting in football, where teams try to gain field position.

As another example, if I am doing well at the scrum, then every time I "knock on," I stand a good chance to get the ball back.

Record times and details of scoring moves.

ASK

▶ Ask the fly half to describe key scoring plays. What play did you call? What did you notice about the defense right before you made the call? Did they react as you expected?

▶ Ask the scrum half to describe the team's performance in rucks and scrums. Were you able to drive them off the ball? Were you able to roll the ball in where you wanted? How did the team's performance in scrums help, or hurt, the team today?

▶ Ask fullbacks to assess the opposing team's backs. How did they compare with other teams in regard to speed? Did they have good moves? Were they tough to tackle?

▶ Ask backs to describe an opponent's defensive abilities. How hard did they tackle? How well did they plug running lanes and fill holes in the line during your runs?

▶ Ask coaches to assess their team's overall performance? What did your team do best? Worst? What was the key play? What bothers you the most about the team's performance?

▶ Ask coaches to assess their opponents as well. Did they scheme to do anything unexpected? Different plays or alignments? What players performed the best on the other team?

▶ To start, reporters might want to just list the scoring plays (including the pass that set the score and the length of this scoring run). For example:

> Samantha Manto took a pass from Molly Clutter and ran 30 yards down the left sideline to score the decisive try in a 90 – 0 victory over Tennessee.
>
> That score was only three minutes into the game. Manto scored four more times, and Brittany Brown scored twice, to keep Eastern Illinois undefeated (4 – 0) on Saturday afternoon.

▶ Don't insert the same clichés others rely upon. Don't make jokes about hookers or refer to blood and guts. Just cover the game.

▶ Focus on decisive plays on offense and defense. Cite the length of scoring runs. Did anybody make a key move – a cut to the inside that left a defender out of position and the ball carrier to run toward the goal unimpeded? How did the opposing team react? Hunched shoulders? Yelling and screaming at one another? Offer some of the emotion of the game as well.

▶ Cite any unanswered runs of points. Did one team score three straight trys? How much time elapsed – five minutes, 35 minutes?

▶ Focus on game-winning scores or defensive plays. How much time was left when a player broke through the middle for a winning score or a fullback made an open-field tackle to prevent a try?

▶ Most people won't understand the insider information about rugby, so find a storyline associated with the game whenever possible.

> CHARLESTON, Ill. – Jamaris DelValle had never heard of rugby before she started playing three years ago in Jupiter, Fla.
>
> Like most Americans, the teen knew little about the sport's rules, traditions or strategies. Still, she was drawn to a sport where she has the opportunity to hit someone in a game.
>
> DelValle quickly fell in love with the game. She is working hard, hoping her efforts will result in a scholarship to play rugby at the collegiate level, something Saturday's game between West Chester (Penn.) University and Eastern Illinois University may remedy – or so organizers hope.

For the record, West Chester defeated Eastern Illinois on Saturday afternoon, scoring a try in the final minutes to win 20 – 19 in the first-ever NCAA women's rugby game, which was held at Eastern Illinois. The final score, though, is inconsequential to those who helped organize the game. Instead, coaches and administrators are more interested in convincing athletic directors that rugby can be a success at the NCAA level.[1]

SOCCER

S occer is probably the most popular sport in the world, although no studies have verified this widely held assumption. We do know that more than a total of 25 billion viewers watched the 2006 men's World Cup tournament. And about 715 million watched the final between Italy and France, attracting seven times more viewers than the 2009 Super Bowl between the New York Giants and New England Patriots. We also know that more than 260 million people, roughly 4 percent of the world's population, are registered to play soccer.

But soccer is considered a second-tier sport in the United States despite having the premier women's program in the world and attracting millions of young people for leagues each year. Soccer's TV ratings are dismal, and most Major League Soccer teams average fewer than 20,000 attendees per game. In the United States, soccer has a bad rap for being a sport where nothing happens, nobody scores, and where players dribble the ball up and down the field without any noticeable strategy – a keep-away, of sorts. Nothing could be further from the truth. Just like basketball, football and baseball, soccer teams employ a variety of strategies, plays and alignments.

Soccer is a flowing game of territory, space and time where teams of 11 attempt to advance the ball downfield in order to fire shots into a net that measures 8 feet by 24 feet. Unlike football, the ball's advancement is not always vertical. Territory is not to be won and held at all costs. Instead, passes frequently go both forward and backward in the players' attempt to find a weakness in an opponent's defense. Teams are trying to break through spaces in time to advance the ball and score.

In soccer, the team with the most goals wins. But how these goals are scored, or prevented, is far more complex than a game of keep-away.

Learn the Basics

▶ Time runs progressively through two 45-minute halves in a match, meaning a goal scored five minutes into the game was scored during the fifth minute while a goal scored with five minutes remaining in the game was scored in the 85th minute.

▶ A referee keeps official time, stopping his watch for goals, substitutions, fouls and injuries, although the scoreboard clock runs continuously. After the clock reaches 45 or 90 minutes, the referee calculates the time added because of earlier stoppages and determines how much time remains. This rule leads to the term "stoppage time."

▶ A player can never receive a pass from a teammate while behind the last line of defenders. When a player first touches a pass, a defender must always be between that offensive player and the goal, otherwise "offside" is called, play is stopped and any score is dismissed.

▶ Teams employ a variety of alignments. Most coaches plan defensively, using more fullbacks than forwards. A 4 – 4 – 2 alignment means a team employs four fullbacks, four midfielders and two forwards. A 4 – 3 – 3 is also a common alignment.

▶ A counterattack occurs when the defenders steal the ball and quickly go in the other direction, hoping they can quickly outnumber the opposing team on the other end of the field. Speed is essential in any counterattack.

▶ Familiarize yourself with the following positions:

▶ ▶ **forwards:** usually the best shooters, players who can create shots and can fire precise shots on goal.

▶ ▶ **fullbacks:** play closest to the goal, in a line directly in front of the sweeper. Most teams will position three players as right, left and center fullbacks. These players are more skilled than forwards at stealing the ball.

▶ ▶ **midfielders:** most diverse players on the field, able to shoot like a forward, pass like a midfielder and defend like a fullback. Midfielders are frequently the busiest players on the field.

▶ ▶ **striker:** a team's most skilled scorer. Strikers are usually positioned farther up field than any other player, usually settled in the center and waiting for a pass.

▶ ▶ **sweeper:** acts like a free safety in football, roaming the field behind the full-backs. This sweeper is the last line of defense before the goalkeeper, sometimes the only player available to stop breakaways. The sweeper's job is to steal the ball (sweep it up) and clear it by kicking the ball far down the field or out of bounds, enabling teammates to get into a better defensive position. Because sweepers can see the field better than anybody else, they often act like coaches, yelling for teammates to adjust as needed.

▶ Three types of free kicks are awarded when an opponent is penalized. On a direct kick a player can kick the ball directly into the goal without anyone touching it, although another player is allowed to make contact on these kicks. On an indirect kick, a player must kick the ball to another player before a shot can be made on goal. Usually, a player slowly rolls the ball to another who fires off a shot. On a penalty kick, a player shoots on goal from just 12 yards out. These are high-percentage shots awarded for penalties inside the penalty box.

▶ Restarts happen in a variety of ways. When a ball rolls out of bounds over the end line, play is restarted either through a goal kick or a corner kick. If the defending team last touched this ball, the attacking team can place the ball at the nearest corner for a shot toward the goal. If the attacking team last touched this ball, the defending team can clear the ball with a long kick from anywhere inside the goal box. Other restarts include throw-ins, kickoffs (after goals) and the three free kicks.

▶ Players try to exploit a team's weak side, or backside, where few defenders are situated. For instance, when a player rushes in with the ball from the right side, most defenders converge, even those from the left side, which may leave an area that is not defended. A skilled team would send a pass to a teammate on that side, hoping this player can fire an unimpeded shot into the net.

ON INTERVIEWING

Don't ask questions about officiating. We can't comment so that should be respected and the question not even be asked. I always enjoy questions regarding the opposition. It is the right thing to do to comment on the good play of the opposing players, if they have had a good match. I think praise always means more when it comes from the opposing coach.

Bob Warming,
men's soccer coach, Creighton University

- Fouls are called for the following – kicking, charging, pushing, holding, tripping and spitting at an opponent.

- Players receive yellow cards for playing too roughly, which also results in fouls. Two yellow cards merit a red card, which results in an immediate ejection. Depending on the league, college or high school rules, this player may receive a suspension of at least one more game. In addition, ejected players cannot be replaced, causing the team to compete with only 10 players on the field.

- Statistics are not as significant in soccer as they are in other sports. For instance, total shots taken does not really illustrate who played better or who won. Players can take shots from all over the field, even from poor angles, that never reach the goal. (Shots on goal better illustrates a team's ability to score.)

- Time of possession can also be misleading. In football, this stat illustrates that a team dominated both offensively and defensively. But in soccer, one team may lure its opponent deep into its own territory before it steals the ball to go on a counterattack.

- Only goalkeepers can use hands, but they may no longer pick up balls passed from teammates. On passes, goalkeepers will usually kick the ball to a teammate on the opposite side of the field, redirecting the flow of the game; or they will clear it, driving the ball deep downfield.

- Games tied after regulation and at least one overtime period are determined by shoot-outs, when each team takes a predetermined number of shots from the penalty kick area. Five players from each team usually shoot once on goal to determine which team wins the match.

- The Federation Internationale de Football Association, or FIFA, is the international governing body of soccer.

- Players earn "caps" for each international game they play for a country, meaning a player who competed in nine international matches for Team USA would have accumulated nine caps.

Get Ready

- Besides a notebook, consider bringing a stopwatch to more accurately record the length of key plays and to determine the correct time during stoppages. Scott French, a senior editor for *The Soccer Magazine,* also brings binoculars and a tape recorder. The binoculars help him gather details about plays across the field (or from high in a press box). He also prefers to use a flexible Mead composition notebook because the pages allow him to record play-by-play and commentary. Notebooks can also serve as a great reference to previous games.

▶ Record both starting lineups and substitutions during a game.

WATCH

▶ Determine how the game flows. Did play go mostly through the middle of the field, where most games are won? Or did the team have to play more down the sidelines? Where did teams push the ball throughout the game? The team that controls midfield usually wins the game.

▶ Describe key plays. Did someone make a tremendous pass? Did an exciting steal start the play? Did the defense fail to shift properly? Explain how the scoring play developed, from pass to location of shooter to goalkeeper's reaction.

▶ Although time of possession may not be as significant in soccer as in other sports, this number could lead to an interesting story angle. Did the team with fewer possession minutes employ a counterstrike strategy? Or was this team fortunate to have scored in its limited shooting opportunities?

▶ Focus on the play of the defense. Do not automatically give credit for a shutout to the goalkeeper unless he or she made a key save or stopped many shots. If the goalkeeper was not really challenged, note a few defensive plays that illustrate how well fullbacks or midfielders played.

▶ Focus on unusual field conditions. Did rain or freezing temperatures create conditions that made playing difficult? How did this affect the teams involved?

▶ Record injuries. Did any player return later from an injury? What was the time lapse between injury and the player's reinsertion?

▶ Cite trends. Did a team win or lose its last four games by a single goal? Did a team record countless corner kicks, yellow cards or headers?

▶ Determine the defensive strategy a coach used – man-to-man, zone coverage or a hybrid. If you are not sure, ask the coach afterward.

▶ During stoppage time, keep a stopwatch going to determine when goals or key plays are made. If a goal is scored two minutes into stoppage time, you can say so. (In the first half, it's best to write: "two minutes into stoppage time." If the goal was scored two minutes into stoppage of the second half, you would write that the goal was scored in the 92nd minute (even though, officially, the goal was scored in the 88th minute). You could also write that a goal in the 88th minute was scored with two minutes remaining in the regulation 90-minute match. You can also refer to a goal being scored in the final two minutes to avoid confusing casual readers.

▶ As you learn more about soccer, start to diagram scoring plays to show which defenders were beaten, to record the passes leading to the goal and to note where the shot was placed.

ASK

▶ Ask players to describe key plays or key moments or to assess their team's performance. "Often, the simplest question is best," says Steve Goff, soccer reporter for *The Washington Post.* "'What was the difference in the final five minutes?' or 'What did you like about what your team did tonight?' or 'What does this result mean for the long run?'"

▶ Ask players to explain how they felt about key plays. Many players cannot describe the plays they've been involved in, yet they can offer an emotional assessment of the overall game. "One of the best quotes on tactics I received was many years ago from Paul Caligiuri, who explained how difficult it was to deal with Russia's 'passing triangles,'" French says. "After Mexico dominated the U.S. in the 1993 CONCACAF Gold Cup final in Mexico City, Cobi Jones talked about how the elevation sapped the Americans as the game wore on, to the point where it seemed 'there were four green (Mexico) shirts for every white (U.S.) shirt.' It's nice to have an array of quotes to use."

▶ Players can offer perspective on many facets of the game. They can describe opponents they directly faced or describe key plays. A forward can discuss the play of a goalkeeper, and vice versa. A midfielder can assess the play of an opposing forward or midfielder. These comments can yield great insights. What did you think of the stops the other team's goalkeeper made? How do the other team's backs compare with other fullbacks you have faced this season? What happened when the opposing player headed into the net?

▶ Coaches can offer a broader perspective on a game, discussing strategies and analyzing the team in far greater depth. How has the team progressed during the last several games? Who has been playing well, or poorly? Who would you like to see more effort from? Which opposing player impressed you the most?

▶ Find your go-to players, people who regularly offer terrific quotes. The best players do not always offer the best comments. On deadline, you may have time to talk with two or three people. Make sure these players have something to say. A midfielder can often describe a player that unfolded in front of her better than other players who were involved in the play. So consider talking with these other players as well.

WRITE

▶ Do not focus only on play-by-play and game stats. Instead, tell the story that unfolds. Find stories within the game. "This is critically important in our new world of communication in which many readers have already watched the game on TV, and/or read the wire services story on the Internet; and/or scoured the box score," Goff says.

▶ Describe key goals, including the play that led to the scores:

> It took Eskandarian a mere 7 minutes 52 seconds to notch his first goal in a Galaxy uniform. He made the start in place of Gordon.
> The goal was deftly worked. It came when defender Todd Dunivant floated a cross in from the left and Eskandarian, timing his run expertly, met the ball and drove it wide of goalkeeper Matt Reis.[1]

▶ Cite the game's significance. Does the game clinch a postseason berth or eliminate a team from the playoffs? Is this a conference or district victory? Does this team advance to the next round in a tournament?

▶ Lead with a snapshot of an important event that might illuminate a turning point in the game or that might focus on a key player – perhaps a last-second shot or a significant penalty. Explain the big picture. "What does it [this game] mean?" Goff says. "How does it affect a team or a league? Are there any particular trends, or the disruption of a trend?"

► Note key saves by goalkeepers.

> Los Angeles did not do much better at creating scoring opportunities, but it did force Reis into two exceptional saves at around the 82nd-minute mark. The first came when the goalkeeper threw himself to his right to deny a Chris Klein header from close range. The second came off the resulting corner kick when Reis tipped a header by Dunivant over the crossbar.[2]

► Read other soccer stories to learn how to describe key plays. For instance: "the forward split two defenders," "a sliding right-footed shot," "the goalkeeper misplayed a crossing shot," "the shot bent inside the goal post."

SOFTBALL

Softball is not just baseball played with a bigger ball. The field is smaller and the game moves more quickly – the average college softball player reaches first base in three seconds. Softball pitchers usually throw for the entire game. And they can concentrate more fully on batters since they do not have to hold runners close to base. Softball rules forbid runners from leaving base until the ball leaves the pitcher's hand. In softball, throwing out base stealers hinges almost entirely on the catcher.

Bunting is used much more frequently in softball. In baseball, designated hitters and aluminum bats have led to high-scoring games and big innings, but softball teams usually try to score one run at a time. "We don't always rely on the three-run homer like many baseball teams," says Kelley Green, softball coach at Lock Haven University, the 2006 National Collegiate Athletic Association Division II champs. "You will have more sacrifice bunts in softball than baseball to move runners into scoring position."

Softball also features the "lefty slapper," a batter who combines blazing speed with great bat control. The slapper can drop a bunt down the lines, slap a hit past a drawn-in third baseman or hit from a regular stance. Check out how frequently a third baseman plays in to defend against bunts. It's scary to see a fielder so close to a batter, but it's very effective.

A designated player (different from a designated hitter) can go in and play any defensive position, and a flex player bats 10th and can play defense or hit for the designated player. Plus, starters can re-enter the game once. In softball, many of the fundamentals are similar to baseball. But the philosophies can differ. In softball, teams play small ball, meaning they sacrifice, do hit and run, and steal more frequently than in higher-scoring baseball games that rely more on big hits.

PREPARE

Learn the Basics

▶ In college and international competition, softball games go seven innings. High school games last six innings.

▶ Players age 10 and under use an 11-inch softball. All other age groups use a 12-inch ball. (Baseballs are 9 inches in circumference.)

▶ The bases are 60 feet apart, 30 feet closer than on a baseball field.

▶ The softball mound is 43 feet from the plate. That's three feet farther back than in the 1980s, a change made to increase scoring. Most youth and high school mounds are still at 40 feet, while international competitions place the mound at 45 feet.

▶ In college, a pitcher must throw within 10 seconds of receiving the ball.

▶ Stealing is allowed, but runners must wait until the ball leaves the pitcher's hand to leave base.

▶ Softball pitchers throw rise curves and flat curves, rise balls, screw balls, changeups and two kinds of drop balls that are like nasty sliders.

▶ There are very few saves in softball because starters usually go the distance. Most softball teams retain three pitchers on staff – unlike baseball, where a roster is likely to have four to five starters plus some middle and late relievers.

▶ A softball pitcher's rotation has three parts: windup, windmill and release.

▶ In softball, pitchers routinely throw more than 100 pitches per game and pitch on consecutive days. The underhanded motion does not put as much strain on the shoulders and arms compared with pitches in baseball. Although pitchers still need to make sure they do not overwork, the windmill delivery does not usually induce as much soreness. But this motion results in pitches that are just as fast.

▶ Pitching speeds in softball need to be converted before comparing them with pitches in baseball, where pitchers throw from 60 feet, 6 inches. The following calculation can offer some perspective: Multiply a softball pitcher's overall speed (say 50 mph) by 60½ (baseball distance), which equals 3025. Divide this by 40 (softball

The *Arizona Daily Star* put together a mini press guide to the Arizona Wildcats softball team. It offers basic details (such as height, position and hometown of each player), along with a brief analysis of accomplishments, a preview of the coming season and video interviews and photos. Check out "On to the Playoffs" at www.azstarnet.com/sbplayoffs/.

On to the playoffs Meet the 2009 Arizona Wildcats softball team

Arizona Daily Star
START OVER | CREDITS

The Arizona Wildcats are back in Oklahoma City, naturally.

For the 21st time in 22 years, Mike Candrea has brought his team to the Women's College World Series, the Round of 8 double-elimination tournament that determines the national championship.

Arizona might be the greatest program in the history of the game. The Wildcats have won eight championships and reached the NCAA tournament for 23 consecutive years.

With the team nearing the pinnacle of the sport, we take a look at the Wildcats' record-setting roster, season outcomes an superlatives, and the team's all-time playoff record, game-by-game.
— *Patrick Finley*

2009 regular season and playoff results

Women's College World Series

DATE	LOCATION	RESULT
May 30	Oklahoma City, Okla.	Alabama 14, Arizona 0
May 28	Oklahoma City, Okla.	Florida 3, Arizona 0

NCAA Super Regionals

DATE	LOCATION	RESULT
May 22	Palo Alto, Calif.	Arizona 6, Stanford 5
May 22	Palo Alto, Calif.	Arizona 7, Stanford 3
May 21	Palo Alto, Calif.	Stanford 6, Arizona 4

NCAA Regionals

Click on a photo below to learn more about each player on the team.

---

distance) to get the conversion. In this case, a 50 mph softball pitch from the high school distance of 40 feet is the same as an 75.62 mph baseball pitch. Use 43 to convert college speeds.

Earned run average means the number of runs a pitcher has allowed per game (every seven innings). Lower numbers are better. Top high school pitchers may have an ERA below 1.00. Anything below 3.00 is very good. Unearned runs scored as a result of errors do not count toward an ERA. An ERA is determined by multiplying the total number of earned runs allowed by the number of innings in a complete game. Then divide this number by the total number of innings pitched. Let's say a pitcher has allowed six earned runs across 20 innings. The ERA would be 2.1 runs per game.

$$(6 \times 7) \div 20 = 2.1$$

Scoring is typically low, especially between top-rated teams. In these games, you will see much more bunting, slap hitting and stealing to manufacture runs. Your reporting can focus on these key plays.

▶ Speed is essential in softball. At the college level, the average batter reaches first base in three seconds. That means fielders have about a half second to field and throw a ball from third base or shortstop.

▶ Double plays are less common in softball than in baseball, mostly because runners can cover the shorter distances faster.

▶ The NCAA now uses the "mercy rule," where games are halted if a home team is ahead by 8 runs after 4½ innings (after 5 innings, if the visiting team is ahead). Youth league and travel games have mercy rules that vary among high school and national associations.

▶ Familiarize yourself with the following terms:

▶▶ **drag bunt:** when a batter tried to reach base on a bunt.

▶▶ **fielder's choice:** when a batter reaches base at the same time a base runner was forced out at another base. This at bat is considered an out, not a hit, meaning this batter would be credited with going 0-for-1.

▶▶ **passed ball:** when the catcher misplays a pitch that rolls away and allows a runner to advance at least one base. If the pitch is uncatchable, the event is recorded as a wild pitch. Passed balls and wild pitches are considered errors.

▶▶ **sacrifice bunt:** when a batter advances a base runner on a bunt.

▶▶ **sacrifice fly:** when a base runner scores by tagging up from third base on a fly ball.

▶ A base runner is considered in scoring position when the runner is on second or third base.

▶ Playing positions are assigned numbers that correspond with their positions, something that makes keeping score easier and more streamlined:
  1 – pitcher
  2 – catcher
  3 – first baseman
  4 – second baseman

5 – third baseman
6 – shortstop
7 – left fielder
8 – center fielder
9 – right fielder

▶ Familiarize yourself with abbreviations used for recording plays. A strikeout can be recorded two ways: a regular note of K can mean the batter struck out swinging. A backwards K can denote a player looked as the third strike landed in the catcher's mitt.

Here are the key abbreviations:

1B – single
2B – double
3B – triple
HR – home run
RBI – runs batted in
BB – base on balls (walk)
HBP – hit by pitch (awarded first base)
PB – passed ball
WP – wild pitch
SF – sacrifice fly
Sac – sacrifice bunt
SB – stolen base
FC – fielder's choice
E – error (batter reaches base on fielder's mistake)
BK – balk
CS – caught stealing (for any base)
DP – double play (although you probably record this as 6-4-3, for example)
DH – designated hitter
IW – intentional walk

▶ Familiarize yourself with these terms:

▶▶ **at bat:** hits and outs count as official at bats, but walks and sacrifices do not. So a batter who walked twice is officially 0-for-0, but a batter who singled and struck out would be 1-for-2. An official at bat is one where a batter has recorded either a hit or an out, something that is recorded for calculating batting averages. Because walks do not count as either an out or a hit, they are not used – neither are sacrifice flies, sacrifice bunts or when a batter is hit by a pitch.

▶▶ **balk:** when a pitcher stutters, fails to stop properly in the stretch or touches his mouth while on the mound, among other things. When this happens, all runners get to advance one base and a ball is added to the batter's count.

▶ ▶ **batting average:** measures a player's ability to collect hits. This is calculated by dividing total hits by total official at bats.

• Someone with 28 hits in 100 at bats would have the following average:

$$28 \div 100 = .280$$

▶ ▶ **catcher's interference:** when a batter hits the glove of a catcher during a swing, usually because a catcher is trying to sneak forward to throw out a base runner attempting to steal. Play is called dead and the batter is awarded first base. All other runners advance one base.

▶ ▶ **earned runs:** runs a team scores without the aid of errors or passed balls.

▶ ▶ **fielder's choice:** the batter reaches base but a force-out is recorded. This counts as an official at bat but not a hit, meaning this batter would be 0-for-1.

▶ ▶ **on-base percentage:** measures a player's ability reach base. Add each time a player reaches base for any reason except by error or fielder's choice. Divide this by total plate appearances.

$$(H + BB + HBP) / (AB + BB + HBP + SF)$$
$$(28 + 12 + 2) \div (100 + 12 + 2 + 8)$$
$$42 \div 122 = .344$$

▶ ▶ **on-base plus slugging percentage:** measures a player's overall offensive value by combining on-base percentage and slugging percentage. The best players will have an average around 1.000. To calculate, add on-base percentage and slugging averages.

$$OBP + SLG = average$$
$$.344 + .535 = .879$$

▶ ▶ **passed ball:** a thrown pitch that the catcher misplays, allowing any runner to advance at least one base.

▶ ▶ **sacrifice fly:** a fly ball hit by a batter that enables a base runner to advance at least one base. A sacrifice bunt also enables a runner to advance an extra base.

▶ ▶ **slugging percentage:** measures a batter's power. To calculate this, add all official at bats (see below), but do not include walks, sacrifices, or hit by pitch. Next add total bases. Next, divide total bases by official at bats.

• Total bases ÷ at bats = slugging percentage

$$221 \div 400 = .552$$

▶ ▶ **total bases:** used to calculate slugging percentage. To arrive at total bases, multiply singles by one, doubles by two, triples by three and home runs by four. Then add the sums together to get this total.

Singles $42 \times 1 = 42$
Doubles $28 \times 2 = 56$
Triples $9 \times 3 = 27$
Home runs $29 \times 4 = 116$
Total bases   241

▶ ▶ **wild pitch:** an errant pitch that allows runners to advance at least one base.

Get Ready

▶ Get to the game early enough to record team lineups. At high school games, you'll need to speak with each team's designated scorekeepers, who are usually in the team dugout. At college and professional games, you can usually get lineups in the press box from the sports information directors.

▶ Get team stats for players by checking team Web sites. For high school games, check the local newspaper or arrive early enough to get the stats from the team's student manager, scorekeeper or coach. Knowing the stats enables you to find interesting angles and stories as the game progresses.

▶ Go through past box scores to find trends in hitting and pitching for individuals and teams. You might find that a team has left more than 10 runners on base during the past six games, or that a team has averaged 2.1 runs per game during the past two weeks. You might also notice that a pitcher has not walked a batter in the past three games pitched or that a hitter has gone 9-for-12 in the past four games.

▶ As you look through stats, check for hitting streaks or streaks that show players are struggling. These will help you see what's different about today's game and help you know what questions to ask.

WATCH

▶ Record how many runners are left on base each inning. You will see the stat "LOB" in many softball box scores. Did a team leave many runners on base because it couldn't deliver clutch hits, or did a team leave many on base because players had so many hits and runs?

▶ Evaluate the pitcher's performance. Has this pitcher won or lost a number of games in a row? Has this pitcher struck out 10-plus hitters a game or walked four-plus each game? How many unearned runs has this pitcher allowed in recent games? How many runs does this pitcher usually allow in the first few innings, or how many does the pitcher allow after 80 or 90 pitches? These are more detailed stats that will be harder to get at the Little League or high school levels unless you are charting every game.

▶ Focus on key plays less obvious than a grand slam or the game-winning single in the bottom of the ninth. Maybe a hard slide in the fourth inning broke up a double play that, in turn, allowed the inning to continue and a run to score in a game determined by a single run. Or maybe a batter fought off a tough pitcher for a 10-pitch walk late in the game before scoring the game-tying run. That could also be a slide that breaks up a double play in the fourth inning or a three-run homer in the seventh inning.

▶ Determine how many outs a pitcher records from fly balls compared with ground outs. Pitchers and managers prefer ground outs, which can lead to more double plays and are less likely to go for home runs. You'll also find these outs reflect the types of pitches thrown. A sinker-ball pitcher is more likely to get many more ground outs than a pitcher who relies on a fastball.

▶ Look for ministreaks. Did a pitcher retire nine batters in a row across four middle innings, or retire the final eight batters? Did a team score a run in five straight innings, or connect for eight straight hits? These events might not be the lead, but they're interesting components, especially if you can connect the streak to the game's overall story.

ASK

▶ Ask coaches what they saw as the key moments in the game.

▶ Ask players what they were thinking during a key moment in the game. Did the batter who struck out get fooled by a riser? Or did a batter who drilled a game-winning double hit an expected fastball?

▶ Ask players to comment on the opposing pitcher. Catchers, who handle pitchers all the time, will usually offer the best insights. Ask catchers about their own pitchers – specifically about ball movement, mechanics and location.

▶ Ask managers and coaches to explain reasons for recent trends. Why has your pitcher been struggling? Any theories on what's caused your shortstop to go on a hitting streak?

WRITE

▶ Use earned run average in first reference. You can use ERA in subsequent references.

▶ Use RBI in first reference, or find other ways to cite this number. For example, you can write that a player "drove in three runs," not just that "he had three RBIs."

▶ Batters go 2-for-3, not two for three.

▶ You can put records in parentheses, especially when they also reflect conference or district marks. For example, you would write that Eastern Illinois (18 – 10, 12 – 2 in the Ohio Valley Conference) is one game away from earning an NCAA bid. If you have mentioned that the game is a conference or district game, you do not need to cite that information in the parentheses. For example: Lake Brantley (15 – 3, 9 – 1) drilled four home runs to rout Lyman (14 – 4, 8 – 2) in a Class 6A, District 3 game.

▶ Here is the Associated Press style for commonly used words and phrases in softball: ballpark, outfielder, center field, center fielder, doubleheader, ground-rule double, home run, line drive, lineup (n.), pinch hitter, RBI (singular), RBIs (plural), strikeout (n.).

▶ Put these elements in the first several paragraph: score, team names, name of field and date.

▶ Game's significance. Does the game clinch a playoff berth or eliminate the team from the postseason? Is this a conference or district victory? Does this advance the team in a tournament?

▶ What does this game mean to the teams involved? How does it affect them?

- For precedes, do not lead with the fact that two teams are going to play each other; instead, find an angle that is more interesting. What's the history between the teams? What's the significance of this game? Does the game have an impact on the conference or district standings? Find something about the upcoming game to introduce the fact the two teams will be playing. Perhaps, this is the first game of a conference schedule.

- In a long season, every hitter struggles at some point, so do not be unfairly harsh on players when this happens. Just cite the stats.

- Yes, we call softball players "man," when it refers to positions, as in first baseman. These terms could change in time, but there are no replacement terms right now.

- Avoid leads and angles that refer to players as "girls" or as "demure." Softball players are trained athletes. Treat them as such.

SWIMMING & DIVING

S wimming is a watery world with its own language (negative splits, leadoff, outside smoke), a world in which athletes are shaved, tapered and suited for major meets. Not sure what all that means? Your readers won't be either, so skip the jargon. "Swimming is not like football or basketball, where you can assume that your audience knows what a sack or dunk means," says Jason Marsteller, managing editor of *Swimming World Magazine.*

Just as you don't want to get too technical in your stories, you don't want to focus too exclusively on winners – unless, of course, that swimmer is winning a record number of gold medals like Michael Phelps.

"It's usually easiest to pick a theme or human interest angle or to focus on one athlete or one race than to weave in the other significant details," says Vicki Michaelis, who covered the 2008 Olympic Games for *USA Today.* "A story that simply listed results would not be well-received, by my editors or readers."

Like track, swimming is about beating an opponent and a time, winning titles and setting records. Like baseball, swimming is also about numbers. Stats, though, can be difficult to find at the high school level. Sports information directors at colleges, in contrast, record all results, making comparisons easier.

Like any sport, swimming has its winners and losers, but it's up to the sports journalist to determine what else readers want before diving in.

PREPARE

Learn the Basics

Swimming

▶ Swim meets are often held in natatoriums, the word for enclosed swimming facilities.

▶ The international governing body for swimming is Federation Internationale de Natation, otherwise known as FINA.

▶ International and National Collegiate Athletic Association championships use pools measured in meters, but most colleges and high schools compete in courses measured by yards. While Olympic trials are usually held in long-course pools of 50 meters, most events at the lower levels rely on 25-yard short-course pools.

▶ The individual medley consists of the following strokes by a single swimmer in the following order: butterfly, backstroke, breaststroke, freestyle. Refer to this as IM in second reference.

▶ In a medley relay, four swimmers swim different strokes over one-fourth of the prescribed distance in the following order: backstroke, breaststroke, butterfly, freestyle. That means that each swimmer races 100 meters in the 400-medley relay.

▶ In relays, the leadoff swims the first leg. The anchor is the final, or fourth, competitor.

▶ Swimmers train so they have their best performances at big meets; this is called peaking. Dual meets are, really, competitive practices.

▶ Swimmers use a variety of kicks during a race – two beat, four beat, six beat, which are counted by how many times the legs kick for each stroke of the arms. A six-beat kick is used in sprints start to finish. Two-beat kicks are seen more often in distance events, with the swimmer changing to a six-beat kick toward the end. Some distance swimmers are starting to use six-beat kicks during the whole race, which takes a lot out of the legs. There is some debate whether a too-fast kick can create negative drag.

▶ A negative split is when a swimmer has a faster time during the second half of a race. That may mean a swimmer clocked in at 28 seconds for the first 50 meters and 26 for the second 50 meters in the 100-meter freestyle.

▶ Touched out means that one swimmer barely edged out another.

Some other terms include: "shaved" – when a swimmer has shaved his or her body for an event; "tapered" – when a swimmer is completely physically and mentally prepared for a specific meet; "suited" – when someone is wearing a high-tech suit. Avoid using most of those terms unless you also define them. Swimming insiders may know what you mean by "outside smoke," but casual readers won't know you are writing that a swimmer won from lanes 1 or 8.

In dual meets, relay teams earn the following points for placing first through fourth: 11 – 4 – 2 – 0. Points for individual events are scored 9 – 4 – 3 – 2 – 1 – 0 (but only three swimmers per team are eligible to earn points).

In tri-meets, the same scoring systems apply except only the top two swimmers for each team earn points.

At college championship meets (using six lanes), relay teams earn points in the following order of finish: 14 – 10 – 8 – 6 – 4 – 2. In individual events, swimmers earn the following points for the top six places: 7 – 5 – 4 – 3 – 2 – 1.

At college championship meets (using eight lanes), points earned for relays are 18 – 14 – 12 – 10 – 8 – 6 – 4 – 2; individual events are scored 9 – 7 – 6 – 5 – 4 – 3 – 2 – 1.

Scoring varies for college championship events that use 12 and 16 lanes.

High school scoring is governed by a rule book published each year by the National Federation of State High School Associations that includes several scoring options. Coaches can use any of them. If coaches cannot agree, the default scoring is based on a six-lane pool where each team may have three swimmers eligible to score. Points are assigned for individual events in this order: 6 – 4 – 3 – 2 – 1. Each team may also enter two teams in relays that are scored: 8 – 4 – 2. Check rules books for other scoring options.

A false start is where a swimmer starts before the gun sounds to start a race. Swimmers are now disqualified on the first false start. The time is not recorded.

At the high school level, swimmers often qualify for state meets by finishing in the top four or six in postseason meets – districts, regionals, sectionals. In some states, high school swimmers qualify simply by reaching a qualifying time standard at any point during the season. At the college level, swimmers qualify for national championships by beating a time prescribed by the NCAA at the beginning of the year, something called provisional time. If too many swimmers surpass these provisional times, the NCAA will adjust times to reduce the number who go to nationals.

sports insider

"Covering the swimming events in Beijing presented an altogether new challenge because of the deadline situation. With finals scheduled for morning in Beijing, night on the East Coast, I was on very tight deadlines every day. Before each finals session, I wrote the framework for two stories – one that had Phelps continuing his quest, the other that had it ending. On the days an American was his top challenger, I wrote a third story on that person in case they won. For most of Phelps' races, my editors needed me to send the story literally as he was climbing out of the pool. So, unfortunately, I would have to watch on monitors near my work station so that I could be typing in race details as it was happening. Then I would run to the mixed zone, where athletes walk through to answer a couple quick questions post-competition. I would send quotes to my editors from there via BlackBerry to be added to my story. After the athletes gave their full press conferences (by then it was usually 2 A.M. on the East Coast), I would write a more complete story to be posted online only. Since we don't have a newspaper on Saturdays and Sundays (therefore no deadline sprint), I did get to see his first race from **Vicki Michaelis,** the poolside press tribune, as well as his *USA Today* last two races."

▶ National Federation of State High School Associations rules limit swimmers to four events in state championships – and no more than two may be individual events.

▶ Athletes compete in qualifying heats (or prelims) before they can compete in the finals. Usually the top eight racers reach the finals.

▶ Backstrokers are the only swimmers who do not start from a platform; instead, they begin the race while in the water.

Diving

▶ Divers start from either concrete platforms or flexible springboards.

▶ Dives have five basic elements – starting position, approach (walk to end of board using no fewer than three steps), take-off (balance, control), flight (smooth, graceful), entry (as close to vertical as possible).

▶ Diving includes four possible positions during flight: free, straight, pike, tuck. In free, a diver is usually twisting and may be using a variation of pike, straight or tuck. The legs must be kept together, toes pointed. In straight, the diver does not bend either the hips or knees. In pike, the body is bent forward and the knees are held straight

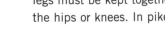

In games, put a video camera on a goalie, catcher, batter, running back or pole vaulter to immerse readers into these players' challenges. This video can run with a feature on these players, or it can complement some audio where these players explain what it feels like to stop a slap shot, to catch a knuckleballer or to navigate narrow openings between 300-pound defensive linemen. Check out "The Diver's View" to see what it's like to leap off a 10-meter platform board. Click on www.nytimes.com/interactive/2008/08/21/sports/olympics/20080821_10M_DIVING.html.

out, nearly parallel. In tuck, the diver looks almost like the cannonball dives made by kids at local pools. Divers grab their bent legs on the shin as they somersault through the air.

▶ Diving is judged subjectively, like figure skating. Judges consider many factors before offering their scores, which must be offered in half-point increments from 1 to 10. Are the knees bent when the diver enters the water? Did the diver stay close to the board on the descent? Were legs together on entry? On entry into the water, was the splash minimal? Judges also like higher bounces in springboard dives.

▶ Most diving competitions use at least three judges, although colleges allow two for dual meets (frequently, both coaches serve in this capacity). At larger national and international meets, five or more judges may be used.

▶ Dives are scored according to two elements: the judges' scores and the degree of difficulty.

- Dives range in difficulty from 1.2 for a forward dive in a tuck position from the 1-meter springboard to 3.8 for a dive that includes a reverse 3½ somersaults in pike on a 3-meter springboard. Each dive is assigned a score by FINA that relies on a formula that includes the following elements: number of twists, level of dive (platform, 1-meter, 3-meter), number of somersaults, position from which the dive is performed (free, pike, straight, tuck), and diver's approach (back, forward, inward, reverse, twisting).

- Dive scores are calculated by first adding the scores of the judges, then multiplying this total score by the degree of difficulty.

  - Sample Scoring for a Five-Judge Panel
    - Scores: 6, 5, 6.5, 6.5, 4.5
    - Low (6.5) and high (4.5) scores dropped
    - Raw score = 17.5 (6 + 6.5 + 5)
    - Raw score (17.5) × Degree of difficulty (3.0)
    - Total score for the dive = 52.5

Get Ready

- Do as much research as you can before arriving at the meet. Which athletes are expected to win? Which ones have struggled recently? Who is returning from an injury? Who has a personal challenge away from the pool? Who has a chance to break a record? And who are the top-rated teams? "Things happen so quickly at a swim meet that you have to stay sharp throughout," says Michaelis.

- For background, ask coaches for information not included in published stories or the press guide. If possible, call coaches days earlier. How many swimmers have returned? How many swimmers graduated the previous year? Who are the leaders on the team? Interview opposing coaches for additional perspectives.

- When you arrive at the meet, get programs and verify factual information with coaches and officials.

- Find out where the official scoring takes place so you can get updates through the meet. If possible, see whether these results can be printed so you can view them. Ask to have the final team and individual results e-mailed to you or your editors at the end of the meet.

- Obtain a heat sheet if possible. Heat sheets cite event, heat, lane and seed times for all swimmers so reporters can learn the top-rated swimmers. They are rarely used in dual meets at high school and college levels, but all championship meets prepare them.

▶ Before finals start, coaches may be more willing to answer questions. What are the team's goals? What are the expectations for this meet? Either ask questions or just chat informally with the coaches to get a perspective that can help you develop story angles and ask better questions later.

WATCH

▶ Right before a race starts, stay quiet and still, as you would when a golfer prepares to swing. When a competitor is about to dive, stop walking if you are close to the diver's line of sight.

▶ Look for races that are most competitive, which usually means races in which times are the closest.

▶ Focus on finals unless someone sets a significant record during prelims.

▶ Take note of a coach's reactions throughout a race. Watch the reaction of competitors, both winners and losers. Did someone toss his goggles, slap the water or thrust a fist in the air? This kind of detail enhances your descriptions.

▶ Focus on split times. Did a swimmer go faster in the second half of the 100-meter breaststroke or 1,000 freestyle? Splits can help illustrate when a swimmer took control or faltered.

▶ Keep track of scoring throughout the meet. If the score is close, start focusing on the events down the stretch that ultimately determine the team champion. Perhaps a team outscores another 39 – 8 in the final few events to win by a few points. Or a team fares particularly well in one or two types of events such as the relays, freestyle races or diving. Or perhaps a team scores not by winning but by compiling points from second-, third- or sixth-place finishes in a larger meet, points that enable it to win despite a lack of individual victories.

ASK

▶ Avoid interviewing swimmers immediately after a race. They're already thinking about their next event. Wait until they are more focused and can speak more lucidly.

- Don't interview swimmers or coaches on the competition deck unless you already know them well. Many complexes have warm-down areas, where you may be able to start a conversation, but tread lightly. Warm-down pools are similar to football practice fields in that athletes are still training. "Media members can't just walk up during practice and start chatting up a position coach during a drill," says Marsteller. "In swimming, you have a bit more leeway, but just make sure you read into what's going on with each person. Don't get the 'media-first' mentality and try to shove a question down someone's throat." Instead, you may have to just ask, "Can we chat after you finish warming down?" Most swimmers will come speak with you later, appreciative that you did not interrupt their training.

- Ask swimmers to rate their competitors. Whom had they been most concerned about? Did those worries prove justified?

- As always, aim for detail. If a swimmer says he or she felt especially strong that day, ask more questions: Strong how, exactly? Were you breathing easier? Did your strokes feel strong? Were you noticing competitors in nearby lanes? When did you know you had won?

- In the IM, ask competitors about the four strokes used for this event. Which stroke does a swimmer like the best? Which stroke is the most challenging?

- Ask divers to describe dives. Which were most difficult? What were they thinking on the board or platform?

WRITE

- For leads, you can focus on several angles – record-setting performances, key match-ups, an impressive overall performance, a turning point in the meet or a significant team victory. For larger events and for larger audiences, though, finding a theme or human interest angle is best. Casual readers do not usually read stories that only cite race results. "The most difficult aspect of writing swimming stories is making them accessible to the *USA Today* readers who don't follow swimming while also making them informative and interesting enough for those that do," says Michaelis. "That's why, yes, it's usually easiest to pick a theme or human-interest angle or to focus on one athlete or one race, then weave in the other significant results."

- Highlight the overall performance of someone who won several events in a dual meet or invitational. Example: "John Barnes won two individual events and anchored another winning relay team to lead Cypress Lake to the Class AAA state championship Saturday."

▶ Offer an opening anecdote that reveals a human interest story:

> When Dan Wilson's right leg was ripped off by a bull shark, he was certain his life was about to end.
> When a lifeguard rescued him, he knew he'd never walk or swim again.
> At best, he figured he would be able to relax in a shallow pool.
> Nine months later, Wilson never dreamed he would compete in a state high school swim meet, but that's exactly what he did Friday night, finishing eighth in a 100-meter breaststroke.
> Jacksonville Bolles, meanwhile, captured the boys high school title for the ninth year, compiling 49 points to edge Miami Lakes (45) and Sarasota Riverview (42) in the Florida High School Swimming and Diving championships.

▶ Cite team scores somewhere in the opening paragraphs, as in this from the Associated Press:

> The Wildcats, who finished second last season, in 1998 and 2000, used five relay titles and two individual champions over the three-day event at Ohio State's McCorkle Aquatic Pavilion to amass 484 points for the win.
> Two-time defending champion Auburn was second with 348. The Tigers won five of the previous six championships and also were second in 2005. Stanford was third with 343 followed by Texas A&M (315) and California (291).

▶ After you focus on the main stories of the meet, list other interesting results by bulleting them:

> Arizona also fared well in several other events:
>
> ▶ Michelle Himmelberg clocked in at 53.49 seconds to take second in the 50-meter freestyle.
>
> ▶ Mary Garber took the lead early to easily win the 200-meter fly in 2:01.24.
>
> ▶ Marjorie Kinder anchored a 200-meter medley squad that finished second. Joan Ryan, Tracy Dodds and Claire Smith teamed up with Kinder to finish in 1:43.91.

▶ Don't forget to include some of the following information in the introductory paragraphs – team names, overall scores, location, name of meet.

- Note the meet's significance. Does any individual performance clinch a postseason berth? Is this a conference or district victory? Does the team have a chance to win at the next level, based on the number of swimmers who just advanced?

- Compare a swimmer's time with previous performances: "Piersoll's 200-meter time was .1 second better than his previous best, but far behind the national record."

- Cite splits: "Shelley Fisher was second at the 50, 100 and 150 splits but could not retain the slim lead she held down the stretch an finished third, .2 seconds behind Tracy Wagner."

- Describe a race: "Natalie Smith took the lead from the start, building a .21 second lead at the wall. After the turn, she was .12 seconds ahead of the state record. Smith held off Janet Evans down the stretch, touching the wall .04 seconds ahead of the state mark and .18 seconds ahead of Evans."

- Refer to events in lowercase – 500-meter freestyle, 100-meter breaststroke, 200-meter butterfly or 50-meter backstroke.

- Cite diving heights in numerals – the 3-meter springboard, 10-meter platform.

- Spell out minutes and seconds the first time you cite race times. After that you can use only numerals. "Janet Evans won the 1,000-meter free in 6 minutes, 12.45 seconds. Lydia Ciurcovich took second in 6:18.25."

- Local results typically trump all other results. That's what readers care most about. If you are covering a meet where no swimmer from your area finished higher than third, that should still be your angle. Focus on your local swimmer's performance, describing how she kicked it in or faltered at the end to take third.

- Look ahead. In longer meets like the NCAA championships, cite the events that key swimmers are scheduled to compete in: "Mark Spitz will compete in the 4×100 free relay and the 200 IM on Monday."

TENNIS

Tennis is that rare athletic event in which one individual directly faces off against another. Only wrestling and boxing can match it for creating intimate one-on-one battles. More than other sports, tennis is about style and personality, especially at the professional level. "That's why fans tune in, for the most part," says *San Francisco Chronicle* columnist Bruce Jenkins, whose tennis coverage has earned several writing awards. "And I find that's what they want to read about."

Personality may not be as significant at the high school and college levels, where team results are emphasized as much as individual accolades. At these lower levels, researching storylines in advance and intently describing key matches will help you produce coverage even casual fans can appreciate.

At any level, tournaments are the main events where writers can cover only a few matches. So carefully pick these out, settle in and describe the action. You've seen one-on-one matchups in football and basketball, or pitcher-hitter duels in baseball, but the team still determines the outcome in those sports. In golf, players compete individually, but they do not play one another directly except during a rare playoff.

"Tennis is a wonderful sport in that way, a bit like boxing, in that you're out there one-on-one against another person, and nobody else can really help you," Jenkins says. "It's always interesting to watch someone rise to the occasion, or fall apart, under severe duress."

PREPARE

Learn the Basics

▶ In tennis, a player must win four points to win a game, but scores are not recorded 1 – 2 – 3 – 4; instead, they are recorded in this succession: 0 (called "love"), 15, 30, 40, and game. As a result, a server who wins two straight points would lead 30 – 0, or 30 – love.

▶ Games must be won by two points. Games tied 40 – 40 require an extension of play that results in scores called "advantages." A player who wins the first point on a serve after 40 – 40 has the "advantage," which is also called "ad-out" and "ad-in." At ad-in, the server leads; at ad-out, the person served to leads. If the server wins the point at ad-out, the score returns to even. If the receiver wins the point at ad-out, the game is over. Scores can go back and forth from ad-in, even and ad-out countless times during a single game.

▶ Some high school sports associations use a no-ad system for scoring tennis matches, which means that the first player to win four points wins each game, regardless of margin of victory. In this system, a player who is ahead 4 – 3 in a game wins.

▶ Sets are won by the player who first reaches six total games. Sets must be won by at least two games, which means there are times a player must win seven games to earn a set. If the score is 6 – 5, at least one more game is required. If the score extends to 7 – 5, then a set is earned. If the score evens to 6 – 6, a 12-point tiebreaker is required. The winner of the tiebreaker would then win the set 7 – 6.

▶ 12-point tiebreakers are used when both players have won six games in a set. The first player to reach seven points wins the tiebreaker and the set.

▶ A tennis match is composed of anywhere from three to five sets. Typical sets are best of three, meaning a player must win two sets before the opponent does. Example: "Venus Williams defeated Maria Sharapova, 6 – 2, 4 – 6, 6 – 4."

▶ Unforced errors are when a player makes a mistake that results in a point for the opposing player. A point can end three ways – in an unforced error, a forced error or a winner. An unforced error is a shot that a player would normally get back into play.

▶ Forced errors are the result of excellent shots from an opponent who has forced the player out of position or who has hit the ball with extra pace. A missed return off a first serve is usually a forced error, but a missed return on a second serve is usually unforced

because second serves are not usually hit with as much pace and speed.

▶ On a serve, a player is given two attempts to serve the ball over the net into the service area. If both serves fail, this is considered a double fault and the receiver wins the point. A double fault is an unforced error.

L. Jon Wertheim,
Sports Illustrated

ON FINDING UNIQUE ANGLES

In some ways, when I cover tennis, the match itself is the least important part of the day. The crucial part of button-holing the coach in the hotel lobby or observing the mannerisms of the losing player as she walks off the court makes the job more challenging, but, ultimately, it's more satisfying than sitting in the press box.

▶ Balls that land on the lines are considered in play.

▶ At many high school and college tournaments, the players themselves make the calls in a match. In professional tournaments, a chair umpire who almost always sits on a raised chair on one side of the court next to the net is the final authority on all calls.

▶ Doubles play is sometimes scored differently from singles competition, using pro-set rules where the first to win eight games earns the match. For example, "Sally Jenkins-Charisse Williams defeated Venus Williams-Steffi Graf, 8 – 6, in doubles action." Rules can vary, especially for small amateur or high school matches, so check with local officials if you notice unusual scores.

▶ Outdoor courts are hard court, grass or clay. A person with a strong serve often does better on grass and hard-court surfaces while a better baseline player might do better on slower clay surfaces.

▶ Professional tennis has four major professional tennis tournaments: Australian Open (hard court), French Open (clay), Wimbledon (grass), U.S. Open (hard court). These are called Grand Slam events.

▶ Keep a running tally of aces. But also record unreturned serves, or "free points," a stat that is not usually kept during matches.

▶ Players are seeded before a major event, like Wimbledon, from 1 to 64. Players are also seeded before high school and college tournaments. You do not need to cite these seedings in stories unless they are significant, such as when the 24th-seeded player defeats the fifth-seeded player.

▶ Familiarize yourself with the following terms:

▶ ▶ **ace:** serve that is not returned and results in a point.

▶ ▶ **backhand:** shot made with the back of the racquet.

▶ ▶ **baseline player:** someone who mostly stays near the backline, preferring to trade ground strokes with an opponent.

▶ ▶ **crosscourt:** when a player hits the ball diagonally over the net, from the left corner to the right corner and vice versa.

▶ ▶ **deuce:** when the score is tied 40 – 40.

▶ ▶ **double fault:** when a server fails to hit the ball in play on two successive serves, resulting in a point for the opponent.

▶ ▶ **fault:** a point is awarded to an opponent when a player breaks any of the following rules – failing to hit the ball before it bounces twice, hitting a ball out of bounds, failing to hit the ball over the net, hitting the ball more than once, touching the net, net post, or ball, and by throwing the racket to hit a ball.

▶ ▶ **foot fault:** on a serve, neither foot can hit the baseline before the ball is hit with the racquet; otherwise a foot fault is called. A foot fault on a second serve results in a point for the other player. This is an unforced error.

▶ ▶ **forehand:** shot made using the front of the racquet.

▶ ▶ **ground stroke:** forehand or backhand hit after the ball has bounced once on the court.

▶ ▶ **let:** serve that hits the net and lands in the service box. The server essentially gets a do-over, allowing for another serve. If a serve falls outside the service box, the serve is considered a fault.

▶ ▶ **lob:** shot hit high and deep into the opponent's court, a shot that is used for both defensive and offensive purposes.

▶ ▶ **lucky loser:** player who loses in qualifying for a tournament but who gets a spot in the tournament after a qualifier withdraws for injuries or personal reasons.

▶ ▶ **serve-and-volley player:** someone with a great serve who gets to the net quickly for the return shot. This person can have a higher number of aces but might also have a higher number of unforced errors.

▶ ▶ **service break:** when the player receiving the serve wins the game.

▶ ▶ **slice:** shot with backspin, which goes back toward the net instead of forward toward the baseline; sometimes called a drop shot.

- ▶ ▶ **smash:** shot that is hit above a player's head by using a service motion, usually near the net or at midcourt. Smashes are usually hit before the ball has bounced on the court.

- ▶ ▶ **topspin:** shot where the ball rotates as if it's rolling in the same direction it's moving, causing it to arc downward after it crosses the net.

- ▶ ▶ **volley:** shot hit before the ball bounces to the ground, usually while the player is near the net.

Get Ready

▶ Check the backgrounds of key players before heading out to the matches. Read about hometowns, experience and recent performances through the season. If this is a youth tournament, go early to speak with officials, coaches and parents.

▶ You can't cover every match at tournaments, so you'll have to determine the best match-ups to watch. Read previously published stories and press guides and interview players and coaches before the tournament to determine which matches will be the most compelling or newsworthy. Your story can focus primarily on a single match or two, but do not forget to offer team champions and other significant results in the story as well.

▶ Create a scoring system you can use to jot down details about key plays, like service breaks, great shots, changes in momentum and displays of emotion. Here's one method: Write the two players on top of a blank page and draw a line down the middle of the page to separate the two players. Then you can put the score down the center. In addition, you can add comments on the sides.

▶ Record details about the scene around the courts, such as noteworthy people in attendance and players' body language. You never know when these details may be useful. In addition, record the name of the chair umpire in case a controversial play becomes newsworthy.

▶ Check on winning streaks for both individuals and teams.

WATCH

▶ Take lots of notes during matches. When *Sports Illustrated's* L. Jon Wertheim covers a tennis match, he goes old school, breaking out pen and paper to take notes amid the aisles of laptops. He divides the page into two vertical halves. On the left side, he scribbles about on-court actions, writing notes like "lots of double faults," "lost four straight after hitting a volley across the court," "looks heavier than normal." On the right side of the page, Wertheim writes what he calls "atmospheric jottings" that include anything from the words on a fan's banner to the weather to the music played on the public address system during breaks in the action. Says Wertheim: "Basically, anything you wouldn't necessarily pick up watching at home on TV." Once he starts developing the game story, Wertheim focuses on themes, trends and news.

▶ Focus on a key play (or a string of plays) that changed the course of the match. This can be a point in the final game, or it could have been set up by a point in the first of several games.

▶ Describe the great shots, especially if these are made during pivotal moments.

▶ Focus on trends in a game: a high percentage of first serves landing in, volleying, double faults, unforced errors, number of points won off the first or second serves or troubles with a backhand return.

▶ If you notice a player missing several backhands, start recording every such error. Does this player usually have troubles with that shot? Did the opponent recognize these struggles?

▶ Determine whether the tournament produced any breaking news. Did anybody get hurt? Were there any upsets? Was anyone fined? Did anything happen off the court between matches?

▶ In early-round matches, focus on major upsets or top local performers.

▶ Record the length of rallies. Matches between serve-and-volley players tend to have shorter rallies than those between two baseliners. Count how many times the ball went over the net in longer, or pivotal, rallies, something you can include in your game stories. For example, "Andre Agassi fired a backhand volley down the right side to culminate a nine-shot rally that left Sampras trailing 4 – 1." Games between players with different styles are always interesting. Which player, for instance, will assert her personality on the court, the volleyer or the baseliner?

▶ Look for displays of emotion. Did a player react to a certain point? Did the player react emotionally to a series of points, or actions, on the court? Describe this. Speak to this player (and this player's opponent) after the match to gain more insight.

▶ Record body language. On the court, watch to see whether a player hunches over after a bad play or whether she smiles and jokes. Does a player bounce on his toes

before a shot. At what point does the player seem less bouncy? You might want to describe the player's game early, then do the same halfway and near the end of the match to see how this player's body language, and perhaps attitude, changed through the match. This can also reveal something about the player's personality. Also, watch players as they walk off the court, regardless of whether they won or lost.

- Focus on weather when it affects play. A blustery afternoon can cause more problems for a baseliner than a serve-and-volley player.

- Describe how injuries affected play on the court.

- Write a few sentences describing a player in general and a few sentences on a few plays. Trust your observations. Here's how author John McPhee does it in *Levels of the Game:* "Left arm up, fist closed, index finger extended, he continues to point at the ball until he has all but caught it. His racquet meanwhile dangles behind his back. Then it whips upward in the same motion as for a serve."[1]

- Left-handers sometimes create problems for righties. If you notice a lefty-righty matchup, see how this affects the game. Ask players and coaches about this afterward.

ASK

- Ask a player to describe her opponent's game. What were the person's strengths and weaknesses? What did she notice most about the other player's game plan or skills? You can also ask these questions of a coach. Try to speak with both player and coach.

- Ask a player to describe her own game.

- Ask how players felt during key moments of the match.

- Ask questions that add more depth to your observations and notes. Players' insights into key plays, emotional displays and other aspects of the game can be illuminating, more so if you are talking with high school and college players. Pros tend to be more guarded. "Afterwards, when the interviews are taking place, you basically get a lot of nothing," Jenkins says. "Players tend to be guarded and cautious, and with good reason. So many stories run worthless quotes like 'I was serving well,' or 'He (she) played better on the important points.' I try not to use quotes unless they are funny, off-the-wall or especially revealing or relevant."

- Ask follow-up questions. If a player says he served well, ask how he knows this. What about the serves felt particularly good? Had he been concerned about serves before the match? If a player says her opponent played better, ask for more details. How in particular did the other player perform better? With returns, footwork, serves? Then follow up on this by asking for more explanations on these specific areas.

- Too often, sports reporters allow a first response to serve as the answer. But these questions are just the starting points. Lob questions back to players and coaches – and continue to do so until you learn more details and gain more insights. Remember, we ask questions for information, not quotes. Don't worry: The quotes will surface if you continue to ask pointed, specific follow-up questions.

- Ask players questions related to your descriptions and notes and observations. Don't be shy. Then listen and ask more questions. That's what we do.

WRITE

- Here are some possible lead angles: major upsets, a decisive play in an important match, or key injuries. Wertheim defines his potential focuses as themes, trends and news.

- Focus on a clash of styles between two players. Here is Jenkins' take on the 2005 Wimbledon:

  > The women's draw lost more than a feared contender when Justine Henin-Hardenne was knocked out in the first round Tuesday. It lost the element of contrast.
  >
  > Henin-Hardenne, upset by 76th-ranked Eleni Daniilidou 7 – 5, 2 – 6, 7 – 5, is the only elite player to fashion a one-handed backhand and take pride in an all-court game. To the shock of a Court 1 crowd, her virtuosity wasn't enough against a powerful, 22-year-old player with a fondness for grass.[2]

- In tournaments, cite whom a player faces in the next round.

- Cite records for players and teams. What is a player's record against an opponent, on a certain surface, or in a specific stadium? What is a player's record on clay or grass? What is a player's all-time record at a specific venue or tournament?

- Put the match winner's scores first, even if the winner has won fewer games in one of the sets. For example, if Serena Williams defeats Maria Sharapova in three sets, you would write: "Williams rallied to defeat Sharapova, 1 – 6, 6 – 4, 6 – 3."

- Cite tournament victories for professional events. If this player has not won a tournament, cite the best previous finish, even if that is 10th or 20th.

- Record rankings properly. A player can be described as being ranked No. 31 or 31st ranked. Avoid writing that someone is a second seed; instead, write that a player is seeded second.

- In the opening paragraphs, city the name and location of the event (city, stadium), and date played.

- Some possible lead angles include major upsets, a decisive play in an important match and key injuries.

TRACK & FIELD

C overing a track meet is like reporting 14 (or more) shorter stories. Reporters almost always wander from event to event around the stadium, watching and recording scores as athletes run, jump and throw things. Unlike in most sports, you can interview athletes and coaches even before the meet ends. The challenge is not only finding a focus in all that action, but also showing people how exciting the sport is. Track and field tends to get lots of attention only in or near an Olympic year; otherwise, it's relegated to second-tier status.

Because few readers understand the rules or know the athletes, a reporter needs to develop an angle that even those who aren't track fans can enjoy. "When you cover track and field and swimming, maybe two out of a hundred readers are really devoted to the sport," says *The New York Times* sportswriter Frank Litsky. "You can't write for two people. You have to pull in the others by focusing on people – like the swimmer with the defibrillator or the runner recovering from cancer. If you tell stories, you can get people to read them."

Research before you arrive; learn as much as you can about the events and athletes. Then watch, listen and interview athletes from as many of the 14-plus events as possible. Covering track can be busy. Like a 5,000-meter runner, you'll need to pace yourself so you can finish strong on deadline.

PREPARE

Learn the Basics

▶ The following individual events are contested in USA Open and Junior Outdoor Track and Field championships: 100-, 200-, 400-, 800-, 1,500-, 5,000-, 10,000-meter races, 20,000-meter walk, 100-, 110- and 400-meter hurdles, 3,000-meter steeplechase, high jump, long jump, triple jump, pole vault, shot put, discus throw, hammer throw, javelin throw.

▶ All world and collegiate running distances are in meters, not yards. To convert kilometers to miles, divide by 1.6 for the longer distances. But you can avoid tough math simply by remembering that 800 meters is about a half-mile, 1,600 meters a mile, and 5,000 meters about 3 miles. Estimate other distances accordingly.

▶ Medleys are relays where runners cover different distances. Unlike the 4 × 400, when each runner sprints 100 meters, medleys rely on athletes with different specialties. For example, a sprint medley requires short- and middle-distance sprinters to run 200 – 200 – 400 – 800 meters, in that order. In a distance medley, runners cover 1,200 – 400 – 800 – 1,600 meters, in that order.

▶ Most state high school associations (and some college conferences) offer the following relays: 4 × 100, 4 × 200, 4 × 400 and 4 × 800 meters. At the international level, the 4 × 200 and 4 × 800 are not run. In relays, each runner races one-fourth of the distance, meaning four athletes run 400 meters each in the 1,600-meter relay. Most states also offer the 3,200 (2-mile) and 1,600 meters (1-mile) for individuals. Races longer than 3,200 meters are not used for state high school championships, neither is the javelin or hammer throw.

▶ In a decathlon, male athletes compete over two days in 10 events: 100 meters, long jump, shot put, high jump, 400 meters, 110-meter hurdles, discus, pole vault, javelin and 1,500 meters, usually in that order.

▶ In the heptathlon, female athletes compete in seven events over two days: 100-meter hurdles, high jump, shot put, 200 meters, long jump, javelin and 800 meters.

▶ Scoring varies at meets, invitationals and championships. For National Collegiate Athletic Association meets, winners earn 10 points, followed by 8 – 6 – 5 – 4 – 3 – 2 – 1 for the next seven finishers. If a meet has fewer than six teams, scoring changes to 10 − 8 − 6 − 4 − 2 − 1.

▶ Athletes get three attempts in field events finals. In events like the long jump, triple jump, shot put and discus, the longest leap or farthest throw is used. In events such as the pole vault and high jump, the highest jump wins. When athletes tie for the highest jump, the winner is determined by a tiebreaker that considers two factors: fewest misses at the height at which the tie occurred and fewest misses throughout the competition.

▶ In the high jump and pole vault, competitors can start jumping at any height. Three consecutive failed attempts at any height eliminates a jumper. Jumpers and vaulters may pass on any attempt at any height (top performers usually don't bother with the lower heights) and move to the next level, even if they failed to reach a previous height. So a high jumper who misses twice at 6 feet, 4 inches can pass on her final attempt and start over with three attempts at 6 feet, 4½ inches.

▶ The term "kick" varies depending on the length of a race. A miler might sprint the final 200 meters, but a 5,000-meter runner might pick up speed during the final quarter mile.

▶ During relays, runners have a short area where they are allowed to hand off the baton to a teammate. Passing the baton outside of the exchange area results in a disqualification, as does a dropped baton from any of the four team members at any time during the race.

▶ Athletes can be disqualified for a variety of reasons − for stepping on either lane line during sprints, for stepping on the inside lane during a distance race, for stepping over the line (or take-off board) during long and triple jumps, and for stepping outside the marked circle while competing in the shot put, among others. False starts also cause disqualifications. In most prep and college races, runners are allowed one false start before getting "DQ'd." A second false start disqualifies an athlete from the event.

▶ FAT refers to fully automated timing, as opposed to handheld timing. FAT is used at most major meets. Handheld times are rounded up to the next tenth of second, so a handheld time of 10.89 for 100 meters should be recorded as a 10.9.

▶ Handheld times are considered less exact, usually 2/10th to 3/10th of a second slower. To compensate, the NCAA adds .24 to events shorter than 300 meters that are timed by hand. Add .14 seconds for distances longer than 300 meters.

The New York Times explained how Usain Bolt set the world record in the Olympic 100 meters, using nine panels to break down the race from start to finish. This includes graphic elements and photos. Check out "Bolt's Record in the 100 Meters" at www.nytimes.com/interactive/2008/08/16/sports/olympics/20080816_mens100_graphic.html.

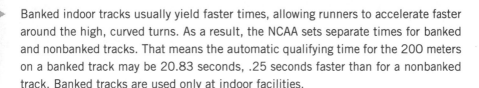

Bolt's Record in the 100 Meters

By SHAN CARTER, SERGIO PEÇANHA, GRAHAM ROBERTS, BEDEL SAGET, MIKE SCHMIDT and JOE WARD
Updated: August 19, 2008

Usain Bolt of Jamaica set a world record of 9.69 seconds in the 100 meters.

✉ E-MAIL

▤ FEEDBACK

ⓑ SHARE

Bolt was nearly last to react to the gun. His large frame and long limbs work against him at the start of races.

		takeoff time in seconds
Frater	0.147	
Patton	0.142	
Bolt	0.165	
Thompson	0.133	
Dix	0.133	
Powell	0.134	
Burns	0.145	
Martina	0.169	

10m

1 **2** 3 4 5 6 7 8 9 NEXT▶

▶ Banked indoor tracks usually yield faster times, allowing runners to accelerate faster around the high, curved turns. As a result, the NCAA sets separate times for banked and nonbanked tracks. That means the automatic qualifying time for the 200 meters on a banked track may be 20.83 seconds, .25 seconds faster than for a nonbanked track. Banked tracks are used only at indoor facilities.

▶ Tracks for indoor meets are usually smaller – 200 meters compared with 400 at outdoor venues – so event distances vary. For example, the 60 meters replaces 100 meters and the 60-meter hurdles replaces the 100 and 110 hurdles.

▶ Before the season begins, the NCAA sets times, heights and distances it believes will limit the field for the national championships, meaning athletes who reach these levels can qualify provisionally. If too many athletes surpass the prescribed levels, the NCAA will decrease the time or increase the distance or height, which means that some who had qualified are no longer eligible. Hence the term "provisional."

▶ The NCAA also prescribes times, distances and heights that give athletes an automatic berth in the national championships, regardless of how many people reach this level. These levels are more difficult to reach. At 60 meters, for example, the automatic time may be 6.62 seconds, .12 seconds faster than the provisional time.

▶ In larger meets, runners usually need to qualify in heats for finals because the lanes limit the number of participants to eight. Distance races do not have this same limitation, so races longer than 800 meters do not usually require qualifying. A runner needs to finish first or second in a heat to advance, along with those who recorded the next-best recorded times.

▶ High school athletes qualify for state meets by finishing among the top runners through a series of postseason meets that usually start at the district level and advance through regionals and sectionals.

▶ "Last chance" meets are competitions held toward the end of the college track season for the main purpose of helping athletes qualify for the NCAA championships. Team points and trophies are not usually awarded at these meets.

▶ Springier surfaces lead to faster times. Research has shown that a running surface made of asphalt and stone base, polyurethane surface and a butyl rubber layer gives the best results.

▶ Tailwinds greater than 2 meters per second (roughly 4.7 mph) nullify most world records.

Get Ready

▶ Go to the event early. Typical field events and preliminary sprint heats start early. Field events for a high school district meet might begin at 4 P.M. and be followed by finals at 6 or 7 P.M. Preliminary races also start early, but you can usually avoid these and focus on the field events finals instead. Coaches tend to have more time to speak during these early events.

▶ Move around the stadium so you can follow the early field events. This is where research comes in handy, knowing where the top matchups and most talented athletes will be competing, because many field events take place at the same time. Should you watch the long jump, high jump or shot put? The triple jump, discus or pole vault? It depends on who's competing. Once there, describe how one athlete performs compared with others. Did the high jumper scrape the bar at 6 feet, 2 inches, before rising several inches over the bar at 6 – 4 or 6 – 5? You not only can describe these efforts; later, you can also determine whether this jumper had to make adjustments, asking if this athlete can walk you through these jumps. The running events are usually held in order, so you won't have to race from place to place although you should find a location to watch the race. You may want to move between the back stretch and finish line for longer events. For the 100, find a spot where you can observe the start and finish and note any unusual movements.

▶ Do research before heading to a meet. Who's in the meet? What's the biographical information? "I never want to go to a meet cold," says *The Times'* Litsky, the author of eight books on sports – including one on track and field. "You can't cover everything at a track event. You can't watch it and interview people at the same time. You have to interview after events have ended and when other events are taking place."

▶ Make a list of what you plan to focus on so you don't get distracted when the action starts. Local coverage is usually paramount in covering larger meets unless you are writing for a national publication or news service.

▶ Pick up brochures or packets that include meet records. You will probably find them useful during the meet. For college events, check the NCAA's Web site for national records. Most NCAA conferences post their schools' best times as either best of the week or as individual performance lists.

WATCH

▶ Focus on athletes who are local, who are contenders for state or national titles, or both.

▶ Describe runners as they battle one another during a race and down the stretch. Cite when runners begin their kicks. Later, ask runners to walk you through their races.

▶ See who gains (or loses) the most ground during handoffs for relay events. Afterward, ask the runners and coaches to walk you through their handoffs.

- Some runners do better when they go out fast and push the time for the entire race. Some runners, especially those who have very strong kicks, do poorly when they are forced to go out too fast. Check runners' quarter-mile splits to determine where runners slowed or quickened their pace.

- Watch for pack running during distance races. Often, certain runners stay together for most of the race, to pull each other along. In some ways, pack running works like the drafting methods used by cyclists and race car drivers. It also eases the psychological burden of running alone.

ASK

- Give athletes time to catch their breaths before you ask questions.

- Use your advance research to focus your reporting. "If I have an interest in some athlete, I'll Google them and then do some other research on my own," Litsky says. "That way I can have questions drawn up. I then listen to their responses to questions."

- Specific questions can coax out athletes' thoughts and fill in the narrative. What were you thinking during the second lap of the mile? What were you thinking when you hit the board for the long jump? Was there a point in the race when you felt particularly strong, or weak? Which competitors were you particularly focused on, and why? What were your goals coming in, and which strategies did you use? "Post-race interviews are really when you pick up about 75 percent of the information you need," says *The Oregonian* track writer Doug Binder. "The competitors can tell you how the race unfolded usually better than your notes can."

- Ask what athletes learned from previous competitions that included any other athletes in today's event.

- Ask coaches to explain strategy and techniques. Sometimes it's better to put down your notepad and just listen, especially if you plan to cover track again. Absorb the information so you can observe events better down the line – and so you can ask better questions. Ask coaches to explain anything that you are not certain about, meaning anything you cannot write in an authoritative voice.

- Talk with coaches early – during prelims and field events. They might have a little more time to talk with you then. After the finals start, they will be cajoling runners and calculating team points. If this is your first meet, ask a coach if you can watch some of the events side by side. You can learn much just by watching and listening.

- Talk to field athletes. Most of the time, these athletes compete almost anonymously. Says Litsky: "There are three events where people are the most interesting – the hammer throw, pole vault and shot put. Here's what they have in common: the public doesn't understand what they're doing. That's a fact. They all talk."

WRITE

- Spell out times in first reference, separating minutes and seconds like this: 15 minutes, 37 seconds. Abbreviate subsequent times like this: 15:41.2. For example, "Aaron Smith won the 5K race in 15 minutes, 20 seconds, followed by Matt McElwee in 15:32."

- Do not use a colon for times in events like the 100 meters given only in seconds. Write 10.12 seconds.

- Spell out distances in first reference, separating feet and inches with a comma like this: 19 feet, 6½ inches. On second reference, write 19 – 4.

- Do not use PR, the abbreviation for personal record. This is a runner's personal best time. Instead, write out "personal best" because such times are not actually records.

- Compare performances by offering gaps in time or geography: Scott Raft sprinted to the finish to win the 800 meters in 1 minute, 51.2 seconds, which was 1.4 seconds ahead of runner-up Glenn Nicholson. Or: Maria Bristol flew past all competitors to win the 100 meters in 10.1 seconds, two full steps ahead of her nearest rival.

- Use distance gaps to compare heights and lengths in a single field event: Sarah Elizabeth leaped six inches farther than her nearest competitor to win the conference long jump title. Elizabeth soared 24 feet, 11 inches for her second title, followed by Lydia Ciurcovich (24 – 5) and Lea Packer (24 – 1).

- Focus on a team performance in your lead.

> The UCLA women ended their long string of near misses with their first NCAA outdoor track and field title since 1983 Saturday night, and Arkansas repeated as men's champions.
>
> The Bruins edged defending champion LSU by one point in a controversial final night of competition at Mike A. Myers Stadium on the University of Texas campus. (Associated Press)

▶ Or you can choose to focus on an individual performance in your lead.

> Alan Webb remains America's best young miler, with a career best of 3 minutes 48.92 seconds. But at 24, he is still learning and still experimenting.
> Sunday's experiment on the final day of the United States indoor track and field championships worked just fine. Webb tolerated a sluggish pace for the first half of the mile, turned on the jets and won in 4:01.07.[1]

▶ Include the name and location of the meet in the opening paragraphs of the story.

▶ Include a paragraph that names team and individual winners. For example: Charleston High took the Class AA state title by compiling 82 points, 11 better than runner-up Mattoon.

▶ Offer a quick summary of key results somewhere in the story, either right after the lead or at the end of the game story. There is no way you can cover every single event. Readers can get that information in the agate, results and stats offered in smaller type. Here's an example of summarizing:

> In other events:
> Clearwater High's Shawana Smith ran 12.21 to win the 100 meters by one-hundredth of a second over Tampa Catholic's Molly Clutter.
> Dunedin's Marlise Davidson set a district record in the 800 meters, clocking in at 2 minutes, 12.29 seconds.
> Countryside's Kristen Lydia set a personal best in the shot put, heaving it 42 feet, 6.75 inches.

▶ Focus on the top runners from your primary readership area. Your readers will be more interested in a local girl who finished third in the high jump than a winner who lives two hours away. Cite the overall winners in the story, but lead with local angles.

TRIATHLONS

In triathlons, technology rules.

Sure, triathletes train hard to prepare to swim 2-plus miles, to cycle 100-plus miles and run a marathon in succession. But they are always looking for an edge – a way to reduce resistance and strain on their bodies.

That may be an electric bar end shifter on a bicycle that saves 15 grams (½ ounce) of drag during those 30 mph rides.

That may be a lighter helmet with a balanced design that eases tension on the neck.

That could be inserts for shoes that help redistribute weight and improve balance, depending on the event.

Or a wetsuit that allows a swimmer to glide through the water.

Every little bit helps ease the burden.

Air flow is also important, especially during the bike portions. Bike cowlings, helmets and handlebars are all tested in wind tunnels, where researchers create elements that have become so small and narrow that bicycles now look like flounders, barely visible when they're directly in front of you. Gloves even get tested and redesigned.

Five seconds separated the gold and silver medalists in the Olympic men's competition in 2008, and 20 seconds separated the top four. Can technology save seconds? Minutes? That's not clear. But triathletes will continue to use every advantage possible.

PREPARE

Learn the Basics

▶ Triathlons include the following in different distances – swimming, bicycling and running.

▶ After the race starts, the clock continues to run until the competitor crosses the finish line. The clock does not stop for changes of clothing or any other reason, so quick transitions to new events are important. Athletes usually have their cycling shoes attached to the pedals of bicycles to save time. These shoes usually have lace locks or are elastic.

▶ Drafting can be significant. In the swim competition, athletes draft off one another, in a slightly less aerodynamic manner than stock-car drivers. But following a lead swimmer can save a swimmer valuable energy in these endurance races. Drafting also enables weaker cyclists to keep up, sometimes in packs. Frequently, weaker runners will try to break away during the cycling portion, surging to create distance from stronger runners who are content to allow that portion to unfold. Cycling directly behind another cyclist is allowed for Olympic competitions, but amateur races usually disallow close drafting like this.

▶ Athletes are spent by the time they cross the finish line – mentally and physically wiped out. That's especially true for those running the longer Ironman races where athletes swim 2.4 miles, bike 112 miles, and run a marathon (26.2 miles).

▶ The world's best triathletes cover this distance in about 8½ hours, enduring dehydration, muscle cramps and mental fatigue. "As soon as you cross the line, for me, my body would complete shut down," six-time Ironman titlist Dave Scott told ESPN. "That mental hold that you have on yourself to continue and persevere becomes pretty acute at the end. You're just thinking about holding the pace that you're doing. The people that are in the front, their intensity is up there. Mentally, you just completely collapse. When I cross the line, I just have this huge feeling of thank goodness, I did it. You're pretty darn spent. That feeling stays with you about an hour or so after the race."

▶ The Olympic Games use the following distances for the triathlon: 1,500-meter swim, 40K bike, 10K run. That translates roughly to a 1-mile swim, a 25-mile bike ride and a 6.2-mile run.

"It is required that all athletes (unless they need to report to the medical tent) go through an area called the "mixed zone" immediately after they cross the finish line and grab some water. Interviews are conducted there with media on the other side of a barricade. In Beijing, this area was around 40 yards long with hundreds of media crowding for access. Rights-holding broadcast media get first dibs (NBC in this case); then other broadcast outlets, followed by print media (the largest contingent). What I tried to do in Beijing was group all of the U.S. print media together (about eight to 10 reporters), so the athletes could do all their interviews in one spot and wouldn't have to answer the same questions over and over again. It's better for the reporter, the athletes and me."

Jason Mucher,
USA Triathlon

► Some terms to familiarize yourself with:

▶ ▶ **bonked:** a term used to describe when exhaustion sets in, usually caused when glycogen stores in the liver and muscles are depleted and an athlete can go no further. Runners also call this "hitting the wall."

▶ ▶ **DNF:** Did not finish.

▶ ▶ **DNS:** Did not start.

▶ ▶ **duathlon:** Races consisting of three legs in which competitors run, then bike and then run again.

▶ ▶ **Ironman:** a race with a 2.4-mile swim, followed by a 112-mile bike race and a 26.2-mile run.

▶ ▶ **lactic acid:** causes muscle soreness; formed from glucose, and used by working muscles for energy.

▶ ▶ **OWS:** open water swim. Smaller races are sometimes held in local pools.

▶ ▶ **transition areas:** a fenced-in pen of bike racks where athletes transfer from swimming to cycling and from cycling to running. These quick changes sometimes determine the winners.

▶ ▶ **USAT:** USA Triathlon, the national governing body for the multisport disciplines of triathlon, duathlon, aquathlon and winter triathlon in the United States.

▶ ▶ **VO₂ max:** highest rate at which oxygen can be used during exercise.

▶ ▶ **World Triathlon Corporation:** organization responsible for running all Ironman races.

Get Ready

▶ Speak with sports information directors to see if they can supply media vehicles to transport you ahead of the competitors in the bike and run sections of the race.

▶ Some recommended viewing areas – swim start, swim finish, transition areas, finish lines. The swim entrance and run exit are often the best places for shooting photos of these events because the athletes are moving slower and are upright, unlike when they are cycling.

▶ Stay outside the fencing of transition areas.

▶ Determine whether spotters will be used for the race you're reporting on, so you can get updates along with officials and other reporters.

▶ The media tent that is used to distribute results and notes is usually set near the finish line. This is where post-race interviews usually take place as well. The medical tent is also located near this area for most competitions.

WATCH

▶ Note who leads each leg of the race.

▶ Describe competitors as they depart the water. Who's in the lead? Who makes the quickest transition?

▶ Chart the positions for those who led coming out of the water, seeing whether anybody in the top 10 moved forward or dropped back significantly. You can verify – and quantify – your observations when you read the split times on the final results.

▶ Describe physical gait during the running leg. Are runners swaying near the middle or end? Have they slowed to a walk? Are their arms pumping hard or just swinging loosely?

Most cycling portions are multiloop, meaning the race circles around the same areas more than once. So you can track the athletes' progress through the cycling portion. At the start, athletes may be in larger packs and cycling up to 30 mph. "The bike is much more of a cat-and-mouse game," says Jason Mucher, editor for usatriathlon.com. "Many athletes just sit back in the group and wait for the run to make their move."

Note how weather conditions affected the competitors. Did rain cause cyclists to skid or fall? Did extremely cold water slow down swimmers, or even cause some to need assistance from medical professionals? Did extreme heat cause runners to pass out during the running stage? Did winds cause higher than normal waves for swimmers? Was the course hilly?

Focus on injuries and medical problems, such as dehydration and pulled muscles when they affect a race's outcome.

ASK

The top finishers are going to need some time at the end of a race to compose themselves, so don't rush in to speak with them. Odds are, you won't be able to anyway. They'll be spent. So tell the race director the names of those you'd like to interview along with your cell phone number in case you're not near the media tent or rest area when the athlete is ready to talk.

All athletes must enter an area called the "mixed zone" right after crossing the finish line, where they can grab and drink much-needed water before interviews. The media are usually on the other side of a barricade near this zone. In Beijing, the mixed zone was about 40 yards in length, holding off hundreds of media.

For smaller local races, you may be the only member of the media attending so immediate access should not be a challenge. At larger televised events, TV rights holders interview first, followed by other TV and then print journalists.

Ask athletes to describe how they felt both physically and mentally, insights you cannot determine just from watching the competition. How were you feeling when you left the water? Did those waves take more energy than you had anticipated? How'd you feel during the cycling? Did you try to conserve energy before the run? What was the most challenging part of the race psychologically?

- Ask athletes about their strategies. Why did you break away from the pack during the cycling portion? What was your strategy? Why did you allow the pack to break away? How did this go with your pre-race plans?

- Ask athletes which competitors they were focusing on during the race. Did you ever feel you were pushing harder to keep up than you had planned? Did you notice the others start to tire? Did you ever push harder because you knew these other racers were tiring?

- Ask athletes to describe the key moments in the race. Why was this moment significant?

- Ask them to offer an overall analysis of their performance. What pleased you the most during the race? What was the most disappointing part of the race?

WRITE

- Focus on key moments in the race. That may be when an athlete made a move to pull away or surged to catch up to the leaders.

- Evaluate how well groups work together, especially during the cycling portion where they may draft off one another. This may be difficult to note for the swimming leg though.

- Focus on a key moment from the race, showing how this helped someone to win. Or focus on key leg for a competitor, as in this report from the Associated Press:

> KAILUA-KONA – Australia's Chris McCormack rallied with a strong marathon run to win the 140.6-mile Ironman Triathlon World Championship on Sunday.
>
> McCormack, known as Macca, was 11 minutes behind leader Torbjorn Sindballe of Denmark at the end of the 112-mile bicycle ride. But the Australian's fast run moved him to the front at the 15-mile mark of the 26.2-mile run.

- Include distances for each leg in the race as you refer to them: 1.2-mile swim, 50-mile bicycle ride and 6-mile run.

- Spell out the winning time in first reference: Johnson's total time was 4 hours, 29 minutes, 19 seconds. All other references can be abbreviated: "Pam Sanz-Guerrero finished second in 4:32:16, followed by Janice Collins (4:34:23) and Leda Brophy (4:35:08)."

- Do not force too much information in the lead. There's no reason to cite both the men's and women's winners in the lead. Focus on the best story, then offer details about the other division.

- If the race is a regular event, cite the year in the story, but events do not become annual until their third year. So you would write "second Great Floridian Triathlon" and "18th annual Ironman Triathlon."

- Describe athletes as they finish: Julie Moss' dramatic finish in the 1982 Ironman event single-handedly inspired thousands to start training for this sport. Ahead with 100 yards to go, she fell several times, teetered as she ran, and collapsed about 20 feet from the finish line. As she crawled to complete the race, another woman passed her – all of which was captured by ABC Sports, captivating a nation and helping to jump-start the sport. Races you cover probably won't have the same drama, but try to detail these final moments during close races or when someone struggles physically, showing the passion needed to complete even the shorter races.

- Describe weather conditions – more so if this greatly affected the competition. For extreme weather, ask the triathletes how conditions like excessive heat, strong head-winds or driving rain affected their performances during the various stages of the race. Collect stories you can tell readers and viewers.

VOLLEYBALL

Why's that player wearing a wrong-colored shirt?

That's the initial thought for many writers, parents and fans attending their first volleyball game.

They're wondering why a player on each team wears a shirt that clashes, or wildly contrasts in color, with those worn by her teammates.

This is done to let the referees and opposing team know this player is a libero, a position introduced by the NCAA in 2002.

The libero (pronounced LEE-beh-ro) is a defensive specialist who does not have to abide by the substitution rule, someone who can be substituted for any back-row player so long as she sits out for a play between changes. The libero is also a proficient passer, much like the team's setter. Everything in volleyball revolves around passing. Teams that pass well win, and those that don't lose. "The setter is sport's unsung hero," said Rich Luenemann, a two-time national coach of the year at Washington University in St. Louis. "Her position is easily the most demanding and analytical in all of sport. She must run down passes and digs, sometimes very errant ones, and make instantaneous decisions where to set the ball."

Fans who have not watched volleyball for many years may be surprised by several other rule changes, such as a rally scoring system that allows teams to earn points even when they have not served. Under the old system, teams could use a strong defensive effort to shut down an opponent until they could run off a string of points. Now teams score on every ball won.

Some other changes: serves count if they hit the net and go into the opposing team's court, games now go to 25 at the college level, and players can move to any spot behind the back line to serve.

On the surface, volleyball appears to be a simple game. A player serves the ball from the back of a court, starting a rally where teams volley the ball back and forth; and teams try to hit the ball into the opponent's floor to score a point. But it's far more complex than that. And much more exciting.

Back-row players frequently make acrobatic dives to keep the ball in play before springing back up. Setters have less than a second to call out plays and to pass the ball to an exact spot for a specific hitter. And front-row hitters then leap high, reach back, and slam a moving ball as it reaches it apex, driving it into a specific spot at more than 70 miles per hour.

Volleyball is also the only team sport that doesn't allow players to catch, or hold, the ball. Nor do teams take possession of the ball. Volleyball is more a game of movement and rebound. Ultimately, though, players are more concerned about one simple idea: hitting the ball into the other team's floor and scoring the most points.

PREPARE

Learn the Basics

▶ Rally scoring is now used at all competitive levels, meaning a team wins a point even if it did not serve. A rally refers to the ongoing play that starts with a serve and concludes when a team hits a ball to the floor of the other team's court or the opponent deflects the ball out of bounds. Points are also recorded when either team is called for the following violations – a body part crossing the line under the net, carrying the ball by hitting it with the palm of the hand, reaching over the net, or failing to return the ball over the net within three touches. Teams that win a rally earn one point.

▶ Teams win a match by winning the best three out of five sets to 25 points at the college level. (In 2008, the National Collegiate Athletic Association decreased from 30 the number of points needed to win a set.) Fifth sets go to 15 points. At the high school level, teams play the best two out of three sets, all to 25 points. At all levels, teams must win by two points to earn a set.

"Coaches typically don't like to be asked questions that are loaded ("Are you going to win your conference championship?") or that have timelines ("How long are you planning on coaching here?" or "How long until you win a national championship?"). I am not sure you ever get an honest answer or a direct answer about any of these questions. The questions that are the best to receive are the ones where you can tell the interviewer both was paying attention and understands the game. Maybe a question like, "In the second set I saw you made this adjustment. What was the reason for the adjustment and did it accomplish what you were hoping?"

Kevin Hambly,
former assistant coach,
USA Olympics; coach, University of Illinois

▶ Teams usually rely on three touches before taking a shot over the net, a process called bump-set-spike. On the first touch, a player usually tries to contain a shot from the opposing team, popping it up for a teammate to hit. The second touch is used to set up the kill shot for a third player. Sometimes, to confuse an opponent, a team will alter this rotation by hitting the ball back over in one or two touches.

▶ A setter runs the offense, reacting to hits and calling plays to teammates like a point guard.

▶ Some typical unforced errors include a player hitting the ball twice in a row, catching the ball, touching the net, stepping under the court or reaching over the net to hit the ball.

▶ Hitting percentage is a stat that's unfamiliar to most readers. Players with an average above .200 have played well. Those over .300 have played tremendously well. Outside hitters often have a lower percentage than inside hitters. A team with five players hitting over .200 has done very well. Address that somewhere in the story. This percentage is determined by taking the number of kills, minus the number of errors, and then dividing by total balls attempted. So a player who has 8 kills and 4 errors in 16 total balls would have the following hitting percentage: $(8 - 4) \div 16 = .250$.

▶ Teams employ many strategies. Coaches want to run their offenses through their best players. The main strategy is to set the ball for the best hitter on the team as frequently as possible until the opposing team can regularly stop this player from scoring. In addition, teams may attempt a blind-side attack in which a front-row hitter comes from the other side of the court to spike the ball. Or teams may try a little misdirection, running their best hitter to a set spot but then setting the ball for another front-row player on the other side of the court.

Teams line up three players in the front and back rows in indoor volleyball. Front-row players comprise the right front, center front and left front while the back row has left, center and right backs. Back-row players may not hit, come to the net to spike or kill the ball. They must remain behind the 10-foot line when they hit the ball over the net. Players rotate clockwise after each sideout.

Familiarize yourself with these rules:

▶ ▶ Players can be replaced, or substituted, at any time. Usually taller front-row players are replaced by quicker, more agile players before they move to the back row, and vice versa. Players can be reinserted only for their substitutes.

▶ ▶ Players cannot hit the ball twice except when returning a serve – and only if this is incidental, as when a ball bounces off a forearm and a shoulder. This counts as two of the team's maximum three hits on each possession.

▶ ▶ Teams are allotted two time-outs per game at the college level. Coaches use these to stop another team's momentum or to correct a problem on their own end.

▶ ▶ Volleyball players no longer call balls that bounce off the forearms "bumps." Instead, they're called "passes."

▶ ▶ A serve must be hit from behind the back line, or end line, with one hand. Serves that hit the net now are in play.

▶ ▶ A served ball cannot be blocked at the net; neither can it be spiked until it is hit by another.

▶ ▶ A ball can be played if it hits off any body part above the waist.

▶ ▶ Balls that do not pass inside the antennae placed on each side of the net are considered out of bounds.

Familiarize yourself with the following terms:

▶ ▶ **ace:** a serve that is either hit out of bounds or that lands directly on the opposing team's floor.

▶ ▶ **block:** when a defender literally blocks a hit at the net, sending the ball back into the opponents' side and resulting in a point for the blocking team. Players do not get credit for a block unless it ends play. The person who hit the blocked ball receives a hit error for stats.

▶ ▶ **bump:** two-armed pass that usually bounces off the forearms to a teammate. "Pass," though, is the preferred term to use for stories.

▶ ▶ **dig:** when a player saves the ball from a spike, keeping it in play for at least one more hit.

▶ ▶ **double-fault:** Players on both teams commit a violation at the same time, such as going over the net.

▶ ▶ **hit:** a ball hit softly over the net. Sometimes referred to as a dink shot.

▶ ▶ **kill:** a spiked ball that results in a point.

▶ ▶ **lift:** a violation called when a ball is held too long (sort of like a basketball player palming a ball.)

▶ ▶ **quick hit:** when a ball is hit over the net on the second touch by a front-row player, usually to surprise the opposing team.

▶ ▶ **sideout:** when the nonserving team wins a point to earn the serve.

Get Ready

▶ Keeping stats for volleyball can be difficult for someone covering a match. Ask an assistant coach or team manager for team stats on aces, digs, assists and total points. At college matches, the sports information director should have these printed out soon after the match ends. At high school events, you'll have to rely more frequently on coaches.

▶ Set up a system to keep play-by-play through the match. You may consider using a basic setup like the one shown below.

Team A		Team B
#12 ace	1 – 0	
#21 block at net	2 – 0	
	2 – 1	#17 kill down back right side
	2 – 2	#12 dig
#9 kill near back	3 – 1	

► Volleyball is a game of momentum. Teams go on many rallies during a match, whether it is an 8 – 0 run or a 10 – 2 run. It is unusual for teams to mount major rallies after they've fallen behind by large margins, especially now that games rely on rally scoring. A team ahead 20 – 10, for example, will usually win. Focus on these scoring runs. Did either team roll off six or seven straight points? Did the run prove to be a turning point? Did a team win despite failing to put together a series of runs in the sets, instead winning a few points at a time?

► More than anything, coaches focus on passing and serving, but they evaluate success much differently from most sports journalists and fans. For example, many game stories focus primarily on the number of aces and service errors, not the location where the serves traveled. In addition, game stories rarely focus on passing, a skill that is much more difficult than it appears. "When passing is going bad, fans don't understand how someone couldn't just simply pass the ball to the target," says University of Illinois coach Kevin Hambly. "The problem is passing is not that exciting and so most of the media don't care about it, or even pay attention to it."

► Focus on the setter. Passing is critical in volleyball, so do not overlook it for flashier kills or acrobatic digs. A calm, precise passing game sets all of these plays in motion.

► Focus on key plays, which could be a solid serve, a block, a dig, or a tricky set.

► Focus on trends within the match. Did a team score more often for certain servers? Did a team rely heavily on a certain player or play? Did one team, or player, have many more blocks than the opponents?

► Cite when coaches call time-outs. What was the score? What was the situation – to stop a rally or to correct an error? How did the team respond after each time-out – by scoring a string of points or by losing several points in a row?

► Focus on a team's strategy. Did a team pass more to the outside hitters? Or did they send two blockers to the net against certain hitters or in certain spots?

► Focus on the first few points of a set. Some teams rely more heavily on emotion, which is most evident at the start of a game. Emotions can much more easily help a team go on an early run; however, teams have difficulty retaining intense emotions throughout an entire game, much less through a three- to five-game match. Ask coaches about this afterward.

- Determine how front-row players hit at the net. A player who leaps off one foot is much more difficult to defend because she can jump at angles as she hits the ball, which means defenders are less certain where to go to block such hits. Players who leap off two feet usually go right to the ball only.

- Look for spacing between players. Sometimes, a team uses two blockers at the net, but this can open other spots on the court. Did the double-blocking work? Did the opposing team exploit this, hitting balls into open areas?

- On the front row, determine which players get more elevated. Check the heights of these players before the matches to see whether one team has a clear advantage. Then determine whether the team took advantage of its height advantage, or did the opposing team do a great job compensating for its lack of height? Record short hits, or tips, that fall over the front line for points.

- Focus on defense. Describe acrobatic dives, diving saves and effective blocks at the net. These plays can illustrate trends and strategies during the game, so take detailed notes. "I always focus on defense right from the beginning," says University of Southern California women's coach Mick Haley, a former U.S. Olympics coach who has won three NCAA titles. "Specifically, the blocking because once that is in synch, we will develop rhythm."

- Sometimes a player hits the ball off two hands, causing it to spin. This is considered a lift, or second contact.

- Focus on fouls when they take away a point, changing momentum or altering the final outcome. How did the team respond right after the foul was called?

- Servers jump and drive balls, float them like knuckleballs, put on a topspin that forces them to shoot down like a slider, and can even hit the ball underhanded

ASK

- Coaches focus on the other team a great deal, evaluating an opponent's systems, determining their tendencies and identifying their weaknesses. After the match, ask coaches to offer their evaluations. Did anything surprise you about today's match? Did you notice whether the opposing team adjusted to any of your set plays?

- Determine the turning point in the match. What play or change in strategy changed the match's outcome?

- Ask coaches what they said during timeouts.

- Ask players to comment on someone who played directly opposite, meaning front-row hitters may comment on one another. Plus, a back-row player can also speak about the velocity and angles of slams from the opposing front line.

- Ask players to describe key plays.

- Ask front-row hitters to describe the play of their own setter. Always ask the reason a coach pulls a setter from the game. If that happens, something is very wrong because a typical team has difficulty adjusting to a new setter.

- Ask players how they adjusted to the other team's style of play. Did the other team tip the ball over the net unexpectedly? Did the team fail to talk and call out plays well during any particular set? Was the team in synch? If not, ask for examples. Did the opposing team exploit any specific weaknesses at any point during the match?

- Ask coaches to clarify main ideas and key points. Consider this quote: "We worked more in our system in the fifth game than we had the entire match." What kind of a system did the team employ? Why did this approach work better in the fifth game than it did in the previous four sets? Is this a difficult system to run? Get the details so you can explain this to readers.

WRITE

- Focus on a key moment that reveals a trend or that affected the match's final outcome.

- Focus on scoring runs. Describe plays that propelled these runs. Did a team record four kills during a 7 – 0 run? Did a player record a string of aces? Did a team continually find an open spot on the opponent's side? "If the score is 15 – 15 and then 25 – 17, fans want to know what the heck happened," said Mike Miazga, editor for *Volleyball Magazine*. "Ask 'What changed?' 'Did the setter hit more spots?' Explain this."

- Certain stats are important, such as the dig-to-kill stats. But avoid using stats to explain a team's success. Unlike baseball, volleyball's stats are not as widely understood. Most readers won't understand the significance of hitting percentages (that .300 is excellent and .125 is poor). So avoid writing: "Rutgers won the opening set convincingly, out-scoring Boston College 25 – 14 thanks in part to a .312 attack percentage." Instead, explain how Rutgers drilled several key shots and made few unforced errors to record the victory. Show what happened; don't just cite stats.

▶ Focus on the impact the game has on conference or postseason possibilities. Does this game put the team in position to reach the conference tournament? Or does it eliminate the team from a tournament? Mention these details in the opening few paragraphs.

WRESTLING

C an't tell a cradle from an inside trip? What about banana splits, chicken wings and ankle picks? Don't worry. Most of your readers can't discern these either. Few sports are as technically oriented as wrestling, which has its own language and relies on very specific rules and guidelines. Even so, you don't need to be an ex-wrestler to cover the sport; you just need to do some homework to pin down the basics.

"Wrestling is really very simple," says Greg Strobel, a two-time National Collegiate Athletic Association champion and coach of the 2000 U.S. Olympics wrestling team. "Try to take your opponent to the mat, try to turn him over, try to control him. On the converse, don't get taken down, get away, don't be controlled."

Rather than the intricacies of various moves and holds – some of which have more than one name – good stories about wrestling focus on the head-to-head struggle, with all its accompanying action and emotion. Too many technical details, in contrast, tend to scare readers away from reading about wrestling.

"Even here in Iowa, where it is very popular, there are a lot of people who have no idea what the sport is about and what some of the finer points are," says Jim Leitner, sports editor for the Dubuque *Telegraph Herald.* "So you have to strike a balance in your story. You have to write a story that will appeal to the die-hard wrestling fans, and, at the same time, you can't make it so technical that a casual sports fan can't follow it."

But if a wrestler has a patented move, you might want to describe it – or even develop a graphic or video that explains how the move works.

PREPARE

Learn the Basics

▶ Matches last three periods unless the match ends prematurely by a pin, technical fall or disqualification.

▶ Wrestlers can be disqualified for various reasons, including a skin disease or viral infection, injury, failure to make weight or flagrant misconduct.

▶ Scoring during matches goes as follows: near fall (2, 3 or 4 points), takedown (2 points), reversal (2 points), escape (1 point), time advantage (2 points).

▶ Points are awarded to teams whose wrestlers win by the following methods:
6 points – fall (or pin), default, forfeit, disqualification.
5 points – technical fall (if near fall was already awarded to winning wrestler).
4 points – technical fall (if near fall is not recorded by winning wrestler).
3 points – for a decision.

▶ An overtime or sudden-death period is required when wrestlers are tied after three regulation periods. In college, the first wrestler to score a point during the one-minute overtime period wins the match.

▶ At the college level, scoring is based on how many places are awarded. If eight places are awarded in a tournament, scoring goes as follows: 16 – 12 – 10 – 9 – 7 – 6 – 4 – 3. For six places, points awarded to each wrestler go as follows: 12 – 10 – 9 – 7 – 6 – 4. For four places, scoring is 10 – 7 – 4 – 2.

▶ The NCAA uses the following weight classes in its championships: 125, 133, 141, 149, 157, 165, 174, 184, 197, heavyweight.

▶ Most high school associations offer several lighter classifications that include the following weights: 103, 112, 119, 125, 130, 135, 140, 145, 152, 160, 171, 189, 215. A few states include another even heavier weight division.

▶ Wrestlers cannot wrestle below their weight, but they may compete above their weight classifications. Rules vary for how much higher athletes can compete. In some states, an athlete cannot compete more than one weight class above, meaning a 119-pounder may not go beyond the 125-pound class.

- Growth allowances are usually granted for high school athletes. In some states, a wrestler can gain two pounds midway through the season and still wrestle in the same weight class. These rules are created so wrestlers won't go on crash diets or starve themselves. "But there are still abuses," says *USA Today's* Gary Mihoces, who has covered the sport at every level, including the Olympics, "and weight-cutting remains an issue that is worth watching and covering."

- The weigh-ins to verify a wrestler's weight happen about an hour before the meet, although they can be done two hours before some NCAA meets.

- Usually tournaments are double-elimination, which means wrestlers who lose can "wrestle back" into the later rounds until they lose their second match.

- Familiarize yourself with some basic wrestling terms:

    - **advantage:** when a wrester is on top and in control of an opponent.

    - **escape:** wrestler escapes from a down position.

    - **near fall:** wrestler has control of an opponent, holding both shoulders near the mat for at least two seconds.

    - **pin:** when both shoulders are held down for at least two seconds.

    - **reversal:** wrestler escapes from under an opponent and controls him in a single move.

    - **takedown:** wrestler takes opponent to the mat.

    - **time advantage:** a wrestler is in control for at least one minute, restraining an opponent from moving.

Get Ready

- Never come to an event empty-handed. Get names and records for all participants. Better still, always come armed with a few unique facts or ideas for sources. For example, if a wrestler is going for 100 victories, talk to his family before coming to the match.

- Check to see what the team's all-time series record is against its opponent.

- Record the names of the game officials in case anything unusual happens. Interview them afterward in such instances.

- Look for trends and statistical streaks, such as a run of eight successive pins or breaking a four-match losing streak.

▶ Introduce yourself to the coaches before the meet, even if it's just to tell them you'd like to talk with them later. In addition, sit or stand by them during matches to listen to their commentary or to ask questions. "You hear things," says Mihoces. "Maybe they know some lower-seeded wrestler who was hurt in the regular season but is healthy at tournament time and likely to pull some upsets."

▶ Pick up bracket sheets for bigger tournaments that list times for the opening-round matches. Look for your local wrestlers. In addition, highlight any matches featuring a No. 1 or No. 2 seed so you can watch them as well (because you never know when an upset is going to take place).

WATCH

▶ A good note-taking system is essential for all sports coverage. You might want to borrow this system used by some reporters who cover wrestling: Divide a notebook page into two columns and put one wrestler's name at the top of each. Then keep track of all scoring moves.

Wrestler A		Wrestler B
Takedown	2 – 0	
	2 – 1	Escape
Near fall	5 – 1	
	5 – 2	Escape

On the side of the page you may also want to record extra details, such as facial expressions, crowd reaction and other information that will help your readers feel as if they were there.

▶ Watch as many matches as possible that involve teams you're interested in, but with eight to 16 matches taking place at bigger meets, this is easier said than done. Then get the results from matches you missed from the official scorers.

▶ Look for something in the meet that is first, biggest or only, such as a wrestler's first pin or only loss, or a team's biggest point total for the season. "If you can use any of those words," says Bryce Miller, who has covered five NCAA championships and the 2004 Olympics for *The Des Moines Register,* "it means your reporting has identified the uniqueness in the event."

Record matches that swing momentum for an entire meet or tournament. If a meet is a blowout, watch for specific ways that one team overwhelmed another. Did the first two wrestlers record pins in less than a minute? Did a wrestler rally in the final minute to win, which led to a string of four straight match victories?

Cover matches that feature top-ranked wrestlers. Did these two ever wrestle before? Who won – and why? What are the two wrestlers' records? Does one wrestler rely more on pins? Did a match between two top wrestlers turn into a dud, where one routed the other? Explain the reasons for this.

Follow the team races so you can watch matches that help clinch a title. Even a loss can clinch a title because of the points system, where a major decision is worth fewer points than a pin. That means a wrestler can help his team by finding a way to fight off a pin – thus preventing an opposing team from scoring additional points. Sometimes, these matches are more interesting to focus on in game stories.

ASK

Wait until the overall competition has concluded before you start interviewing wrestlers and coaches. Coaches often want to keep their teams focused on their teammates.

Some reporters prefer to speak with coaches first, to develop better questions to ask their wrestlers.

Make sure you have names and records for all wrestlers. Then you're ready to ask a coach questions like these: What were your goals today? Did any wrestler surprise you? What were you thinking during (a match you've identified as key)? How has the team progressed during the last several meets?

Ask wrestlers to describe their matches. What was your strategy entering the match? What concerns did you have? Did your opponent prove stronger or weaker than you'd expected? Did either wrestler make any adjustments?

Do not get discouraged if someone does not talk to you right away. "It truly depends on the individual and the situation," says Miller. "I've known NCAA champs who seemed unapproachable, but were just fine talking right after they were finished. I know others who needed a small amount of time to decompress. You must know the athletes/teams you cover, since there's no one answer that applies to every situation."

WRITE

▶ Make sure key information is placed high – team scores, key match results. If this is a postseason tournament, cite which wrestlers and teams advance to the next round

▶ Show, don't tell. Rather than simply labeling a freshman as "the player of the game," describe how he performed. Rather than saying a wrestler "appeared fatigued," show what made you think that. Was he unable to fight off several attacks? Did he move slowly to get back into position after being pulled off the mat?

▶ Here are a few other things to focus on:

▶ ▶ A key match that altered momentum or secured a team victory.

▶ ▶ An individual performance, particularly by a wrestler with a terrific human interest story; mention the name of a top-ranked wrestler's next opponent.

▶ ▶ A coach's decision or strategy. Was a wrestler moved up a weight class or did the match begin at a mid-weight class?

▶ ▶ A stats leader. Did a wrestler pin his ninth opponent or did a wrestler win his 10th decision by two points or fewer?

▶ ▶ The team's performance. Is this a team's worst loss or biggest margin of victory? Cite the last time the team won or lost by such a margin. Did a team rally to win three of the final four weight divisions to earn a tournament win?

▶ ▶ If the match is a blowout, focus on how – and why – one team dominated. Did one team record pins in six matches? Did two points or fewer determine five matches?

▶ Put team records in parentheses within the first few paragraphs. Lake Brantley (14 - 2, 8 – 1 in the Apollo Conference) recorded six pins to rout Apopka (10 – 6, 6 – 4).

▶ Include records for individual competitors. For example: Jerry Duffy (21 – 2) pinned Stan Packer (17 – 8) in 1 minute, 9 seconds to win the 184-pound title.

▶ Spell out times in first reference, such as in those citing pins. Example: Oklahoma's James Tidwell pinned Brian Poulter 2 minutes, 12 seconds into the second period.

▶ Cite wrestlers who have earned a previous title.

WORKING WITH SPORTS INFORMATION DIRECTORS

Before Sarah Jones can interview an athlete for her university's newspaper, she must contact the athletic department and let them know about the scheduled meeting. As sports editor of *The Equinox,* the campus newspaper of Fairleigh Dickinson University, Jones is required to cite the date, time and place where she will interview the player.

At the University of Texas in Austin, reporters are usually limited to speaking with athletes brought to press conferences after basketball and football games. During this time, sports information associates may even tell players: "You don't have to answer that."

More and more, sports information directors are trying to control access to players and coaches, requiring journalists to schedule interviews through their offices in what the SID at Baylor calls "hard-and-fast rules."

Sports information associates at many schools also frequently listen in on interviews, serving as chaperones who can turn a private conversation into an awkward prom date.

Sports writers at some schools face challenges like that at Boise State University, which limits football players to one interview per week and requires members of the sports media to schedule through the SID's office in advance. And once the time for this athlete is scheduled, other media are allowed to attend as well.

Student sports journalists cause many of their own problems by not reporting properly and by dressing unprofessionally. Few student reporters attend practices or check in each day with players and coaches when athletes are more readily available. Student sports journalists admit they do not usually introduce themselves before interviews.

Student reporters are sometimes chastised for scheduling their own interviews, which has happened at Ball State and other schools.

And players get chewed out for speaking candidly.

"They [SIDs] program athletes to only things that follow with the company line, leading to the usual quotes that appear in every paper, every day," says Mike McCall, sports editor for *The Independent Florida Alligator.* "It's tough to get people to open and be honest when they know they'll get a lecture afterward if they speak their minds."

Access is getting tighter than ever, thanks in part to policies that advisers and college sportswriters have called arbitrary, rigid and a violation of free speech that limits the athletes' ability to speak their minds. Sports information directors say these accusations are not fair, that they take their role as liaison between athletics and the media seriously, but that their primary responsibility is to student-athletes, assisting them with time management and education. Even more, SIDs say their role is to control the image of their athletes, coaches and programs. Listening to interviews is just a way to protect this appearance.

"They [college sports reporters] don't take the time to know/understand who we are and what our jobs are," says Luke Reid, assistant sports information director at California State University, Chico. "They don't get that we work for the university. They don't get that relationship goes two ways. In order to get a little, you need to give a little, in other words."

Trust, or truth, is also a major concern for SIDs who face growing pressure from fans posing as online journalists. Frankly, the SIDs do not know whom to trust. Doug Dull, associate athletics director for media relations at the University of Maryland, says stalkers have posed as journalists to try to get phone numbers and e-mail addresses of female players. Many policies, he says, are implemented to protect players, not to cause problems for legitimate reporters, and SIDs have to err on the side of caution.

Dull says that rule of thumb applies to news media across the board. "It's naive to assume that any media relations professional, in sports or otherwise, would allow 24-hour access to our sources and clients," he said. "If that's a hindrance to those people who can't plan ahead or work with us to manage accessibility, then so be it."

Contributing to the friction is that many student reporters are undergoing Journalism 101 on the fly. One editor said newer college reporters usually come in with a far less objective approach, more freely mixing opinion with their stories. No doubt, young journalists are watching more and more of their role models vent, argue, opine and yell on the air. "Our young journalists usually want to be either rah-rah or mud-sling," writes another sports editor. "But we can usually train them within a month or to be neutral and to 'ca

ON GAINING CREDIBILITY

"A sports reporter should know the basics of the team and the sport before going out for an interview. The coach or A.D. or sports info writer should not have to educate you on stuff you should already know. Use them to fill in the details, to explain the nuance, to get beyond the stats. I think that kind of prep work can lend credibility to the student journalist when she or he goes out on the beat. If the A.D. or coach respects your knowledge, chances are she or he will be more willing to help you. It's a matter of mutual respect."

Merv Hendricks,
director of student publications, Indiana State University

it as they see it.' We are very good about teaching not to cheer in the press box and about not editorializing in stories."

Even in the best of circumstances, staffing shortages, scheduling conflicts and publishing cycles contribute to the difficulties in meeting the expectations of many SIDs. Regardless of the causes, student sports journalists can borrow trouble by not maintaining a consistent reporting presence – by not regularly attending practices and games, in other words.

The nature of the collegiate press, even at its best, puts it at a general disadvantage when it tries to emulate its professional counterparts. And the increasing control that sports information departments are exerting to try to control the flow of information exacerbates the tensions that would exist under the best of circumstances.

SUGGESTIONS FROM SIDs

1. Introduce yourself to the sports information director before starting a beat. Explain your deadlines.

2. Don't copy pictures from a school Web site, which is protected by copyright laws. Do additional reporting to supplement any news releases posted on these sites.

3. Show up early to games so the SID can fill you in on any notes on the game and players or fill you in about post-game protocol.

4. Dress in a neat, professional way. Show that you're taking the job seriously.

5. Give SIDs more than a few hours to set up interviews. Call a few days ahead. Better yet: Head out early to practice so you can speak with players on your own. If needed, wait until practice concludes so you can talk with players as they walk back to the training rooms or their dorms.

6. Bring a pad and recorder to all interviews.

7. Concentrate on campus events, not on professional teams.

8. Don't assume that because you've written about a team for six months you have the same access as established beat writers. Earn your status.

C overing fantasy sports is much more challenging than playing in them. You can't just review a manual or Web site or put your draft on automatic.

As with any beat, fantasy sports writers need to immerse themselves in their topic. Drew Silva, who covers baseball for Rotoworld.com, reads as many as 300 articles a day, scouring news wires and Web sites to find information on players, depth charts, injury updates and real-time stats, among other things. Fantasy writers may also call baseball beat writers and agents for inside information.

"And I'm still not on top of everything," Silva says. "It takes an insane commitment to form respectable opinions."

That's because readers are equally fanatical.

"There is no limit to the minutiae," says Rob Bolton, golf editor for Rotoworld.com. "And there is at least one reader out there that needs every scintilla of information. Anything short of attempting to meet this expectation is falling short."

About 30 million people play in fantasy sports leagues, generating more than $3 billion a year, according to the Fantasy Sports Trade Association.

As a result, numerous Web sites and blogs now cover fantasy sports. And ESPN's web-cast, "Fantasy Football Now," won an Emmy for its coverage in 2008, further legitimizing the profession.

Leagues are offered for every professional sport, everything from football to NASCAR to golf – and even bass fishing. A Kentucky man recently won $1 million when the fisher-men he selected caught the most bass across six tournaments. Obviously, fantasy sports readers have a little more on the line than casual fans. They want information that reveals their players' true statistical value.

Fans expect fantasy sports writers to provide this.

"Every time you write, try and answer the question, 'Why does this matter?'" says Bolton. "This is what separates the writers you trust from those you don't."

Here are 10 things to consider if you want to cover fantasy sports.

1. Start a blog. That's where you'll practice essential writing skills, develop clips for potential employers and prove that you can regularly post on a topic.

2. Play in several types of leagues so you can learn both the terminology and changes in scoring formats. "You have to be an expert player before you can be an expert writer," says Mike Beacom, president of the Fantasy Sports Writers Association. "You have to know where to dig for stats. In some ways, fantasy writers work like handicappers or gamblers, looking for the separation points – in this case, to find the stats that make a difference."

3. Scrutinize stats. Your readers do not care so much about a running back's overall performance; instead, readers want to know whether this player is going to get enough carries to be worth starting. "Readers want information that is quick, clear and understandable," Silva says, "If a player is injured, who is going to take his place? And is that guy worth grabbing in fantasy leagues? It's a combination of knowledge and good sense."

4. Pay attention to trends. Perhaps, you've noticed a goalie on a hot streak (going 4 – 0 with a .942 save percentage) or that a pitcher is about to face a team that strikes out frequently. "I think that aspiring fantasy writers think that it's a piece of cake to project results," says Rob Bolton, golf editor for Rotoworld.com, "but it requires years of experience in analyzing trends to establish credibility."

5. Be accurate. Unlike regular fans, fantasy sports readers are hurt when they use incorrect information. Keep messing up and these fans will find someone else to follow. "Readers want to know they are reading legitimate thoughts from someone who has already researched everything for them," says Jon Rascon, a writer for Fantasyfootballtrader.com.

6. Improve writing skills. Produce copy that is free of grammar errors and typos, something fantasy sports editors emphasize more than nearly any other trait.

7. Be available. Fantasy sports fans actively seek a connection with writers, so read your e-mails and always respond. This helps build the community for your blog or Web site.

8. Don't be afraid to be controversial. At times, take risks if you want to distinguish yourself. And don't just repeat what others are saying. Evaluate match-ups, stats and breaking news in order to offer unique insights.

9. Write with authority. You don't have to be infallible, but you should not diminish your advice either. After all, if you do not believe in yourself, who else will? Cite sources for all information, which further builds credibility and prevents plagiarism.

10. Develop your own style. Find a way to stand out. In fantasy sports writing, the entertainment value is more important than it is for traditional print and online media. The best fantasy sports writers, like ESPN's Matthew Berry, who also writes under the pseudonym "The Talented Mr. Roto," insert a great deal of humor.

AVOIDING
CLICHÉS

J im O'Connell says clichés and jargon should be kept on the bench.

Clichés, says the AP's national college basketball writer, are a sign of laziness.

That lesson was drilled into him from Associated Press sports editor Darrell Christian, who lambasted anybody who used them and any editor who allowed them to remain in copy sent over the wires—especially jargon like "Cinderella" and "back to the wall."

"God help anybody who couldn't come up with something better to describe an underdog's victory or a tough situation," O'Connell says.

Broadcasting, no doubt, has influenced many of today's sports writers. Thanks to SportsCenter and sports talk radio, we have phrases like "cool as the other side of the pillow," "en fuego," and "aloha means goodbye." And games are played with "pigskins" and "rawhides," rebounds are "caroms," tight games are "nail biters" or "pressure cookers," and where teams play "with a sense of urgency," "dodging bullets" to knock down "treys," hit "dingers," and record "hat tricks." Sigh.

"I believe a lot of cliché use comes from trying to prove that you know the latest sports speak or that you might be trying to dumb it down for the reader," O'Connell says. "Don't do either."

Sports has always had an esoteric language, one that includes insider terms and phrases that fans like to use during conversations—as if they were part of a secret code. But save these terms for your buddies. Clichés and jargon should be avoided. (Yes, like the proverbial plague.)

"None of us are above this, but the writer who resorts to cliché is like the basketball player who doesn't get back on defense or the baseball player who doesn't run out the ground ball," says *Sports Illustrated's* L. Jon Wertheim. "Clichés are lazy displays that often fail the audience. Saying that an athlete 'gets going when the going gets tough,' or 'fires all cylinders,' or 'gives 100 percent,' or 'gets it done during crunch time' doesn't tell us much. The sports world is, unfortunately, loaded with clichés, but let the athletes traffic in 'taking it one at a time' or 'having a gun for an arm.'"

AP national golf writer Doug Ferguson suggests sports writers observe more and take note of specific details that can replace these meaningless terms.

You can also tweak a cliché, suggests Wertheim, and give an old saying a fresh twist. Perhaps, two basketball players worked so well together that they were on the same paragraph. Or, maybe a coach needs to wake up and smell the frappuccino.

In addition, writers should avoid comparing sports to war or economic struggles—or any other serious issues.

Sports writers are translators, explaining the action in games for fans and interpreting the language for those who are not fluent.

There's nothing creative about using clichés. Plain, clear, accurate language is difficult to beat when you're trying to "step up to the next level."

CLICHÉS

It's impossible to narrow clichés to a top 10 (or 100) list. Yet, here are some words and phrases that can wreak havoc with your writing IQ.

Cliché	Explanation
biscuit in the basket	goal
bounce back	a player or team is getting ready to play after a poor performance
came up big	played very well
charity stripe	free-throw line
dinger	home run
heartbreaker	tough loss
hooked up	completed pass
payback game	a team is set to play a team it lost to the last time
pigskin	football
rawhide	baseball
star player	talented player
threw a pick 6	threw an interception returned for a touchdown

ETHICS:
SPORTS WRITERS CAN'T
ACT LIKE FANS

Fans don't really understand sports journalists.

Fans' vision of the profession: hanging out with sports stars, getting into games for free, receiving autographs and team jerseys and rooting for the home team.

Reality: dealing with athletes who sometimes don't want to speak with you, getting to games several hours early and staying several hours afterward, arguing with folks at the front gate who still want to charge you, declining all memorabilia offers and rooting for the best story. Oh yeah, and driving hours through back roads to cover prep sports, and walking the sidelines or sitting in the bleachers when it's raining, freezing or sweltering.

Obviously, covering sports for a living has many more advantages than disadvantages – watching sports, talking with interesting people and being outside (most of the time) – far, far from cubicles and cranky bosses.

But sports writers certainly have to act much differently than fans, whose instincts are to get a "piece" of their favorite players and teams. Sports writers should take only notes.

"Covering sports presents the constant challenge of rejecting offers of meals, tickets and gifts," says Vicki Michaelis, sports writer for *USA Today.* "I follow the twenty-five dollar rule in these circumstances. I don't accept anything more than twenty-five dollars. And the majority of what I do accept (usually because it comes to me in the mail so it's difficult to return), I give to charity."

Sports writers should adhere to both the Sports Editor Ethics Guidelines of the Associated Press and the Code of Ethics of the Society for Professional Journalists, but these do not cover every ethical challenge faced by sports journalists. Here are a few more daily ethical challenges to consider.

1. Do not cover any team you play for. Yes, this is a challenge for smaller high school and college staffs, but you'll face dilemmas both as a journalist and as an athlete. Do you write about teammates fumbling the ball in the fourth quarter, or striking out four times in a key game, or missing several free throws down the stretch? How do you interview your coach, the person who decides whether you'll be playing? And do you really think coaches and players from other teams are going to speak to someone wearing an opponent's jersey? This says "fail" all over it.

2. Do not work simultaneously for the sports information office and the college newspaper, a job arrangement that will split your allegiance. You hear in the sports information director's office that a coach is going to get fired. Do you report it? In the newsroom, you hear the paper is starting to investigate a volleyball player. Do you give the SID that tip? This creates far more problems than it's worth. In the end, your credibility can be destroyed – and nobody will trust you.

3. Cite others' work. If you learn something from another reporter or news organization, give credit for others' efforts. Do not rewrite the information and act as though you broke, or reported, the story. You may trick some readers, but you'll hurt your reputation among your peers (and, ultimately, more savvy readers will catch on to this practice).

4. Don't accept gifts. Decline team jerseys, hats and anything else offered to you by anyone associated with the organizations and teams you cover. News organizations sometimes set a dollar figure for gifts, which usually covers meals or items that cannot be returned.

5. Don't be a homer, openly rooting for your team. Refrain from cheering both in the press box and in your own stories. Leave that to the sports information office. You do not work for the teams but for readers, many of whom may not care for this team. In addition, don't wear team memorabilia when you are working as a sports journalist. That's a major credibility killer. (For that matter, do not wear ripped jeans or T-shirts that promote any team, beer or ridiculous statement. Dress professionally, even at practices.)

6. Don't attack coaches or players who refuse to speak with you or who have angered you. Cover them the same as you would any other person associated with the team. And columns are not a place to vent about confrontations on the beat. First, readers don't care about your problems. (Remember: fans think you have a dream job, hangin' with their favorite players.) Second, you'll destroy your reputation in the locker room, prompting coaches and players to stop speaking directly with you.

1. The newspaper pays its staffer's way for travel, accommodations, food and drink.

   (a) If a staffer travels on a chartered team plane, the newspaper should insist on being billed. If the team cannot issue a bill, the amount can be calculated by estimating the cost of a similar flight on a commercial airline.

   (b) When services are provided to a newspaper by a pro or college team, those teams should be reimbursed by the newspaper. This includes providing telephone, typewriter or fax service.

2. Editors and reporters should avoid taking part in outside activities or employment that might create conflict of interest or even appearance of a conflict.

   (a) They should not serve as an official scorer at baseball games.

   (b) They should not write for team or league media guides or other team or league publications. This has the potential of compromising a reporter's disinterested observations.

   (c) Staffers who appear on radio or television should understand that their first loyalty is to the paper.

3. Writers and writers' groups should adhere to APME and APSE standards: No deals, discounts or gifts except those of insignificant value or those available to the public.

   (a) If a gift is impossible or impractical to return, donate a gift to charity.

   (b) Do not accept free memberships or reduced fees for memberships. Do not accept gratis use of facilities, such as golf courses or tennis courts, unless it is used as part of doing a story for the newspaper.

(c) Sports editors should be aware of standards of conduct of groups and professional associations to which their writers belong and the ethical standards to which those groups adhere, including areas such as corporate sponsorship from news sources it covers.

4. A newspaper should not accept free tickets, although press credentials needed for coverage and coordination are acceptable.

5. A newspaper should carefully consider the implications of voting for all awards and all-star teams and decide if such voting creates a conflict of interest.

6. A newspaper's own ethical guidelines should be followed, and editors and reporters should be aware of standards acceptable for use of unnamed sources and verification of information obtained other than from primary news sources.

(a) Sharing and pooling of notes and quotes should be discouraged. If a reporter uses quotes gained secondhand, that should be made known to the readers. A quote could be attributed to a newspaper or to another reporter.

7. Assignments should be made on merit, without regard for race or gender.

Guidelines can't cover everything. Use good judgment when an ethical dilemma arises that is not already covered by these recommendations.

Source: "APSE Ethics Guidelines," http://apse.dallasnews.com/main/codeofethics.html.

7. Don't accept favors given because of your job as a sports journalist. That means you can't purchase extra tickets to the Rose Bowl from someone in the athletic department, an offer that is probably made because you cover the team or work as the sports editor. Ask yourself: Could anybody else purchase these tickets at this price? Or would they have to pay far higher fees from ticket agents – if they could even find someone to sell one? If the answer is no, then you should decline such offers as well.

8. Give people the opportunity to respond to charges, whether it's one coach saying another cheats or one player saying another one plays dirty. If you must publish a claim like this, refrain until you contact the person getting criticized.

9. Use social networks to contact athletes if you cannot find another way. Even though information on MySpace and Facebook is frequently published for public consumption, you should find other ways to speak with these players. Develop a professional relationship at practices and after games. You may use these social networks to introduce yourself and to set up an interview, but avoid using Facebook for the interview – except, perhaps, during a deadline of a serious, late-breaking event (and that does not mean writing a feature or preview story on deadline).

10. Of course, the big question is – can you eat from the buffet in the press box? A plate of Swedish meatballs, a ham sandwich or a hamburger will probably not sway a reporter to cover the team differently. At some venues, sports writers are stuck, unable to depart and purchase a meal elsewhere. That is one reason buffets are offered at larger sports events. Eating the food should be acceptable (unless you try sneaking out additional meatballs in your backpack).

BROADCASTING
GAMES ON
RADIO

Listeners hate it when announcers fail to offer the score during radio broadcasts. They also hate when announcers predict plays, act like homers, and forget to offer the time left in a game. Here are some suggestions from Warren Kozireski, past president or College Broadcasters, Inc., a nonprofit organization that promotes the profession and develops training. Kozireski also teaches broadcast journalism at SUNY College in Brockport.

1. Offer time and score frequently. "That is the number one complaint," said Kozireski, who is also the general manager for a radio station in Brockport, N.Y. The key is to have a system that reminds announcers to add these key elements. In baseball and softball, for example, some announcers offer the score after every batter, while others offer it after the second out in the inning. Some offer it every three minutes, using an egg timer. Also note time left in games.

2. Know team rosters, including the names and numbers of key players. Saying that a pass has been completed to No. 48 (even if you add the name after a brief glimpse at the roster) reveals you did not do your homework. "The moment 48 catches the ball, you need to know the name," Kozireski said. Study key players first. In football, that means the quarterback, running backs and receivers. In hockey or basketball, that may mean the leading scorers – players who will touch the ball, or puck, most frequently. Ask team managers and assistant coaches to verify names.

3. Don't predict. That means you should say what has happened, not what is going to happen. Don't say that a quarterback is going to pass or that a running back is going

to get a first down as he runs. Instead, say that a quarterback is in the pocket and that a tailback ran for a first down.

4. Don't be a homer. Networks are not interested in biased announcers on national broadcasts where there are no home teams. Be more excited about key plays regardless of which basketball team makes them.

5. Drink lots of water. Not Red Bull, Gatorade or vitamin water. Milk is the worst thing because it coats the throat. "By the third period of a hockey game, your throat is rough," Kozireski said. "If the games goes into overtime, you can be in trouble." For sore throats on game day, drink hot tea with lemon.

6. Read books on sports broadcasting. Helpful books include Josh Lewin's *Getting in the Game,* Marv Albert's *Yesss,* and Keith Olbermann and Dan Patrick's *The Big Show* – all of which offer tips, suggestions and insights into the profession.

7. If you're an analyst, shut up! Give the play-by-play announcer time to do the job. The game is not about you. Know as much about the teams and players as possible, more than you can ever share during the game. Analysts should not follow the ball. That's the play-by-play announcer's job. Instead, look at other parts of the field or rink. And do not be a Monday morning quarterback, saying what a player or coach should have done; if you must, offer suggestions before these plays.

Here are a few other brief suggestions:

▶ Don't limit yourself to covering a single sport.

▶ Avoid jargon when you translate a sport's terminology.

▶ Sit down and talk with coaches to learn the game better.

▶ Dress the part. Keep those worn jeans and torn T-shirts at home. Dress professionally to be treated as such.

ASSIGNMENT DESK

GAME ASSESSMENT

The following exercises test a sports writer's ability to read a box score, to analyze play-by-play, to find key moments, to utilize quotes and to write game stories for different audiences. Some of these exercises are intended for a class setting where students are expected to write on deadline.

Exercise—BASKETBALL

Directions—You can write the following game story from one of three perspectives—as a reporter who covers Eastern Illinois University, who covers Austin Peay State University or who writes for the Associated Press. Include at least three links for any online stories.

WHAT	Ohio Valley Conference women's basketball championship
WHERE	Nashville, Tenn.
WHEN	This afternoon
NOTES	Austin Peay Governors. Eastern Illinois Panthers. . . . Austin Peay won OT game vs. EIU in team's final regular-season game. . . . EIU ends season 24–9, Austin Peay is 17–15. . . . Galligan is EIU's all-time leading scorer with 1,891 career points. In this game, she also broke single-season record held by JoAnn Archer, who had 575 points in 1981. Galligan now has 582 points. . . . Pollock's previous season-high was nine points. . . . Eastern Illinois had defeated Austin Peay twice in regular season, both times by double digits. . . . Austin Peay advances to the NCAA Tournament next week. . . . EIU had 25 turnovers. Had averaged 17.6 per game during season. . . . EIU may still be able to play in the National Invitational Tournament, a 48-team tournament that begins in 10 days. The tournament's selection day is March 16. Austin Peay was ranked fifth entering the tournament. The Governors defeated No. 4 Morehead State in the first round, No. 1 Murray State in the semifinals. Eastern was ranked No. 2. . . . EIU lost to Murray State in the previous year's OVC title game.
QUOTES	"They [his players] kept fighting, that's what they do."—Austin Peay coach Carrie Daniels. . . . "We got down to the end and the needle was on E."—Eastern Illinois coach Brady Sallee. . . . "We ran into a hot basketball team that

had a lot of confidence and they played like it tonight. I'm very proud of my kids' effort. Their heart, their determination. If we take a little bit better care of the ball and there's not an 18-free throw attempt discrepancy, things might've been different."—Sallee. . . . "As the season went on, we started thinking 'if we keep pushing through, keep pushing through and keep playing we'll be OK.' "—Austin Peay's April Thomas said. . . . "Nobody thought we'd be here. We had confidence. We knew it was going to be hard, but we fought."—April Thomas. . . . "It was just adrenaline flowing through me. I think we all thought we could do it."—Austin Peay's Emily Pollock. . . . "It just wasn't our day. They made more plays than us."—senior forward Lindsey Kluempers.

INDIVIDUAL STATS

AUSTIN PEAY

Player	FG-FGA	3pters	FTs	Rebs	Fouls	Pts	Assists
HANLEY, Whitney	0–8	0–6	0–0	1	2	0	1
FAULKNER, Brooke	3–13	1–9	2–4	6	4	9	2
THOMAS, April	4–10	0–1	5–8	8	3	13	0
HERRING, Ashley	9–16	2–5	1–4	2	4	21	1
JAMEN, Nicole	2–9	0–0	3–5	13	3	7	2
RAYNER, Jasmine	1–2	0–0	1–1	1	0	3	0
WARNER, Darcie	0–1	0–1	0–0	0	0	0	0
JONES, Lauren	1–2	0–0	1–2	0	0	3	0
POLLOCK, Emily	4–5	1–1	4–8	3	2	13	3
TEAM							
Totals	24–66	4–23	17–32	39	18	69	9

EASTERN ILLINOIS

Player	FG-FGA	3pters	FTs	Rebs	Fouls	Pts	Assists
CANALE, Ellen	1–7	0–2	2–2	6	5	4	3
EDWARDS, Megan	3–11	2–6	1–2	1	2	9	8
SIMS, Dominique	3–10	0–2	1–2	8	4	7	4
KLUEMPERS, Lindsey	3–9	1–5	0–1	8	3	7	4
GALLIGAN, Rachel	12–15	0–0	0–1	4	3	24	0
WALKER, Pilar	0–0	0–0	0–0	0	1	0	0
THOMAS, Ashley	2–3	2–3	0–0	5	4	6	3
KLOAK, Maggie	2–3	0–0	4–6	4	3	8	0
PRESSLEY, Chantelle	0–0	0–0	0–0	1	1	0	0
TEAM	5						
Totals	26–58	5–18	8–14	37	26	65	22

PLAY-BY-PLAY

FIRST OVERTIME

Eastern Illinois	Time	Score	Austin Peay
TURNOVR by SIMS, Dominique	04:58		STEAL by HERRING, Ashley
REBOUND (DEF) by (TEAM)	04:31		MISSED JUMPER by JAMEN, Nicole
JUMPER by EDWARDS, Megan	04:14	50–48	
ASSIST by SIMS, Dominique	04:14		
REBOUND (DEF) by GALLIGAN, Rachel	03:56		MISSED JUMPER by THOMAS, April
MISSED JUMPER by KLUEMPERS, Lindsey	03:23		
REBOUND (OFF) by KLUEMPERS, Lindsey	03:23		
JUMPER by KLUEMPERS, Lindsey	03:04	52–48	
ASSIST by EDWARDS, Megan	03:04		
REBOUND (DEF) by CANALE, Ellen	02:40		MISSED 3 PTR by FAULKNER, Brooke
MISSED JUMPER by KLUEMPERS, Lindsey	02:25		REBOUND (DEF) by HERRING, Ashley
	02:14	52–50	LAYUP by HERRING, Ashley [PNT]
JUMPER by SIMS, Dominique [PNT]	01:43	54–50	
	01:27	54–52	JUMPER by HERRING, Ashley
	01:27		ASSIST by POLLOCK, Emily
	01:27		TIMEOUT 30sec
TURNOVR by SIMS, Dominique	01:06		
	01:05		STEAL by POLLOCK, Emily
	01:03	54–54	LAYUP by POLLOCK, Emily [FB/PNT]
MISSED JUMPER by GALLIGAN, Rachel	00:48		
REBOUND (OFF) by KLUEMPERS, Lindsey	00:48		
MISSED FT SHOT by KLUEMPERS, Lindsey	00:46		FOUL by FAULKNER, Brooke (P3T8)
	00:46		REBOUND (DEF) by THOMAS, April
	00:23		MISSED JUMPER by THOMAS, April
	00:23		REBOUND (OFF) by FAULKNER, Brooke
REBOUND (DEF) by (TEAM)	00:17		MISSED 3 PTR by HERRING, Ashley
TIMEOUT 30sec	00:07		
MISSED JUMPER by GALLIGAN, Rachel	00:03		
REBOUND (OFF) by KLUEMPERS, Lindsey	00:03		
MISSED JUMPER by EDWARDS, Megan	00:01		
	00:00		REBOUND (DEF) by (DEADBALL)

SECOND OVERTIME

Eastern Illinois	Time	Score	Austin Peay
	04:33	54–56	LAYUP by POLLOCK, Emily [PNT]
LAYUP by GALLIGAN, Rachel [PNT]	04:12	56–56	
ASSIST by SIMS, Dominique	04:12		
	03:52	56–59	3 PTR by POLLOCK, Emily
	03:52		ASSIST by JAMEN, Nicole

MISSED 3 PTR by EDWARDS, Megan	03:37		REBOUND (DEF) by THOMAS, April
	03:06		TURNOVR by FAULKNER, Brooke
	03:06		FOUL by FAULKNER, Brooke (P4T9)
TURNOVR by SIMS, Dominique	02:43		
	02:22	56–62	3 PTR by HERRING, Ashley
	02:22		ASSIST by FAULKNER, Brooke
MISSED 3 PTR by CANALE, Ellen	01:59		
REBOUND (OFF) by CANALE, Ellen	01:59		
MISSED 3 PTR by EDWARDS, Megan	01:54		REBOUND (DEF) by FAULKNER, Brooke
FOUL by SIMS, Dominique (P3T14)	01:41	56–63	FT SHOT by POLLOCK, Emily
REBOUND (DEF) by (TEAM)	01:41		MISSED FT SHOT by POLLOCK, Emily
	01:40		TIMEOUT 30sec
MISSED JUMPER by GALLIGAN, Rachel	01:20		REBOUND (DEF) by THOMAS, April
FOUL by KLUEMPERS, Lindsey (P2T15)	01:18	56–64	GOOD! FT SHOT by THOMAS, April
REBOUND (DEF) by CANALE, Ellen	01:18		MISSED FT SHOT by THOMAS, April
MISSED 3 PTR by KLUEMPERS, Lindsey	01:10		REBOUND (DEF) by POLLOCK, Emily
FOUL by CANALE, Ellen (P5T16)	01:05	56–65	FT SHOT by POLLOCK, Emily
	01:05	56–66	FT SHOT by POLLOCK, Emily
SUB IN : THOMAS, Ashley	01:05		
SUB OUT: CANALE, Ellen	01:05		
MISSED FT SHOT by EDWARDS, Megan	00:55		FOUL by HERRING, Ashley (P4T10)
REBOUND (OFF) by (DEADBALL)	00:55		
GOOD! FT SHOT by EDWARDS, Megan	00:55	57–66	
	00:48		TURNOVR by FAULKNER, Brooke
STEAL by EDWARDS, Megan	00:47		
GOOD! LAYUP by GALLIGAN, Rachel [PNT]	00:45	59–66	
ASSIST by EDWARDS, Megan	00:45		
TIMEOUT 30sec	00:45		
FOUL by THOMAS, Ashley (P3T17)	00:44		MISSED FT SHOT by FAULKNER, Brooke
	00:44		REBOUND (OFF) by (DEADBALL)
	00:44	59–67	FT SHOT by FAULKNER, Brooke
TURNOVR by EDWARDS, Megan	00:36		
	00:35		STEAL by POLLOCK, Emily
FOUL by THOMAS, Ashley	00:34		MISSED FT SHOT by POLLOCK, Emily
	00:34		REBOUND (OFF) by (DEADBALL)
	00:34	59–68	FT SHOT by POLLOCK, Emily
3 PTR by EDWARDS, Megan	00:20	62–68	
ASSIST by SIMS, Dominique	00:20		
FOUL by SIMS, Dominique	00:16		MISSED FT SHOT by FAULKNER, Brooke
	00:16		REBOUND (OFF) by (DEADBALL)
	00:16	62–69	FT SHOT by FAULKNER, Brooke
3 PTR by THOMAS, Ashley	00:07	65–69	
ASSIST by EDWARDS, Megan	00:07		
FOUL by KLUEMPERS, Lindsey	00:06		MISSED FT SHOT by THOMAS, April
	00:06		REBOUND (OFF) by (DEADBALL)
REBOUND (DEF) by GALLIGAN, Rachel	00:06		MISSED FT SHOT by THOMAS, April
MISSED 3 PTR by SIMS, Dominique	00:01		REBOUND (DEF) by (DEADBALL)

Directions—Use the following information to write a story for *The News-Gazette* in Champaign, Ill. If writing for online editions, include at least three links in the story.

WHAT	Midwest NCAA women's cross country regional
WHERE	Stillwater, Okla.
WHEN	This morning
DISTANCE	6,000 meters
NOTES	The top three teams and 10 individuals qualify for the NCAA Division I Cross Country Championships that will be held next week in Terre Haute, Ind. . . . Minnesota won its second straight regional title. . . . 27 teams competed. . . . Illinois' Angela Bizzarri finished second at this meet for the third consecutive year. . . . Illinois qualifies for nationals for fifth year in a row. . . . Katie Engel's time was a career best.
QUOTES	"Overall the girls did a great job. Now we just need to go back and make sure that we recover properly and get ourselves feeling as fresh as possible for next Monday. We want to try to be a top-10 team at the NCAA Championships and we need to make sure that we are ready to go."—Illinois coach Jeremy Rasmussen.

OVERALL INDIVIDUAL RESULTS: TOP 75 WOMEN

Place	TmPl	Name	Year	Team	3km	Finish	Pace	Bib#
1	1	Racheal Marchand	SR	Iowa	10:16	20:32.05	3:26	89
2	2	Angela Bizzarri	JR	Illinois	10:16	20:39.20	3:27	48
3	3	Pasca Cheruiyot	SO	Missouri State	10:08	20:40.70	3:27	152
4	4	Megan Duwell	JR	Minnesota	10:17	20:45.25	3:28	139
5	5	Kellyn Johnson	SR	Wichita State	10:17	20:50.80	3:29	278
6	6	Beverly Ramos	JR	Kansas State	10:17	20:52.95	3:29	126
7	7	Lara Crofford	SO	Nebraska	10:26	20:57.60	3:30	160
8	8	Rachel Carrizales	JR	Nebraska	10:31	21:06.05	3:32	159
9	9	Katie Engel	SR	Illinois	10:22	21:07.25	3:32	52
10		Kelly Waters	SO	Oklahoma	10:30	21:09.05	3:32	203
11	10	Mihaela Susa	SO	Oklahoma State	10:30	21:13.95	3:33	211
12	11	Gabriele Anderson	SR	Minnesota	10:30	21:24.35	3:35	136
13	12	Amy Laskowske	JR	Minnesota	10:32	21:26.55	3:35	140
14	13	Mallory Van Ness	JR	Minnesota	10:32	21:26.85	3:35	143
15	14	Chantelle Groenewoud	SO	Illinois	10:32	21:27.15	3:35	53
16	15	Lauren Bonds	JR	Kansas	10:32	21:29.70	3:35	104
17	16	Kristin Sutherland	FR	Illinois	10:34	21:29.90	3:35	57
18	17	Felicitas Mensing	SR	Minnesota	10:33	21:29.90	3:35	141
19	18	Heather Dorniden	JR	Minnesota	10:37	21:31.15	3:36	138
20	19	Natalja Zarcenko Callah	SR	Nebraska	10:45	21:31.55	3:36	172
21	20	Terry Phillips	FR	Missouri State	10:38	21:33.25	3:36	157
22	21	Sarah Perry	SR	Iowa	10:39	21:33.95	3:36	91

23	22	Jennifer Pancoast	SR	Nebraska	10:46	21:34.25	3:36	169
24	23	Elizabeth Boyle	JR	Illinois	10:38	21:37.40	3:37	49
25	24	Colleen Donovan	JR	Loyola (Ill.)	10:45	21:38.35	3:37	129
26	25	Jamie Cheever	JR	Minnesota	10:37	21:42.15	3:38	137
27	26	Jamie Vest	SR	Missouri State	10:42	21:45.05	3:38	158
28		Jessica Engel	SO	Oklahoma	10:42	21:48.60	3:39	199
29	27	Genevieve Binnie	SR	Loyola (Ill.)	10:44	21:48.60	3:39	127
30	28	Liliani Mendez	SR	Kansas State	10:45	21:49.85	3:39	122
31	29	Brooke Eilers	FR	Iowa	10:32	21:50.25	3:39	82
32	30	Laura Hermanson	SR	North Dakota St.	10:48	21:52.30	3:39	177
33	31	Nicole Braunsdorf	SR	Drake	10:46	21:52.55	3:39	30
34	32	Paige Ties	JR	Iowa State	10:50	21:53.45	3:39	101
35	33	Amanda Miller	SO	Kansas	10:47	21:53.90	3:39	109
36	34	Tone Hjalmarsen	JR	Oklahoma State	10:34	21:55.65	3:40	207
37	35	Meaghan Nelson	FR	Iowa State	10:50	22:01.45	3:41	96
38	36	Caedryn Schrunk	SR	Northern Iowa	10:43	22:02.55	3:41	185
39	37	Hannah Roeder	JR	Iowa	10:48	22:03.70	3:41	92
40	38	Betsy Flood	FR	Iowa	10:47	22:06.55	3:42	85
41	39	Casey McDermott	SO	Drake	10:50	22:08.50	3:42	36
42	40	Kinsey Farren	SO	Missouri	10:51	22:09.50	3:42	148
43	41	Victoria Fratczak	FR	Oklahoma State	10:49	22:11.60	3:42	205
44	42	Leah Schroeder	JR	Oklahoma State	10:53	22:12.45	3:43	210
45	43	Sydney Messick	SO	Kansas State	10:58	22:13.05	3:43	123
46	44	Sophie Ewald	FR	Northwestern	10:43	22:16.35	3:43	192
47	45	Carly Brown	SR	Northwestern	10:42	22:16.50	3:43	188
48		Sheilah Ndasym	FR	Oral Roberts	10:53	22:16.80	3:43	213
49	46	Kimber Lemon	SR	Wichita State	10:48	22:17.85	3:43	281
50	47	Kristen Heckert	JR	Illinois-Chicago	10:53	22:19.25	3:44	74
51	48	Fionna Fallon	JR	Iowa	10:49	22:21.05	3:44	84
52	49	Marcellee Fullwood	SR	Northwestern	10:56	22:21.55	3:44	193
53	50	Danielle Nowasell	FR	Northern Iowa	10:55	22:22.90	3:44	183
54	51	Theresa Brokaw	JR	Illinois	10:55	22:24.50	3:45	50
55	52	Megan-Anne Perrin	JR	Kansas State	10:57	22:25.25	3:45	125
56		Lauren Watson	JR	Oklahoma	10:51	22:25.40	3:45	204
57	53	Layne Moore	SO	Missouri	10:55	22:26.90	3:45	149
58	54	Emily Toennies	SO	Southern Illinois	11:01	22:27.95	3:45	250
59	55	Caitlin Berry	SR	South Dakota St.	11:07	22:29.05	3:45	232
60	56	Anna Florzak	SO	Iowa State	11:04	22:30.00	3:45	95
61	57	Natalia Kovtun	JR	Oklahoma State	10:56	22:32.55	3:46	209
62		Kristen Randcliff	SO	Oral Roberts	10:57	22:34.00	3:46	214
63	58	Stephanie Baliga	JR	Illinois	10:54	22:34.60	3:46	46
64	59	Megan Hoelscher	SO	Southern Illinois	11:01	22:35.35	3:46	247
65	60	Kara Windisch	SO	Kansas	11:06	22:36.65	3:47	117
66	61	Emily Baker	JR	Missouri	11:00	22:36.75	3:47	146
67	62	Kirsten Lang	SO	Illinois State	11:06	22:37.30	3:47	67
68	63	Brittani Johnson	FR	Oklahoma State	11:00	22:38.85	3:47	208
69	64	Aisha Praught	FR	Illinois State	11:07	22:40.20	3:47	65
70	65	Alison Knoll	JR	Kansas	11:07	22:40.40	3:47	108
71	66	Jessica Armstrong	SO	Missouri	10:56	22:41.30	3:47	145
72	67	Sarah Glowacki	SO	Illinois State	11:10	22:42.00	3:47	63
73	68	Betsy Miller	SR	Nebraska	11:13	22:42.65	3:48	168
74	69	Olivia Myers	SO	Illinois State	11:04	22:42.80	3:48	68
75	70	Irene Kosgei	JR	Wichita State	10:59	22:45.00	3:48	280

Directions—Use the following information to write a story for a newspaper near Cocoa, Fla. If writing online, include at least three links in the story.

WHAT   Class 3A Florida state football championship

WHERE   Citrus Bowl, Orlando, Fla.

WHEN   This evening

NOTES   Cocoa finished 14–1, Tallahassee Godby finished 12–3. . . . Title is first for Cocoa. Godby has won three state titles but none since 1987. . . . Teams played to first scoreless tie during regulation in Florida finals history. . . . In overtime, each team gets possession at the other team's 10-yard line. . . . Willie Downs caught TD in left corner of end zone. . . . Wilson followed blockers up the middle and stretched ball across goal line for TD. . . . Bell, a sophomore, had missed FGs of 34, 27, 4 and 42 yards. His PAT barely made it inside the right upright. . . . Graham had thrown nine interceptions in previous 14 games. . . .

QUOTES   "Amazing. It was fitting that it came down to that extra point. I missed four field goals. I kept pushing them to the right. I just had a bad day."—Bell

SCORE BY QUARTERS

	1	2	3	4	OT Score
Godby..............	0	0	0	0	6—6
Cocoa..............	0	0	0	0	7—7

SCORING SUMMARY

GODBY—Willie Downs 10 yd pass from A.J. Graham (Billy Mueller kick blocked)
    2 plays, 10 yards

COCOA—Anthony Wilson 5 yd run (Cody Bell kick)
    2 plays, 10 yards

	GODBY	CHS
FIRST DOWNS.................	**15**	**11**
Rushing.............................	2	7
Passing.............................	11	3
Penalty.............................	2	1
NET YARDS RUSHING..............	**8**	**115**
Rushing Attempts.....................	20	43
NET YARDS PASSING..............	**218**	**37**
Completions-Attempts-Int.............	20–35–4	3–14–0

TOTAL OFFENSE YARDS.	226	152
Total offense plays.	55	57
Fumbles: Number-Lost.	5–2	1–1
Penalties: Number-Yards.	9–92	7–59
Interceptions: Number-Yds-TD.	0–0–0	4–132–0
Possession Time.	20:20	27:40
1st Quarter.	5:12	6:48
2nd Quarter.	5:06	6:54
3rd Quarter.	4:20	7:40
4th Quarter.	5:42	6:18
OT Quarter.	0:00	0:00
Third-Down Conversions.	2 of 10	4 of 15
Fourth-Down Conversions.	1 of 3	1 of 1
Red-Zone Scores-Chances.	1–2	1–5
Sacks By: Number-Yards.	2–11	2–7
PAT Kicks.	0–1	1–1
Field Goals.	0–0	0–4

RUSHING: Godby—L. Johnson 11–35; A.J. Graham 5-minus 2; Willie Downs 2-minus 7; TEAM 2-minus 18. Cocoa—Anthony Wilson 9–45; Chevelle Buie 14–38; Matt Younger 11–15; W. Strickland 4–14; Marquise Dixon 5–3.

PASSING: Godby—A.J. Graham 20–35–4–218. Cocoa—Matt Younger 3–14–0–37.

RECEIVING: Godby—Willie Downs 7–82; Kessey Graham 5–100; C. St. Hiliare 3–16; William Davis 3–14; K. Bin-Salamon 1–9; L. Johnson 1-minus 3. Cocoa—Chevelle Buie 2–32; Tyler Anderson 1–5.

INTERCEPTIONS: Godby—None. Cocoa—EJ Johnson 3–132; W. Strickland 1–0.

OVERTIME PLAY-BY-PLAY

Godby on 10	A.J. Graham pass incomplete intended for Willie Downs
Godby on 10	A.J. Graham completes pass to Willie Downs in end zone
	(Billy Mueller kick attempt blocked by Anthony Session)
Godby ahead 6–0	
Cocoa on 10	Penalty (5 yards for delay of game)
Cocoa on 15	Chevelle Buie runs 10 yards
Cocoa on 5	Timeout
Cocoa on 5	Anthony Wilson runs 5 yards for TD (Cody Bell kick is good)
Cocoa wins 7–6	

Directions—Use the following information to write a story for a newspaper in Tampa, Fla. If writing online, include at least three links in the story.

WHAT   Class A Florida high school state softball championships

WHERE   Plant City, Fla.

WHEN   This afternoon

NOTES   Class 1A includes the smallest schools among the six classifications. Class 6A has the highest student enrollment. . . . Canterbury's softball team is the first sports team from the school to make a state title game. . . . Canterbury's nickname: Crusaders. . . . Eagle's View Academy's nickname: Warriors. . . . Canterbury was the first Class A school to score more than one run against Eagle's View all season. . . . Both teams finish season at 22–7. . . . Eagle's View is defending state champion. . . . Fleming stole second, and scored on error in first inning. Hall thrown out at third on double steal attempt in first inning. After Longstreet walked, Crosswait picked off at second. . . . Eagle's View scored its second run after Ashley Moore flied out to center. Fleming made a strong throw to home to keep the runners from advancing. Hall tried a pickoff throw to second that was not in time and the Warriors' Amber Thrush stole home.

QUOTES   Canterbury coach Jody Moore: "We'll continue to grow and build. I'm just really proud we gave everything we had today. Softball is a game of statistics, and they just didn't fall on our side today." . . . "I think that they blocked the bases very well, and we weren't used to getting blocked." . . . "We came in expecting them to hit," Moore said. "I kind of pride myself that we have a great defense. The hits just kind of fell in there today." "She [Ketchie] never threw the same pitch twice." . . . "I'm proud of this program. We are the team that works the hardest and we are the ones who deserved the first (state trophy)."—Canterbury senior catcher Macey Hall. . . . Sara Ketchie is 7–3 for the season. She pitched no-hitter in last year's title game. "It's probably more special than last year," said Ketchie. . . . "This is it, but it's just the most awesome feeling to go out like this. We've been together a long time. We grew together, and I'll miss each and every one of them."—senior Nicole Casaletto.

#	PLAYERS	POS	1	2	3	4	5	6	7	8	9	10	AB	R	H	RBI

VISITOR: Eagle's View Warriors

Date: ___ Time: ___

Place: Plant City Stadium

Players:
1. Brittney Silcox — 7
2. Amber Phillips — 6
3. Aaron Cribb — 3
4. Kristin Brown — 2 / Haley Wilds (PR)
5. Amber Thrush — 5 / Haley Wilds (PR)
6. Nicole Casaletto — 8
7. Brooke Evans — 9
8. Ashley Moore — DP / Jessie Casaletto
9. Sara Ketchie — 1
10. Jessie Casaletto — 4
11.
12.

| Total RUNS | | 0 | 2 | 2 | 1 | 0 | 0 | 2 | | | |
| Total H/E/LOB | 0/0/0 | 2/ / | 4/ /3 | 2/0/ | /0/ | 2/ /2 | /2/ | / / | / / | / / |

#	PITCHERS TOTALS	W	L	IP	AB	R	H	SO	BB	BR
	Ketchie									

FINAL SCORE	RUNS	HITS	ERRORS
Visitor	7	12	2
Home	2	6	5
Umpires			
Scorer			

Field Positions

FIELD GUIDE TO COVERING SPORTS Copyright © 2010 by CQ Press.

Canterbury Crusaders

VISITOR

Date:		Place:
Time:		Plant City Stadium

#	PLAYERS	POS	1	2	3	4	5	6	7	8	9	10	AB	R	H	RBI
1	Sarah Fleming	8	SB E5	X	4-3		F3									
2	Macey Hall	2	2-6 E4		K		SB RBI		K							
3	Jennifer Crosswait	6 / 1			5-3		5-3		K							
4	Kris Longstreet	3		X		X	F4	X								
5	Chelsea Weiland	7	5-4-3		5-3											
6	Savannah Mitchell	4	X	5-6		K		2-6								
7	Emily Winesett	3 / 1				K		6-3								
8	Kirstyn Smith	DP		K		X	K-4	X	F6							
9	Julia Cieutat	9		K-3			SB									
10	Lacey Adams	5														
11																
12																

Total RUNS	1	0	0	0	1	0	0			
Total H/E/LOB	1/2/1	0/0/1	0/0/0	1/0/1	2/0/1	0/0/1	2/0/2	/ /	/ /	/ /

#	PITCHERS TOTALS	W	L	IP	AB	R	H	SO	BB	BR
	Longstreet			3						
	Winesett			4						

FINAL SCORE	RUNS	HITS	ERRORS
Visitor	7	12	2
Home	2	6	5
Umpires			
Scorer			

Field Positions

LEARNING MORE ABOUT SPORTS WRITING

1. Research two teams set to play at any level. Gather team and individual statistics, read published stories and, perhaps, speak with athletes and coaches. Then, determine key matchups, such as a cornerback against a wide receiver, two front-row volleyball players set to face off or a pitcher against a batter. Next, compare stats between the two teams, determining which numbers best illustrate who should win. You often find the best stories just by hanging out at practices or in the coaches' offices, so list information you have learned in conversations. Ultimately, determine what should be the main angle for this story, along with a potential lead.

2. Evaluate a box score or game summary from an event you did not watch, assessing the stats to determine an angle that could be addressed in a game story.

3. Watch a game on TV. Then develop a list of things you'd like to learn from players and coaches during post-game interviews.

4. Invite a coach or player to class to get an insider's perspective on sports, something that will educate sports writers on aspects of the game that few, if any, fan s realize. Treat this like a press conference, where students take notes and ask questions at the conclusion of the talk. Then ask students to write a story that addresses the most significant or interesting ideas.

5. Invite a sports reporter or editor to class in order to get an insider's perspective on covering sports. Treat this like a press conference, where students take notes and ask questions at the conclusion of the talk. Then ask students to write a story that addresses the most significant or interesting ideas.

6. Watch the final five minutes, last several points or final inning of a game that has been taped. Then review the game's total stats summary in order to write the first several paragraphs of a game story.

7. Start a blog where a class covers one or more local high school teams; offer game stories, game precedes, notes, sidebars and features. Advertise this blog to the community.

8. Find clichés and slang in stories. Using clichés and slang is a lazy approach to writing unless the writer uses these phrases or words in a new manner. Rewrite the clichés and slang with more precise and creative language. Compare the sentence and discuss the strengths and weakness of the edited sentences.

9. Evaluate sources in stories, determining whether reporters fully explored all angles related to this topic. If this is a game story, did the reporter speak to coaches and players on both teams? If this is a profile, did the reporter speak with teammates, coaches, players and coaches on opposing teams, along with people who know this person away from the field? If not, what might be the reasons? Suggest other possible sources who could have been used for each of these stories.

10. Read a game story about a local high school or college team to determine possible sidebar angles if none were offered.

11. The best-written stories use active, vivid language. Evaluate several sports stories, highlighting all active verbs. Then underline all passive verbs, such as "was," "were," "is" and "are." Rewrite these passive sentences by using more vibrant, evocative verbs.

12. The best-written stories rely heavily on nouns and verbs, words that evoke a picture in the mind's eye. Highlight adjectives and adverbs in sports stories in order to determine whether the reporter offered enough specific details for a reader to "see" what happened. If not, rewrite the sentences or passages.

13. Count the number of words in leads to several sports stories. Which ones did you prefer, the longer or shorter leads? Did length make a difference? Which characteristics do you like best and worst in leads?

14. Find leads that are longer than 35 words. Rewrite them in fewer than 20 words.

15. Find a person you'd like to profile. First, research the person. Then develop a list of things you'd like to know about the person. Evaluate these questions with the help of others.

NOTES

CHAPTER 2: WRITING GAME STORIES

1. Associated Press, "Villegas Opens with a 63 in Bid for Odd Hat Trick," Golf.com, Feb. 6, 2009.
2. Associated Press, "United States Wins the Men's 4 × 40 at Worlds," usposttoday.com, Aug. 23, 2009.
3. Jason Grodsky, "Two overtimes not enough for Illini," *Daily Illini,* Feb. 8, 2008.
4. Michael Katz, "Return to the Top," *The Diamondback,* Nov. 24, 2008.
5. Dave Caldwell, "Fourth-Down Conversion Key to Victory for Harvard," *The New York Times,* Oct. 25, 2008.
6. Vahe Gregorian, "Tigers Rout Buffs: Colorado's Bumbling Helps Mizzou to Its First Shutout of a Big 12 Team," *St. Louis Post-Dispatch,* Oct. 26, 2008.
7. Tyler Kepner, "Teixeira Helps Yankees Leave West Happy as Red Sox Await," *The New York Times,* Aug. 20, 2008.
8. Danny O'Neil, "Seahawks Handle Broncos, 27-13," *The Seattle Times,* Aug. 23, 2009.
9. Stu Durando, "Postgame: Illini 76, Indiana 45," stltoday.com/blogzone, Jan. 10, 2009.
10. Tyler Kepner, "Phillies 5, Rays 4; Late Into the Night, the Phillies Claim Series Lead," *The New York Times,* Oct. 26, 2008.
11. Fluto Shinzawa, "Lucic's Hat Trick Pumps Up the Bruins," *The Boston Globe,* Oct. 26, 2008.
12. Jeremy Fowler, "Florida Gators Win 2nd National Championship in 3 years," *Orlando Sentinel,* Jan. 9, 2009.
13. Jeff Mills, "Marino Gets Hot at Wyndham Despite a Cold," *News & Record* (Greensboro, N.C.), Aug. 23, 2009.
14. Associated Press, "Angels' Weaver Gets Second Career Shutout," Aug. 19, 2009.
15. Karen Crouse, "On the Brink of Defeat, Jankovic Rallies Past Dementieva," *The New York Times,* Aug. 15, 2009.
16. "Mountaineers Picked to Finish No. 2 in Conference," *The Daily Athenaeum,* Aug. 5, 2009.
17. "Saban Pleased with First Two Units in Tide's First Scrimmage," Rolltide.com, Aug. 15, 2009.
18. "They Said It," *Sports Illustrated,* March 10, 2008.
19. "They Said It," *Sports Illustrated,* Feb. 11, 2008.
20. Paul Forsyth, "If You Lick the Lollipop of Mediocrity, You Suck," *The Sunday Times,* March 30, 2008.
21. "GMAC Bowl Recap," USAToday.com, Jan. 6, 2008.
22. Vaughn McClure, "Jay Cutler Directs Three Scoring Drives in 17-3 Victory," *Chicago Tribune,* Aug. 23, 2009.
23. Rick Stroud, "Tampa Bay Buccaneers Rookie Sammie Strougter Shines on Offense and Special Teams against Jacksonville Jaguars," *St. Petersburg Times,* Aug. 23, 2009.

CHAPTER 5: BEYOND GAMES

1. Kurt Streeter, "A Surprise in the Ring," *Los Angeles Times,* July 10, 2005, http://www.latimes.com/news/local/la-me-boxing10jul10,0,6352350.story.
2. Dave Hyde, "Where's Jake Scott?" *South Florida Sun-Sentinel,* Nov. 19, 2006.
3. Pamela Colloff, "She's Here. She's Queer. She's Fired." *Texas Monthly,* July 2005.
4. John Koblin, "For the Old-Fashioned Sports Columnist, It's Game Over," *The New York Observer,* Aug. 18, 2009.

CHAPTER 6: BLOGGING

1. Jason Sobel, "Masters Live Blog, Round 2," ESPN.com, April 6, 2007.
2. Ibid.
3. Mallary Jean Tenore, "Live Blogging: How It Makes Us Better Journalists," PoynterOnline.org. April 10, 2008.
4. Tommy Craggs, "Venezuela Defeats Upstart Dutch. Good," Deadspin.com, March 14, 2009.

AUTO RACING

1. Seth Livingstone, "Daytona Strategies Take Shape: Drivers Split on When to Pass," USAToday.com, Feb. 11, 2009.
2. Nate Ryan, "Carmichael Getting Used to Two Extra Wheels in Truck Tour," *USA Today,* Feb. 12, 2009.

BASKETBALL

1. "Mavs Stun Spurs to Force Game 5," Associated Press, May 12, 2001.
2. Grant Wahl, "A Quartet of Powerhouse Teams, Each with a Uniquely Skilled Star, Is Set for a Showdown in San Antonio in the Strongest Final Four Ever," *Sports Illustrated,* April 1, 2008.
3. Kate Fagan, "Magic Rally Shoots Down Sixers," *The Philadelphia Inquirer,* March 1, 2009.

CROSS COUNTRY

1. Doug Binder, "Rupp, Oregon Men Win NCAA Meet; UO Women Second," *The Oregonian* (Portland, Ore.), Nov. 24, 2008.
2. Dick Patrick, "Rupp, Oregon Win NCAA Cross Country Title," *USA Today,* Nov. 25, 2008.
3. Robbie McCallum, *Oregon Daily Emerald,* www.dailyemerald.com.

FIELD HOCKEY

1. "Maryland Field Hockey Needs Double Overtime to Advance to the National Title Game," UMTerps.com, Nov. 21, 2008.
2. Stephen Whyno, "Field Hockey Captures National Title," *The Diamondback,* Nov. 21, 2005.
3. "#2 Maryland Takes Down #9 American in Field Hockey," UMTerps.com, Sept. 19, 2007.
4. Peter Berlin, "Dutch Women Win Field Hockey Gold by Beating China, 2-0," *The New York Times* Olympics blog, Aug., 22, 2008.

FOOTBALL

1. Kyle Boller, "Ravens Survive Comeback by Kurt Warner and Cardinals, 26–23." ESPN.com (Associated Press), Sept. 24, 2007.
2. Jim Thomas, "Week 3: Same Plot Line, Same Ending," StlToday.com, Nov. 19, 2008.

GOLF

1. Chuck Culpepper, "Tiger Woods Trailing Tim Clark," *Los Angeles Times,* Feb. 27, 2009.

ICE HOCKEY

1. Phil Coffey, "Giving Credit Where Credit Is Due," NHL.com, Feb. 26, 2009.

LACROSSE

1. Pete Thamel, "Goal in Final Seconds Puts Duke in Men's Final," *The New York Times,* May 27, 2007.
2. "MDI Semifinal: Virginia Races Past Syracuse 17-10," *Lacrosse Magazine,* May 27, 2006.

ROWING

1. Brett Johnson, "Guerette Wins Silver Medal at 2008 Olympic Games," Rowing.teamUSA.org, Aug. 16, 2008.
2. Sean Ingle, "Olympics: Gold Standard Soars Thanks to Hunter and Purchase," *The Guardian* (London), Aug. 18, 2008.

RUGBY

1. Joe Gisondi, "First-ever NCAA Women's Rugby Match Increases Sport's Exposure," ESPN.com, Sept. 18, 2007.

SOCCER

1. Grahame Jones, "Understaffed Galaxy Isn't Overmatched," *Los Angeles Times,* July 4, 2009.
2. Ibid.

TENNIS

1. John McPhee, *Levels of the Game* (1969).
2. Bruce Jenkins, "Wimbledon Notebook: Eleni Daniilidou's Win of a Lifetime," *San Francisco Chronicle,* June 22, 2005.

TRACK

1. Frank Litsky, "Webb Toys with Tactics and the Field in Winning the Mile," *The New York Times,* Feb. 26, 2007.

INDEX

Boxes, figures, and tables are indicated by b, f, and t following the page number.

baseball, 70, 78
rotation, softball, 206
softball, 206, 212
Pitching speeds, softball, 206–207
Pitchout, 82, 142
Pit stops, 59–60, 64–66
Place-kickers, 142
Place kicks, 142
Plaschke, Bill, 48–49
Plateaus, career stats, 164
Play-action, 130
Play-by-play sheets, 138
Player advantage, 158
Player background, 229
Playing fair, 30
Playoffs, 82
Plot, story, 20–23
Plus/minus score, 158
Pocket, bowling, 102
Point after touchdown (PAT), 130
Point attempts, basketball, 96
Point guard, 85
Point of view, 20–23
Pole position, auto racing, 62
Poles, lacrosse, 167–168
Pole vaults, 236
Pooling of notes, 277
Port side of boat, 180
Posting interviews on blogs, 26f
Post-race interviews, cross country, 110, 111b
Post-race interviews, track and field, 240
Post up, 89
Power 10 strategy, 180
Power forward, 86
Power play assists, 171
Power play goals, 171
Power plays, 158, 162, 165
Practices, importance of attending, 47–48, 63, 86b, 173, 265, 267, 278, 290
Precedes, 43b, 46, 214
Predictions, reporter's, 279–280
Pre-game reporting, 74b
Prep beat. See High school sports
Pre-race workouts, cross country, 115
Press boxes, 36, 64, 74, 278
Press guides, 207b
Press tent, golf, 150–151
Preview guides, 207b
Preview packages, 10f
Preview stories, 79. See also Precedes
Probing questions, 11, 27–30
Professional Bowlers Association (PBA), 100, 102
Professional codes of conduct, 2, 274–278

Professional dress. See Dress, appropriate
Professional Golfers' Association of America (PGA), 148
Profiles, 40, 44, 46–47, 47b, 149, 160. See also Feature stories; Human interest stories
Props, rugby, 191
Pro Stock cars, 62
Protagonists, 43–44
Provisional qualifying times, heights, and distances, track and field, 237–238
Publicists, 27b
Puddles, 180
Punts, football, 127, 130, 135, 138, 140, 142
Pushing, soccer, 200
Putting, 150
Putts per round, 145
Pylons, 130

Quad sculls, 179
Qualifying
swimming, 217
track and field, 237–238
Quarterbacks, 142
Questions
feature story, 42
follow-up, 29, 231
interview, 27–30, 27b, 29b
neutral, 28
open-ended, 27
probing, 11, 27–30
targeted, 27
Quick hits, volleyball, 254
Quotations, 5, 18–19, 31, 202–203, 231

Race cars. See Auto racing
Radio broadcasting, 279–280
Rallies
baseball, 76
tennis, 230
Rally scoring system, 250–252, 255
Rascon, Jon, 270
Readers' expectations, 11
Reading out loud, 55
Rebounds, 91, 95
Records, players', 232, 239b
Recovery, rowing stroke, 178
Red auto racing flags, 60–61
Red cards
field hockey, 119
lacrosse, 171
soccer, 200
Red shirts, 130
Red zone, 130